MAN'S WORLDLY GOODS

MAN'S WORLDLY GOODS

The Story of the Wealth of Nations

By

LEO HUBERMAN

MONTHLY REVIEW PRESS

NEW YORK

TO

MY MOTHER AND FATHER

Preface

THIS book has a double purpose. It is an attempt to explain history by economic theory, and economic theory by history. This tie-up is important—and necessary. The teaching of history suffers when too little attention is paid to its economic aspect; and economic theory is dreary when it is divorced from its historical background. The "dismal science" will remain dismal so long as it is taught and studied in a historical vacuum. Ricardo's law of rent, by itself, is difficult and dull. But place it in its historical context, see it as one battle in the struggle between landlord and industrialist in the England of the early nineteenth century, and it becomes exciting and meaningful.

The book does not claim to be comprehensive. It is neither an economic history nor a history of economic thought—but a bit of both. It tries to explain, in terms of the development of economic institutions, why certain doctrines arose when they did, how they originated in the very fabric of social life, and how they were developed, modified, and overthrown when the pattern of that fabric was changed.

I wish to express my deep obligation to the following: my wife, who helped in ways too numerous to mention; Dr. Meyer Schapiro, for his critical reading of the manuscript and stimulating suggestions; Miss Sybil May and Mr. Michael Ross for their constant advice and constructive criticism which kept me from making many errors of judgment and fact. I am especially indebted to Miss Jane Tabrisky, whose careful research and wide knowledge in the fields of history and economics were invaluable aids. Without her assistance the book could not have been written.

LEO HUBERMAN

New York, July, 1936.

Contents

PART I

From Feudalism to Capitalism

PART II

From Capitalism to ?

PART I

FROM FEUDALISM TO CAPITALISM

I

Prayers, Fighters—and Workers

THE directors of the earliest movies often did queer things. One of the most curious was their habit of showing you people riding about in a taxi, then piling out and walking away without paying the driver. They'd ride all over town, have fun, or go to a place of business, and that was the end of that. No payment necessary. It was very much like most of the books on the Middle Ages that go on for pages and pages about knights and ladies all decked out in shining armour and gay dresses, at tournaments and games. They always live in splendid castles and have plenty to eat and drink. You get very little hint that some one had to provide all these things, that armour doesn't grow on trees, and that food that does grow has to be planted and looked after and worked over. But it does. Just as you do have to pay for a ride in a taxi, so some one, in the tenth to twelfth centuries, had to pay for the fun and good things the knights and ladies enjoyed. Some one also had to provide the food and clothing for the clerks or priests who did the praying, while the knights did the fighting. Besides these prayers and fighters in the Middle Ages, there existed another group, the workers. Feudal society consisted of these three classes, the prayers, the fighters, and the workers, with the men who worked providing for both the church class and the military class. This was quite plain to at least one person who lived at that time, and who commented on it this way:

3

"For the knight and eke the clerk
Live by him who does the work."

What kind of work was it? In factory or mill? No, simply because these did not exist then. It was work on the land, raising crops
for food or tending sheep for wool for clothing. It was farm work
but so different from that of today that we could hardly recognize
it.

Most of the farm land of western and central Europe was divided
into areas known as "manors." A manor consisted simply of a village and the several hundred acres of arable land around it on which
the people in the village worked. At the edge of the arable land there
was usually a stretch of meadow, waste, woods, and pasture. Manors
varied in different places in size, organization, and relationships between the people on them, but their main features were somewhat
similar.

Every manorial estate had a lord. It was commonly said of the
feudal period that there was "no lord without land, no land without
a lord." You have probably seen pictures of the medieval lord's
house. It's always easy to recognize because, whether it was a grand
castle or just a good-sized farmhouse, it was always fortified. In
this fortified dwelling the lord of the manor lived (or visited, for
often he owned several manors; some lords even owned several
hundred) with his family, his servants, and his officials who managed his estate.

The pasture, meadow, woods, and waste, were used in common,
but the arable land was divided into two parts. One part, usually
about one-third of the whole, belonged to the lord and was called
his "demesne"; the other part was in the hands of the tenants who
did the actual work on the land. One curious feature of the manorial
system was that every farmer's land was not all in one piece, but
was scattered into strips something like this (see p. 5):

Notice that Tenant A's land is spread over three fields, and is
divided into strips, no two of which are next to each other. Tenant B
likewise, and so with the others. In the early days of the feudal sys-

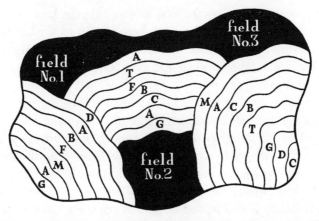

tem this was also true of the lord's demesne; it too was split up into scattered strips intermingled with the others, but in later years it tended to become one big piece.

Strip-farming was typical of the feudal period. It was obviously very wasteful and after a few hundred years it was given up entirely. Nowadays we have learnt a good deal about crop rotation, about fertilizers, about a hundred and one ways of getting more out of the soil than the feudal peasant knew. The big improvement for that day was the change from the two-field to the three-field system. Though the feudal peasants had not yet learnt what crops best follow each other so the soil would not be starved, they did know that planting the same crop each year in the same place was bad, so they moved their crops from field to field every year. One year the food crop, wheat or rye, might be in field I, alongside the drink-crop barley, in field II, and field III meanwhile would lie fallow, "laid off," for a one-year rest. Three-field farming worked out something like this:

	1st Year	2nd Year	3rd Year
Field I	Wheat	Barley	Fallow
Field II	Barley	Fallow	Wheat
Field III	Fallow	Wheat	Barley

These, then, were two important features of the manorial system. First, that the arable area was divided into two parts, one belonging to the lord and cultivated for his benefit alone, while the other was

divided among the many tenants; second, that the land was cultivated not in compact fields as we know them today, but by the
scattered strip method. There was a third marked characteristic—the
fact that the tenants worked not only their own holdings, but
the lord's demesne as well.

The peasant lived in a hovel of the most wretched type. By working long and hard on his scattered strips of land (which all together
averaged fifteen to thirty acres in England, and forty to fifty in
France), he managed to scratch a miserable living from the soil. He
would have lived better but for the fact that two or three days each
week he had to work *on the lord's land* without pay. Nor was this
the only labour service he had to give. When there was a rush such
as occurred at harvest time, he had first to harvest the crop on the
lord's demesne. These "boon days" were in addition to the labour
services. Nor was that all. There was never any question as to whose
land was more important. The lord's demesne had to be ploughed
first, sowed first, and reaped first. Did a storm arise which threatened to spoil the crop? Then it was the lord's grain that must first be
saved. Was it the harvest time when the crop had to be gathered
quickly? Then the peasant must leave his own fields and harvest the
lord's. Was there any produce left over which might be sold at the
small local market? Then it must be the lord's grain and wine which
the peasant carried to the market and sold—first. Did a road or
bridge need repairing? Then the peasant must leave his own work
and attend to it. Did the peasant want his wheat ground at the mill,
or his grapes crushed in the wine-press? He could do so—but it was
the lord's mill or press, and payment was demanded for the use of
it. There was almost no limit to what the lord of the manor might
impose on the peasant. According to a twelfth-century observer, the
peasant "never drinks the fruit of his vine, nor tastes a scrap of good
food; only too happy is he if he can keep his black bread and some
of his butter and cheese. . . .

> If he have fat goose or hen,
> Cake of white flour in his bin,
> 'Tis his lord who all must win."

Was the peasant then a slave? As a matter of fact most of the tenants were called "serfs," from the Latin word "servus" which means "a slave." But they were not slaves in the sense that we have in mind when we use the word. Even if there had been newspapers in the Middle Ages, no such "ad" as the following, which appeared in the *Charleston Courier* on April 12, 1828, would have been found in their pages: "As valuable a family . . . as ever was offered for sale, consisting of a cook about 35 years of age, and her daughter about 14 and son about 8. *The whole will be sold together or a part of them, as may suit a purchaser.*"

This breaking up of a family of negro slaves at the wish of the owner could not have happened to a serf's family. The serf had a right to keep his family together, regardless of the will of the lord of the manor. Where the slave was a piece of property which could be bought or sold anywhere, any time, the serf could not be sold apart from his land. His lord might transfer possession of the manor to another, but that simply meant that the serf would have a new lord; he himself remained on his bit of land. This was an important difference because it gave the serf a kind of security which the slave never had. No matter how badly he was treated, the serf had his family and a home and the use of some land. Because serfs did have security, it sometimes happened that a person who was free, but who was down and out for one reason or another, and had no home or land or food, would "offer himself [to some lord as a serf], a rope around his neck and a penny on his head."

There were several degrees of serfdom, but it has been difficult for historians to trace all the shades of differences between the various kinds. There were "demesne serfs," who were permanently attached to the lord's house and worked in his fields all the time, not just two or three days a week. There were very poor peasants, called "bordars," who held small two- or three-acre holdings at the edge of the village, and "cotters" with not even a small holding but only a cottage, who might work for the lord as hired hands, in return for food.

There were "villeins" who, it seemed, were serfs with more personal and economic liberties. They were farther along the road to freedom than the serfs and had more privileges, and less duties to the lord. One important difference, too, was that the duties they did have were more fixed than were those of the serfs. This was a great advantage because then the villeins knew where they were all the time. No new demands could be made of them whenever the lord took a notion to do so. Some villeins were exempt from "boon days" and gave only the regular labour services. Others gave no services at all, but paid the lord a part of their produce, much as our share-croppers do today. Still others gave no services, but made payments in money instead. This custom grew as the years went on and became very important later.

Some villeins were almost as well off as free men, and might be able to rent a part of the lord's demesne in addition to their own holdings. Then there were some freemen who were independent proprietors and had never owed labour services, but simply paid a tax to their overlord. Free, villein, and serf tenure faded into one another through many stages. It is difficult to establish exactly which was which, and exactly what the position of each class really was.

No picture of the manorial system can be strictly accurate, because conditions varied so much in different places. Nevertheless, we can be certain about some fundamental points in regard to practically all of the unfree labour of the feudal period.

The peasants were all more or less dependent. It was believed, by the lords, that the peasants existed for the sake of the lords. There was never any question of equality between lord and serf. The serf worked the land and the lord worked the serf. As far as the lord was concerned there was very little difference between the serf and any of the live-stock on his demesne. As a matter of fact, in the eleventh century a French peasant was valued at 38 sous, while a horse was worth 100 sous! Just as the lord would be worried about the loss of any of his oxen because he needed them to work on his land, so he would be worried about the loss of any of his serfs—human cattle needed to work his land. Therefore, while the serf could not be sold off his land, neither could he leave it. "His holding was called a 'tenure' (from Latin 'tenere,' 'to hold') but in law the tenure held the serf, not the serf the tenure." If the serf did try to run away and he was caught, he might be punished severely—there was no question but that he had to return. In the Court Rolls of the Manor of Bradford for 1349-1358 there is this extract. "It is presented that Alice, daughter of William Childyong, the lord's bondwoman, dwells at York; therefore let her be taken [arrested]."

Again, because the lord did not want to lose any of his labour, there were rules that serfs or their children could not marry outside the demesne, except with special permission. When a serf died his direct heir could inherit the holding, on payment of a tax. Here is one such case as reported in those same Court Rolls. "Robert son of Roger son of Richard, who held a toft and 8 acres of bondage land there, is dead. And hereupon came John, his brother and heir, and took those tenements [holdings], to hold to him and his heirs according to the custom of the manor . . . and he gives to the lord 3s. [shillings] of fine for entry."

In the above quotation the words "according to the custom of the manor" are important. They are the key to an understanding of the feudal set-up. The "custom of the manor" meant then what laws passed by a city or county government would mean today. Custom in the feudal period had the force that laws in the twentieth century have. There was no strong government in the Middle Ages that was able to take charge of everything. The whole organization was based on a system of mutual obligations and services from top to bottom. Possession of the land did not mean that you could do with it what you pleased to the extent that you can today. Possession implied obligations to some one that had to be carried out. If not, the land could be taken away from you. The services which the serf owed the lord, and those which the lord owed the serf—for example, protection in case of war—were all agreed upon and enforced according to custom. It happened, of course, that the custom was sometimes broken, just as laws are broken today. A quarrel between two serfs would be settled in the lord's court—according to custom. A quarrel between serf and lord was very apt to be decided in favor of the lord, since he would be judge of the dispute. Nevertheless, there are cases on record where a lord who violated the custom too often, was called to account by his overlord. This was particularly true in England, where peasants might be heard in the king's court.

What would happen in case of a dispute between one lord of a manor and another? The answer to that question is a clue to another interesting fact about the feudal organization. The lord of the manor, like the serf, did not *own* the land, but was himself a tenant of another lord higher up in the scale. The serf, villein, or freeman "held" his land from the lord of the manor, who in turn "held" the land from a count, who in turn "held" the land from a duke, who in turn "held" the land from the king. And sometimes it went even farther, and one king "held" the land from another king! This network of overlordship is well shown in the following extract from the records of an English court of justice in 1279: "Roger of St. Germain holds one messuage [piece of land] from Robert of Bedford on the service of paying 3d. [pence] to the aforesaid Robert from whom he holds, and of paying 6d. to Richard Hylchester in place of the said Robert who holds from him. And the said Richard holds from Alan de Chartres, and pays him 2d. a year, and Alan from William the Butler, and the same William from lord Gilbert de Neville, and the same Gilbert from the lady Devorguilla de Balliol, and Devorguilla from the king of Scotland, and the same king from the king of England."

This does not mean, of course, that this particular piece of land was all that Alan, or William, or Gilbert, etc., "held." Not at all. The manor itself might be the only property a knight possessed, or it might be one small part of a great domain which was itself a part of a fief, or huge grant of land. Some nobles possessed a few manors, others possessed several domains, and others possessed a number of fiefs scattered in different places. In England, for example, one rich baron owned estates which were made up of over 790 holdings. In Italy a few great lords owned over 10,000 manors.

Of course the king, who nominally was the owner of all the land, owned vast estates spread all over the country. The people who held directly from the king, whether they were nobles or just ordinary freemen, were called tenants-in-chief.

As time went on, the larger estates tended to be broken up into smaller holdings held by more and more nobles of one rank or another. Why? Simply because every lord found it necessary to attach to himself as many vassals as he could, and the only way to do that was to give away part of his land.

Nowadays, land, factories, mills, mines, railways, boats, and machinery of all kinds are necessary to produce the goods that you and I use, and we call a man wealthy or not, depending on how much of these he owns. But in feudal times, just the land produced practically all the goods that were needed and so land and land alone was the key to a man's fortune. The measure of a man's wealth was determined by only one thing—the amount of land he possessed. Naturally there was a continual scramble for the land, so you won't be surprised to learn that the feudal period was a warring period. In order to win the wars, the trick was to get as many people on your side as possible, and the way to do that was to pay fighters to help you. You got them to make certain payments and promise to help you when you needed it, and in return you gave them a grant of land. Thus, from an old French document of the year 1200, we learn that, "I, Thiebault, count palatine of Troyes, make known to those present and to come, that I have given in fee to Jocelyn d'Avalon and his heirs the manor which is called Gillencourt. . . . The same Jocelyn, moreover, on account of this has become my liegeman."

As "liegeman" to the count, Jocelyn was probably expected, among other things, to give military service to his lord. Perhaps he had to supply a certain number of men fully armed and equipped, for a specified number of days. A knight's service in England and France usually consisted of forty days, but you might be contracted to give only one-half a knight's service, or one-fourth of a knight's service, etc. In the year 1272 the French king was at war, so he sum-

moned his military tenants to the royal army. Some came and
served their time, and others sent substitutes. "Reginald Trihan,
knight, appeared for himself and goes [into the army]. William de
Coynères, knight, sends for himself Thomas Chocquet, for ten days.
John de Chanteleu, knight, appeared saying that he owed 10 days
for himself, and that he also appeared for Godardus de Godard-
ville, knight, who owes 40 days."

The princes and nobles who held land in return for military
service, granted it, in turn, to others on similar conditions. The
rights retained and the obligations incurred varied considerably, but
they were roughly the same over western and part of central Europe.
The tenants could not dispose of the land exactly as they pleased,
but had to have their overlord's consent and pay certain dues if
they transferred the land to some one else. Just as the heir of a serf's
holding had to pay a tax to the lord of the manor on taking possession of his inheritance, so the lord's heir had to pay an inheritance
tax to his overlord. If a tenant died and the heir was under age,
then the overlord had control of the property until the heir came of
age. The theory was that the heir who was under age might not be
able to perform the duties under which the land was held, so the
overlord took charge until he came of age—and in the meantime
kept whatever revenues came in.

Female heirs had to get the overlord's consent to their marriage.
In 1221 the Countess of Nevers acknowledged the fact: "I, Matilda,
Countess of Nevers, make known to all who shall see this present
letter, that I have sworn upon the sacred gospels to my dearest lord,
Philip, by the grace of God the illustrious king of France, that I
will do him good and faithful service against all living men and
women, and that I will not marry except by his will and grace."

If a widow wanted to remarry, a fine had to be paid to her overlord, as we learn from this English record dated 1316, concerning
the widow of a tenant-in-chief: "The king to all to whom etc. greet-
ing. Know ye that by a fine of 100 s. which . . . has [been] made
with us for Joan, who was the wife of Simon Darches, deceased,
who held of us in chief as of the honour of Wallingford, we have

given licence to the same Joan that she may marry whomsoever she will, provided that he be in our allegiance."

On the other hand, if a widow did not want to remarry, she had to pay for *not* being forced to do so at the will of her overlord. "Alice, countess of Warwick, renders account of £1000 and 10 palfreys to be allowed to remain a widow as long as she pleases, and not to be forced to marry by the king."

These were some of the obligations a vassal owed to his liege lord in return for the land and protection which he received. There were others. If the overlord was held for ransom by an enemy it was understood that his vassals would help to pay for his release. When the overlord's son was knighted it was the custom that he receive an "aid" from his vassals—perhaps to pay for the expenses of the celebration festivities. In 1254, a man named Baldwin objected to making this payment because, he argued, the king, whose son was being knighted, was not his immediate overlord. He won his case on that ground according to the English Exchequer Rolls: "Commandment is given to the sheriff of Worcester, that if Baldwin de Frivill does not hold from the king in capite [that is, in chief] but from Alexander de Abetot, and Alexander from William de Beauchamp, and William from the Bishop of Worcester, and the bishop from the king in capite, as the same Baldwin says, then the said Baldwin is to have peace from the distraint which has been made upon him for the aid to make the king's son a knight."

Now notice that between Baldwin and the king there was the usual series of overlords. Notice, too, that one of them was the Bishop of Worcester. That's an important fact, because it shows that the Church was part and parcel of this feudal system. In some ways it was not so important as the man at the top of the heap, the king, but in other ways it was much more important. The Church was an organization which extended over the whole of the Christian world. It was more powerful, more extensive, more ancient and continuous than any Crown. This was a religious age, and the Church, of course, had tremendous spiritual power and prestige. But besides that, it had wealth in the only way it existed at that time—in land.

The Church was the largest landowner in feudal times. Men who were worried about the kind of life they had led and wanted to get on the right side of God before they died, gave lands to the Church; people who felt that the Church was doing a good job in caring for the sick and the poor and wanted to help in that work, gave lands to the Church; some nobles and kings made it a practice, whenever they won a war and took over their conquered enemy's lands, to give part of those lands to the Church; in this and in other ways the Church added to its lands until it came to own from one-third to one-half of all the land in western Europe.

Bishops and abbots took their places in the feudal structure much as counts and dukes did. Witness this grant of a fief to the Bishop of Beauvais in 1167: "I, Louis, by the grace of God king of the French, make known to all present, as well as to come, that at Mante, in our presence, Count Henry of Champagne conceded the fief of Savigny to Bartholomew, Bishop of Beauvais, and his successors. And for that fief the said bishop has made promise and engagement for one knight, and justice and service to Count Henry; and he has also agreed that the bishops who shall come after him will do likewise."

And just as it received land from an overlord, so the Church acted as overlord itself. "Abbot Fauritius also granted to Robert, son of William Mauduit, the land of four hides in Weston . . . to be held as a fief. And he should do this service for it, to wit: that whenever the church of Abingdon should perform its knight's service, he should do the service of half a knight for the same church."

In the early period of feudalism the Church had been a progressive, live element. It had preserved a good deal of the culture of the Roman Empire. It encouraged learning and set up schools. It aided the poor, took care of homeless children in its orphanages, and established hospitals for the sick. In general, the ecclesiastical (Church) lords managed their estates better and got more out of their land than did the lay nobility.

But there was another side to the picture. While the nobles split up their domains in order to attract followers, the Church acquired more and more land. One reason that priests were forbidden to marry was simply that the heads of the Church did not want to lose any Church lands through inheritances to the children of its officers. The Church also added to its property through the "tithe," which was a tax of ten per cent on everyone's income. One famous historian says of it: "The tithe constituted a land tax, income tax, and death duty far more onerous than any known to modern times. . . . Not only were the farmers and cottagers bound to render a strict tenth of all their produce. . . . Tithes of wool were held to include even the down of geese; the very grass which he cut by the roadside was to pay its due toll; the farmer who deducted working expenses before tithing his crops damned himself thereby to hell."

As the Church grew enormously wealthy, its economic tended to outweigh its spiritual importance. Many historians argue that as a landlord it was no better and in some cases far worse than the lay landlords. "So great was the oppression of its serfs by the Chapter of Notre Dame de Paris in the reign of St. Louis that Queen Blanche remonstrated 'in all humility' whereto the monks replied that 'they might starve their serfs as they pleased.' "

Some even think its charitable work was overrated. They grant the fact that the Church did help the poor and the sick. But they point out that the Church was the richest and most powerful landowner of the Middle Ages, and argue that in proportion to what it could have done with its tremendous wealth, it did not do even as much as the lay nobility did. While it pleaded and demanded help from the rich for its charitable work, it was careful not to dig too deeply into its own resources. Also, these critics of the Church point out, if the Church had not worked its serfs so hard, if it had not exacted so much from the peasantry, there would have been less need for charity in the first place.

The Church and the nobility were the ruling classes. They seized the land, and the power that went with it. The Church gave spiritual aid, while the nobility gave military protection. In return for this they took payment from the working classes in the form of labour. Professor Boissonnade, an able historian of the period, has summed it up this way: "The feudal system in the last resort rested upon an organization which, in return for a protection, which was often illusory, placed the working classes at the mercy of the idle classes, and gave the land not to those who cultivated it, but to those who had been able to seize it."

II

Enter the Trader

NOWADAYS very few rich people keep boxes full of gold or silver. People with money don't want to hold it. They want it to work for them, so they look about for a profitable way to invest it. They try to find places to put their money which will bring them the best return, the highest interest. Their money may go into a business, or it may buy shares in a steel company, or it may buy government bonds, or it may do countless other things. Today there are a thousand and one ways of using wealth in an attempt to get back more wealth.

But in the early period of the Middle Ages such possibilities were not open to the people with money. Very few people had money to use, but those who did had little use for it. The Church had its coffers full of gold and silver which it either kept in its strong boxes, or used to buy ornaments for altars. It had a great fortune, but it was idle capital, not continually at work as fortunes are today. Church money could not be used to create more wealth because there was no outlet for it. This was likewise true of whatever money the nobles had. If any money came into their hands through dues or fines, the nobles could not invest it in business enterprises because there was very little business. Whatever capital the prayers and the fighters had was inactive, fixed, motionless, unproductive.

But wasn't money needed every day to buy things? No, because almost nothing was bought. A little salt, maybe, and some iron. For

17

the rest, practically all the food and clothing that people needed was obtained on the manor. In early feudal society economic life went on with very little use of money. It was an economy of consumption, in which each manorial village was practically self-sufficing. If some one asks you what you paid for your new overcoat, the chances are a hundred to one that you will give him an answer in dollars and cents. But if that same question were asked you in the early period of the Middle Ages, the chances are equally as good that you would have answered, "I made it myself." The serf and his family grew their own food, and with their own hands made what-ever furniture they needed. The lord of the manor soon attached to his household those serfs who were good craftsmen to make the things he needed. Thus the manorial village was practically com-plete in itself—it made the things it required, and consumed them.

Of course there was some exchange of goods. Perhaps you didn't have the wool necessary to make that overcoat, or perhaps there was no one in your family with enough time or skill. In that case your answer to the overcoat question might have been, "I paid five gal-lons of wine for it." This transaction probably took place at the weekly market held outside a monastery or castle, or in a near-by town. These markets were under the control of the bishop or lord, and here any surplus products produced by their serfs or artisans, or any serf's surplus, was exchanged. But with trade at a very low level there was no reason to produce a large surplus. People make or grow more of a product than they themselves need only when there is a steady demand. When that demand is absent there is no stimulus for the production of a surplus. Therefore trading at the weekly markets was never very large and always local. Another obstacle to its becoming more extensive was the bad condition of the roads. They were narrow, rough, muddy, and generally unfit for travelling. Then too, they were frequented by two kinds of robbers —ordinary brigands, and feudal lords who stopped the merchants and made them pay tolls for travelling over their abominable roads. The lords' tolls were such common practice that "when Odo of Tours in the eleventh century built a bridge over the Loire and

permitted free crossing of it, his conduct created astonishment."
There were other difficulties in the way of trade. Money was scarce,
and what money there was differed in different places. Weights and
measures, too, varied from place to place. Long-distance hauling of
goods under these circumstances was obviously uncomfortable,
dangerous, difficult, and annoyingly expensive. For all these reasons,
trading at these local feudal markets was small.

But it did not remain small. There came a time when trading
grew and grew until it profoundly affected the whole life of the
Middle Ages. The eleventh century saw commerce take big strides;
the twelfth century saw western Europe transformed because of it.

The Crusades gave a great impetus to trade. Tens of thousands of
Europeans crossed the continent by land and sea to wrest the Holy
Land from the Moslems. They needed supplies all along the route
and merchants accompanied them to cater to their wants. Those
Crusaders who returned from their Eastern journey brought back
with them an appetite for the strange and luxurious food and clothing they had seen and enjoyed. Their demand created a market for
these goods. Moreover, there had been a sharp increase in population after the tenth century and the additional people needed additional goods. Some of these additional people were landless and
saw in the Crusades a chance to better their position in life. Often
border wars against the Moslems on the Mediterranean and against
the tribes of eastern Europe, were dignified by the name of Crusades
when in reality they were wars for plunder and for land. The
Church gave these foraging expeditions a veil of respectability by
making it appear that they were wars whose purpose it was to
spread the gospel or exterminate unbelievers or defend the Holy
Land.

There had been pilgrimages to the Holy Land from early times
(there were 34 in the eighth to tenth centuries and 117 in the
eleventh century). The desire to rescue the Holy Land was genuine
and it was supported by many with no axe to grind. But the real
strength of the Crusade movement and the energy with which it

was conducted were largely based on advantages which could be won by certain groups.

First, there was the Church. It had, of course, an honest religious motive. It had, too, the sense to realize that it was a warring age, and so it seized upon the idea of transferring the violent passions of the warriors to other countries which would be made Christian, if the fighters were victorious. To Clermont, in France, in 1095, came Pope Urban II. On an open plain, since no building was large enough to hold all the people who wanted to hear him, he urged his hearers to embark on a Crusade, in these words, according to Fulcher of Chartres, who was present: ". . . Let those who have formerly been accustomed to contend wickedly in private warfare against the faithful fight against the infidel. . . . Let those who have hitherto been robbers now become soldiers. Let those who have formerly contended against their brothers and relatives now fight against the barbarians as they ought. Let those who have formerly been mercenaries at low wages now gain eternal rewards. . . ." The Church wanted to extend its power, and the greater the area of Christendom, the greater became the power and wealth of the Church.

Second, there was the Byzantine Church and Empire with its capital at Constantinople, very near the centre of Moslem power in Asia. While the Roman Church saw in the Crusades an opportunity to extend its power, the Byzantine Church saw in the Crusades a means of checking the Moslem advance on to its own territory.

Third, there were the nobles and the knights who wanted booty or were in debt, and younger sons with either a small inheritance or none at all—all of whom thought they saw in the Crusades a chance to acquire land and wealth.

Fourth, there were the Italian cities of Venice, Genoa, and Pisa. Venice had always been a trading city. Any city situated on a group of islands was bound to be. If the streets of a city are canals, you can expect the people who live there to be as much at home on a boat as on land. This was true of the Venetians. Then, too, Venice was ideally located at a time when the trade that counted was Eastern trade, with the Mediterranean as an outlet. One glance at a map will be enough to show you why Venice and the other Italian cities became such great trading centres. What the map does not show, but what was also true, was that Venice had remained tied to Constantinople and the East after western Europe had broken away. Since Constantinople had for some years been the greatest city in the Mediterranean area, this was an added advantage. It meant that Eastern spices, silks, muslins, drugs, and carpets would be carried to Europe by the Venetians who had the inside track. Because they were primarily trading cities, Venice, Genoa, and Pisa wanted special trading privileges with the towns along the coast of Asia Minor. In these towns lived the hated Moslems, the enemies of Christ. But did that make any difference to the Venetians? Not at all. Italian trading cities looked upon the Crusades as a chance for them to gain commercial advantages. So it was that the Third Crusade had for its object not the regaining of the Holy Land, but the acquisition of trading benefits for the Italian cities. The Crusaders passed up Jerusalem for the trading towns along the coast.

The fourth Crusade was begun in 1201. This time Venice played the most important and profitable part. Villehardouin was one of six ambassadors who came to the Doge of Venice to ask for aid in transporting the Crusaders. He tells of an agreement made in March of that year:

" 'Sire, we have come to you in behalf of the noble barons of France who have taken the cross . . . they pray you, for God's sake . . . to endeavor to furnish them transports and ships of war.'

" 'Under what conditions?' asked the doge.

" 'Under any conditions that you may propose or advise, if they are able to fulfil them,' replied the messengers. . . .

" 'We will furnish huissiers [vessels having a door, 'huis', in the stern which could be opened so as to take on the horses] for carrying 4,500 horses and 9,000 esquires, and vessels for 4,500 knights and 20,000 foot soldiers. The agreement shall be to furnish food for nine months for all these horses and men. That is the least that we will do, on condition that we are paid four marks per horse and two marks per man. . . .

" 'And we will do still more: we will add fifty armed galleys, for the love of God; on the condition that as long as our alliance shall last, of every conquest of land or money that we make, by sea or land, we shall have one-half and you the other.' . . .

"The messengers . . . said: 'Sire, we are ready to make this agreement.' "

You can see from the agreement that while the Venetians were willing to help this crusade along "for the love of God," they didn't let that great love blind them to a fat share in the booty. They were great business men. From the point of view of religion the results of the Crusades were short-lived, since the Moslems eventually took back the kingdom of Jerusalem. From the point of view of trade, however, the results of the Crusades were tremendously important. They helped to wake western Europe from its feudal slumber by spreading prayers, fighters, workers, and a growing class of merchants all over the continent; they increased the demand for foreign goods; they snatched the Mediterranean route from the hands of the Moslems, and made of it once again the great trade route between East and West which it had been in ancient times.

If the eleventh and twelfth centuries saw a revival of trade on the Mediterranean in the south, they saw a great awakening to trading possibilities in the seas of the north. On those waters commerce was not revived. For the first time it became really active.

On the North Sea and the Baltic, ships hurried from place to place to pick up fish, lumber, tallow, skins, leather, and furs. One centre of this northern seas trade was the city of Bruges in Flanders. Just as Venice, in the south, was Europe's contact with the East, so Bruges was its contact with the Russo-Scandinavian world. It only remained for the two far-off centres to find their best meeting-place, where the bulky northern necessities could be most easily exchanged for the costly luxuries of the East. Since commerce, given a good start, grows like a snowball rolling downhill, it was not long before such a trading centre was found. The merchants carrying the goods of the north met those who had crossed the Alps from the south, on the plain of Champagne. Here great fairs were held at a number of cities, the most important taking place at Lagny, Provins, Bar-sur-Aube, and Troyes. (If you've ever been puzzled as to why we use "troy" weight, here's your answer. This was the system of weights used in Troyes centuries ago at the big fairs.)

Today trade goes on all the time, all around us. Our means of transportation are so perfected that goods from the far ends of the earth come in a steady flow to our big cities, and all you and I need do is go to the store and select what we want. But in the twelfth and thirteenth centuries, as we have seen, the means of transport were not so highly developed. Nor was there a continuous steady demand for goods everywhere that would warrant all-year-round-stores selling every day. Most towns, therefore, could not have permanent trade. The periodic fairs in England, France, Belgium, Germany, and Italy were a step towards permanent steady trade. Places that had in the past depended upon the weekly market to satisfy their simple needs now found that market inadequate to meet the growing trading opportunities. Poix in France was one such place. It asked the king to grant his permission for the establishment of a weekly market and two fairs a year. Here is a part of the king's letter telling about it: "We have received the humble supplication of our dear and well-beloved Jehan de Créquy, Seigneur of Canaples and of Poix . . . informing us that the said village and faubourgs of Poix are situated in good and fertile country, and the said village and faubourgs are well constructed and furnished with houses, people, merchants, inhabitants, and others, and also that there come there, passing and repassing, many merchants and merchandise of the country around and elsewhere, and that it is requisite and necessary to have there two fairs each year and a market each week. . . . For which reason is it that we . . . have created, ordained, and established for the said village of Poix . . . two fairs each year and a market each week." As a matter of fact, the more important Champagne fairs were so arranged that they lasted over the whole year—when one finished the other began, etc. The merchants with their goods moved on from fair to fair.

It is important to note the difference between the local weekly markets of the early Middle Ages and these great fairs of the twelfth to fifteenth centuries. The markets were small, dealing with local goods, most of them agricultural. The fairs, on the other hand, were huge, dealing with wholesale goods that came from all over the known world. The fair was the distributing centre where great merchants, as distinguished from small wandering pedlars and local artisans, bought and sold the foreign goods that came from east and west, north and south.

Witness this proclamation of 1349, concerning the fairs of Champagne: "All the companies of merchants and also individual merchants, Italians, Transalpines, Florentines, Milanese, Lucchese, Genoese, Venetians, Germans, Provençals and those from other countries, who are not of our kingdom, if they wish to trade here and enjoy the privileges and good customs of the said fairs . . . shall safely come, dwell, and depart, they, their merchandise, and their guides, in the safe conduct of the Fairs, into which We take and receive them from henceforth, together with their merchandise and goods, without their ever being subject to seizure, arrest, or hindrance by others than the guards of the said fairs. . . ."

Notice that besides inviting merchants from anywhere and everywhere to come to the fairs, the ruler of Champagne offers them safe conduct to and from the fair. You can easily guess how important this was in a period when robbers infested the roads. Often, too, the merchants going to the fair were exempt from the irksome dues and tolls ordinarily demanded by the feudal lords en route. All this was arranged for by the lord of the province where the fair was being held. What happened if a group of merchants were attacked by a band of robbers on the road? Then the merchants of the particular province where the robbery had taken place were themselves barred from the fairs. This was, of course, a terrible punishment, since it meant that the commerce for that locality was stopped.

But why should the lord of the town where the fair was held go to all the trouble of making these special arrangements? Simply because the fair brought wealth to his domain and to him personally. The merchants who did business at the fairs paid him for the privilege. There was a tax for entry and for departure, and for warehousing the goods; there was a sales tax and a booth tax. The merchants did not object to these payments, because they were well-known, fixed, and not very heavy.

The fairs were so big that the ordinary guards of the town were not sufficient; they had their own fair police, special guards, and courts. When a dispute arose it was handled by fair policemen and settled in fair courts. Everything was carefully and efficiently organized.

The program of the fairs was usually the same. After a few days of preparation in which goods were unpacked, the various booths set up, payments made, and all the other odds and ends taken care of, the great fair opened. While dozens of entertainers tried to amuse the people who were moving about from booth to booth, the sales went on. Though goods of every nature were sold all the time, certain days were set aside for trading in special classes of goods such as cloth and leather and skins.

From a document dated 1429 concerning the fair at Lille, we learn about another important feature of these great trading centres: ". . . to the said Jehan de Lanstais we have of our especial grace granted and accorded . . . that at any place in the said market in our said town of Lille or wherever money-changing has been carried on, he may set up, occupy, and employ a counter and exchange money . . . for as long as it shall please us . . . in return for which he shall pay us each year through our receiver at Lille the sum of twenty livres parisian."

These money-changers were so important a part of the fair that just as there were special days devoted to the sale of cloth and leather, so the closing days of the fair were set aside for dealings in money. The fairs were thus important not only because of trade but also because of the financial transactions conducted there. At the centre of the fair in the money changers' court, the many varieties of coins were weighed, valued and exchanged; loans were negotiated, old debts paid, letters of credit honoured, and bills of exchange circulated freely. Here were the bankers of the period carrying on financial dealings of tremendous scope. By joining together they had command of vast resources. Their operations covered business stretching across an entire continent from London to the Levant. Among their clients were popes and emperors, kings and princes, republics and cities. Of such great consequence had dealing in money become that it was a separate profession.

This fact is important because it shows how the development of trade brought with it a change from the old natural economy in which economic life went on practically without the use of money. There were disadvantages in the barter of the early Middle Ages. It sounds simple to have exchanged your five gallons of wine for an overcoat, but actually it wasn't that easy. You had to seek out a person who had what you wanted and wanted what you had. Introduce money, however, as a medium of exchange, and what happens? Money is acceptable to everybody, no matter what they actually need, because it can be exchanged against anything. When money is widely used, you don't have to carry your five gallons of wine around until you happen to strike some one who wants wine and has an overcoat to exchange for it. No, all you need do is to sell your wine for money, then with that money buy an overcoat. Though the single exchange transaction has now become a double transaction through the introduction of money, nevertheless, time and energy are saved. Thus the use of money makes the exchange of goods easier and so trade is stimulated. The growth of trade, in turn, reacts on the extent of the money transactions. After the twelfth century the economy of no markets was changed to an economy of many markets; and with the growth of commerce, the natural economy of the self-sufficing manor of the early Middle Ages, was changed to the money economy of a world of expanding trade.

III

Going to Town

As THE irregular trickle of trade became a broad stream, every small shoot of commercial, agricultural, and industrial life received nourishment and flourished. One of the most important effects of the increase in trade was the growth of towns.

Of course, there had been towns of a sort before this increase in trade, the military and judicial centres of the country, where the king's courts were held and there was a good deal of coming to and fro. They were really rural towns, with no special privileges or town government to distinguish them. But the new towns which grew up with the growth of trade, or those old towns which took on a new life under its stimulus, acquired a different character.

If towns grow in places where commerce is expanding rapidly, in the Middle Ages you would look for growing towns in Italy and the Netherlands. That's precisely where they were first to be found. As trade continued to expand, more towns grew up in those places where two roads came together, or at the mouth of a river, or where the slope of the land was suitable. Such were the places that merchants would seek out. In such places, moreover, there was usually a cathedral, or a fortified place called a "burg" which would afford protection in time of trouble. Wandering merchants resting between their long journeys, or waiting for a frozen river to thaw

out, or a muddy road to become passable again, would naturally
stop near the walls of the enclosed fortress, or in the shadow of the
cathedral. As more and more merchants congregated at these places,
a "faubourg," or "outside burg," was created. It wasn't long before
the faubourg became more important than the old burg itself. Soon
the merchants in the faubourg, desiring protection, built around
their town protecting walls, which probably looked like the pali-
sades of the American Colonists. Then the older walls became unnecessary and fell to pieces. The older burg did not expand outward,
but was absorbed by the newer faubourg where things were happening. People began to leave their old manorial villages to begin life
anew in these active growing towns. Expanding trade meant work
for more people and they came to town to get it.

Now understand we don't *know* that any of the above is true.
It's simply the guess of certain historians, particularly Mr. Henri
Pirenne, whose collection of clues to prove that that was the way
cities in the Middle Ages grew up is as fascinating as any detective
story. One of his more obvious proofs that the merchant and city
dweller were one and the same is the fact that down to the beginning of the twelfth century the word "mercator," meaning merchant, and "burgensis," meaning one who lives in the town, were
used interchangeably.

Now if you recall the set-up of feudal society, you will see that
the expansion of trade leading to the growth of towns inhabited
largely by a rising merchant class, was sure to lead to conflict. The
whole atmosphere of feudalism was one of confinement, whereas
the whole atmosphere of merchant activity in the town was one of
freedom. Town land belonged to feudal lords, bishops, nobles, kings.
These feudal lords at first looked upon their town land in no different light from that in which they looked on their other land.
They expected to collect dues, enjoy monopolies, impose taxes and
labour services, and run the courts of justice, as they did on their
manorial estates. But this could not happen in the towns. All these
forms were feudal, based on the ownership of the soil. And all

these forms had to be changed as far as the towns were concerned. Feudal regulations and feudal justice were fixed by custom and difficult to alter. But trade by its very nature is active, changing, and impatient of barriers. It could not fit into the rigid feudal frame. Town life was different from life on the manor and new forms had to be created.

At least the merchants thought so. And thinking, with these enterprising traders, was soon translated into action. They had learned the lesson that in union there is strength. When they travelled on the roads they joined together to protect themselves against brigands, when they travelled on the sea they joined together to protect themselves against pirates; when they traded at markets and fairs they joined together to make a better bargain with their increased resources. Now, faced with feudal restrictions that cramped their style, they again joined together into associations called "gilds," or "hanses," to win for their towns the freedom necessary to their continued expansion. Where they got what they wanted without fighting, they were content; where they had to fight to get what they wanted, they fought.

Exactly what did they want? What were the demands of these merchants in these growing towns? Where did their changing world run head on into the older feudal world?

The townspeople wanted their freedom. They wanted to come and go as they pleased. An old German proverb, true all over western Europe, *Stadtluft macht frei* ("Town air makes a man free"), proves that they got what they wanted. So true was this proverb that many town charters of the twelfth and thirteenth centuries contained a clause similar to this one, granted to the town of Lorris by King Louis VII in 1155: "Any one who shall dwell a year and a day in the parish of Lorris, without any claim having pursued him there, and without having refused to lay his case before us or our provost, shall abide there freely and without molestation." If Lorris and the other towns had had our twentieth-century roadside advertising technique, they might have posted signs like this:

The townspeople wanted more than their own freedom. They wanted freedom of the land. The feudal custom of "holding" the land from So-and-so, who in turn "held" it from So-and-so, was not to their liking. The townsman regarded land and the houses on it in a different light from what the feudal landowner did. The townsman might suddenly need some ready cash in a business enterprise, and he liked to think that he could mortgage or sell his property in order to get it, without asking permission from a series of overlords. That same charter of Lorris dealt with this in so many words: "Any burgher who wishes to sell his property shall have the privilege of doing so." You have only to remember the land system described in the first chapter to realize what a change trade and towns had brought about.

The townspeople wanted to judge themselves in their own courts. They objected to the slow manorial courts which had been designed to deal with a static community, and were totally unfitted to handle the new problems that arose in a lively trading town. What, for example, did a lord of a manor know about mortgages, or a letter of credit, or business law in general? Precisely nothing. And anyway, if he did understand these things it was a cinch that he would use his knowledge and position to his own advantage, not that of the townsmen. The townspeople wanted to set up their own courts equipped to handle their own problems in their own interests. They wanted, also, to make their own criminal law. Keeping the peace in the small manorial village was not to be compared with the problem of keeping the peace in the growing town with its greater wealth and its shifting population. The townspeople knew the problem as the overlord did not. They wanted their own "city peace."

The townspeople wanted to tax themselves in their own way and have done with it. They objected to the multiplicity of feudal dues, payments, aids, and fines, which were irritating, and in their changing world had only a nuisance value. They wanted to do business and so they strove to abolish tolls of any kind that hampered them. If they failed to abolish the tolls entirely, they did succeed in modifying them one way or another so they would be less objectionable.

Control over the towns was usually not given all at once, but bit by bit. At first the lord would sell some of his rights in the town to the townsmen, then later sell some more, and so on, until finally the town became practically independent of him. This is apparently what happened in the German town of Dortmund. In 1241 the Count of Dortmund sold to the citizens some of his feudal rights in the town:

"I, Conrad, Count of Dortmund, and my wife, Giseltrude, and all our legitimate heirs sell . . . to the burgesses and city of Dortmund our house situated next to the market place . . . which we leave to them completely in perpetuity, together with the rights which we have held from the Holy Roman Empire in the slaughter-houses and in the cobblers' benches . . . and in the bakehouse and in the house which is above the courthouse, for the price of 2 denarii for the slaughter-house, and also 2 denarii for the cobblers' benches, and for the bakehouse and the building above the courthouse one pound of pepper, to be given to us annually."

Eighty years later another Count Conrad sold for an annual rent "to the council and citizens of Dortmund, to their exclusive lordship, half of the county of Dortmund," which included the courts, tolls, dues and revenues, and everything within the walls, with the exception of the count's own house, his personal bondmen, and the Chapel of Saint Martin.

You might suppose that the feudal bishops and lords would have seen that social changes of great import were taking place. You might suppose that some of them would have realized that they could not stand in the way of these historical forces. Some of them did, but many did not. There were some who were smart enough to sense what was happening, made the best of it, and came off well in the end. But it didn't always work out peacefully in a give-and-take manner. It seems to be true throughout history that those who are in power, those who are well off, will use any means to keep what they have. A dog will fight for his bone. And in many cases the feudal lords and bishops (particularly the bishops) dug their teeth into their bones and wouldn't let go until they were forced to do so by the violence of the townspeople. With some it wasn't only a matter of hanging on to their ancient privileges solely because of the benefits they received. Again, as often happens in history, many of those people who were well off with things as they were, honestly thought that unless things stayed as they were the whole social order would be smashed. And since the townspeople did not believe that, many towns gained their freedom only after violence had broken out. This seems to prove the truth of Justice Oliver Wendell Holmes' statement that, "when differences are sufficiently far-reaching, we try to kill the other man rather than let him have his way."

As a matter of fact, the fighting townspeople led by the organized merchant gilds, were not revolutionists in our sense of the word. They were not fighting to overthrow their overlords, but merely to get them to ease up on some of the outworn feudal practices that were a definite hindrance to expanding trade. They would not have written, as did the American revolutionists, that "all men are created free and equal." Not at all. "Personal liberty itself was not claimed as a natural right. It was sought only for the advantages it conferred. This is so true that at Arras, for example, the merchants tried to have themselves classed as serfs of the Monastery of St. Vast in order to enjoy the exemption from the market tolls which had been accorded to the latter."

The towns wanted freedom from interference with their expansion, and after a few centuries they got what they wanted. The degree of freedom varied considerably, so it is just as difficult to give a comprehensive picture of the rights and liberties and organization of the medieval town, as of the manor. There were completely independent cities, like the city republics of Italy and Flanders; there were free communes with varying degrees of independence; and there were towns which just barely managed to wrest a few privileges from their feudal overlords, but in some measure remained under their control. But whatever the rights of the town, its inhabitants made certain to have in their possession the charter confirming them. This would help to prevent disputes if ever the overlord or his agents happened to forget about those rights. Here is the beginning of a charter given by the Count of Ponthieu to the town of Abbeville in 1184. In the very first line the count himself states one reason why the townspeople prized their charters so much and kept them carefully under lock and key—sometimes even inscribing them in letters of gold on the wall of their city hall or church. "Since what is put down in writing remains more easily in the memory of man, I, Jean, Count of Ponthieu, make known to all present and to come that my grandfather Count Guillaume Talvas, having sold to the burgesses of Abbeville the right to have a commune, and the burgesses not having an authentic copy of this sale, have granted to them . . . the right to have a commune and to maintain it in perpetuity. . . ."

One hundred and eighty-six years later, in 1370, the citizens of Abbeville appear to have a new overlord, the king of France himself. Evidently the movement for town freedom had been progressing rapidly in the intervening years, because the king, in an order to his officers, goes quite far in his promises: "We have given and granted them certain privileges, by which it appears, inter alia [among other things], that never for whatsoever reason or occasion it may be, shall we place, assert, fine or impose, nor shall we cause or suffer to be placed, asserted or fixed, imposed on our said town of Abbeville, nor on the other towns of the county of Ponthieu, any impositions, aids, or other subsidies of any kind, if it is not to the profit of the said towns and at their request . . . for which reason we, considering the true love and obedience shewn us by the said petitioners, command you and all of you and straitly enjoin that you shall allow all the burgesses, inhabitants of the said town to trade, to sell and to buy, to bring and to take through all the towns, countries and limits of the said county, salt and all other merchandise of any kind, without compelling them to pay to us and our men or officers any salt tax, claims, exactions, impositions, or subsidies. . . ."

This exemption from taxation which the king of France granted them in the document above, was only one of the privileges the merchants fought for. In the struggle for town freedom the merchants took the leadership. They were the most powerful group in the towns and they won for their gilds or hanses all kinds of privileges. Merchant gilds often exercised a monopoly over the wholesale commerce of the towns. If you weren't a member of the merchant gild you were out of luck when it came to trading. In 1280, for example, in the town of Newcastle in England, a man named Richard complained to the king that ten fleeces of wool belonging tc him had been seized by several merchants. He wanted his wool back. The king summoned the several merchants and asked them why they had taken Richard's wool. They said in their defence that King Henry III had granted them "that the burgesses of the said town might have a Gild Merchant in the said borough with all liberties and free customs belonging to such a Gild. . . . Being asked what liberties they claim to have pertaining to the aforesaid Gild, they say that no one, unless he should be of the liberty of the Gild, can cut cloth to sell in the town, nor cut up meat and fish, nor buy fresh leather, nor purchase wool by the fleece. . . ." Richard evidently was not a member of the gild which had the exclusive right to trade in woollen fleece.

In Southampton, it seems, non-members might buy goods—but the merchant gild had first chance, "and no simple inhabitant nor stranger shall bargain for nor buy any kind of merchandise coming to the town before burgesses of the Gild Merchant, so long as a Gildsman is present and wishes to bargain for or buy it; and if anyone does and is found guilty, that which he buys shall be forfeited to the King."

Just as the gilds tried to keep local non-members' fingers out of their pie, so they were equally successful in keeping foreign merchants from butting in on their trading province. Their whole object was to have complete control of the market. Whatever goods went in or out of the town were to pass through their hands. Competition from outsiders was to be eliminated. Prices of goods were to be determined by the gilds. At every stage of the game they were to play the leading rôle. Control of the market was to be their exclusive monopoly.

It is obvious that in order to exert such power, in order to obtain this monopoly of trade in the various towns, the merchant gilds had to be "in" with the authorities. They were. Since they were the most important people in the town, the merchants had a great deal to say about who would be officials in the town. In some places the officials were under their influence; in other places, they themselves became the officials; and in some few places the law expressly stipulated that only members of the gild could take office in the town government. This was rare, but that it did happen is proven by the regulations of the town of Preston in England, drawn up in 1328: ". . . . all manner of burgesses the which is made burgesses by court roll and out of the Gild Merchant, shall never be Mayor, nor Bale, nor Sergeant, but only the burgesses the which the name be in the Gild Merchant last made before; for the King gives the freedom to the burgesses which are in the Gild and to none other."

The merchant gilds which were so eager to obtain monopolistic privileges, and were so watchful of their rights, kept their own members in line by a whole series of regulations that each one had to obey. If you were a member of the gild you had certain advantages, but you could remain a member only by carefully abiding by the rules of the association. These rules were many and strict. For breaking them you could be kicked out of the gild entirely or punished in other ways. One method, particularly interesting to us,

is that employed by a gild in Chester, England, over three hundred
years ago. In 1614 the Company of Mercers and Ironmongers of
Chester, finding that T. Aldersley had violated their rules, ordered
him to shut up his shop. He refused. "So day by day two others
[of their company] walked all day before the said shop and did
forbid and inhibit all that came to the said shop for buying any
wares there, and stopped such as came to buy wares there."

It's a safe guess that Mr. Aldersley could not stop this picketing
by getting an injunction against it in twentieth-century style, because the gild was too powerful. As a matter of fact, the gilds
were powerful not only in their own particular locality, but also far
afield. They accomplished this by their old familiar method of joining together. The famous Hanseatic League of Germany is the outstanding example of a union of separate hanses into a powerful
organization. It had trading-posts, which were fortresses as well as
warehouses, stretching from Holland to Russia. So powerful was
this league, which at the height of its power included over one hundred towns, that it practically monopolized the trade of northern
Europe with the rest of the world. It was a state in itself in that it
made commercial treaties, protected its merchant fleet with its own
warships, cleared the northern seas of pirates, and had its own governmental assemblies which made its own laws.

The rights which merchants and towns won reflect the growing
importance of trade as a source of wealth. And the position of the
merchants in the town reflects the growing importance of money
wealth as opposed to landed wealth.

In the early feudal period, land alone was the measure of a man's
wealth. After the expansion of trade a new kind of wealth made
its appearance—money wealth. In the early feudal period money
had been inactive, fixed, motionless; now it had become active,
live, fluid. In the early feudal period the prayers and the fighters
who owned the land were at one end of the social scale, living on
the labour of the serfs who were at the other end of the social
scale. Now a new group had made its appearance—the middle

class, living in a new way, by buying and selling. In the feudal period the possession of the land, the only source of wealth, brought with it the power to govern for the clergy and the nobility. Now the possession of money, a new source of wealth, brought with it a share in government for the rising middle class.

IV

New Ideas for Old

MOST business today is done with borrowed money on which interest is paid. If the United States Steel Company should want to buy up another steel concern that has been competing with it, it would probably borrow the money. It could do so by issuing bonds which are simply promises to pay back, with interest, whatever sum of money the bond-buyer lends. When the owner of the candy store on your corner wants to buy new and expensive fixtures for his store, he goes to the bank to borrow the money. The bank lends him the money and charges him interest for it. The farmer who wants to buy the piece of land adjoining his property may take a mortgage on his farm in order to raise the money. A mortgage is simply a loan to the farmer on which he pays an annual interest. We are so accustomed to this payment of interest for money that is loaned, that we tend to think it is a "natural" thing that has existed always.

But it hasn't. There was a time when it was considered a grave offence to charge interest for the use of your money. In the early Middle Ages there was a power which forbade the lending of money at interest. A power whose word was law all over Christendom.

That power was the Church. To lend money at interest, said the Church, was usury, and usury was SIN. That's in capital letters because that is the way any pronouncement by the Church was regarded in those days. And a pronouncement which threatened damnation to those who violated it was particularly important. In feudal times, the hold of the Church on the minds of people was much greater than it is today. But it wasn't only the Church that frowned on usury. Town governments and later state governments passed laws against it. A "Bill against usurie" passed in England read, "But Forasmuch as usury is by the word of God utterly prohibited, as a vice most odious and detestable . . . which thing by no godly teachings and persuasions can sink in to the hearts of divers greedy, uncharitable and covetous persons of this Realm . . . be it enacted . . . that . . . no person or persons of what Estate, degree, quality or condition so ever he or they be, by any corrupt, colourable or deceitful conveyance, sleight or engine, or by any way or mean, shall lend, give, set out, deliver or forbear any sum or sums of money . . . to or for any manner of usury, increase, lucre, gain or interest to be had, received or hoped for, over and above the sum or sums so lent . . . upon pain of forfeiture . . . of the sum or sums so lent . . . as also of the usury . . . and also upon pain of imprisonment." This law was a reflection of what most people in the Middle Ages felt about usury. They agreed that it was bad. But why? How had this attitude toward the taking of interest grown up? We must look back to relationships in feudal society for the answer.

In that society where trading was small, and the chance of investing money at a profit practically non-existent, if a man wanted a loan, it was certain that he wanted it not to enrich himself, but because he had to have it to live. He was borrowing simply because some misfortune had overtaken him. Perhaps his cow had died, or a drought had ruined his crops. He was in a bad fix and needed help. It was the medieval notion that in such circumstances the person who helped him was not to make a profit out of his misfortune. The good Christian helped his neighbour without thought of profit. If you loaned some one a sack of flour, you expected to get back a sack of flour and no more. If you took back more than the sack of flour you loaned, it was felt that you were cheating the other fellow—which wasn't fair. It was right to get only what was coming to you, no more and no less.

The Church taught that there was a right and wrong in *all* man's activities. The standard of right and wrong for man's religious activities was no different from the standard for his social activities or, more important still, from the standard for his economic activities. The Church rules for right and wrong went for all of these in the same way.

Nowadays a person might do something to a stranger in a business deal which he would not do to a friend or neighbour. We have different standards for business from what we have for our other activities. Thus a manufacturer will do everything in his power to squeeze out his competitor. He will undersell, engage in a trade war, get special rebates for his concern, try every way possible to force his rivals into a tight corner. These activities will ruin the other fellow. The manufacturer knows that, but goes ahead nevertheless, because "business is business." Yet this same person would not for a minute allow a friend or neighbour to starve. This having one standard for economic actions and another for non-economic actions was contrary to Church teaching in the Middle Ages. And what the Church taught was, in general, what most people believed.

The Church taught that if what was good for a man's pocketbook was bad for his soul, his spiritual welfare came first. "What shall it profit a man if he gain the whole world and lose his own soul?" If you got more than was your just due in any transaction you did so at the expense of some one else and that was wrong. St. Thomas Aquinas, the greatest of the religious thinkers of the Middle Ages, condemned the "lust for gain." While it was grudgingly admitted that trading was useful, traders were denied the right to get more out of a transaction than would pay them for their labour.

Churchmen of the Middle Ages would have strongly denounced the middleman, who some centuries later had become, according to Disraeli's definition, "a man who bamboozles one party and plun-

ders another." The modern notion that any business deal is legitimate so long as you can get away with it, was not part of medieval
thinking. The successful business man of today who buys for as
little and sells for as much as he can, would have been damned
twice over in the Middle Ages. For performing a necessary public
service a trader was entitled to a fair reward—but nothing beyond
that.

Nor was it considered ethical to accumulate more money than
you needed to support yourself. The Bible was clear on this point,
"It is easier for a camel to go through the eye of a needle than for
a rich man to enter into the Kingdom of Heaven."

A writer of the time put it this way: "He who has enough to
satisfy his wants, and nevertheless ceaselessly labours to acquire
riches, either in order to obtain a higher social position, or that
subsequently he may have enough to live without labour, or that
his sons may become men of wealth and importance—all such are
incited by a damnable avarice, sensuality, or pride."

People who were accustomed to the standards of a natural economy simply applied those standards to the changing money economy
in which they found themselves. Thus if you loaned a man £100,
it was argued that all you had a moral right to take back was
£100. If you charged interest for the use of your money you were
selling time which was not yours to sell. Time belonged to God
and you had no right to sell it.

Furthermore, to lend your money and receive back not only the
principal, but also a fixed interest payment, would mean that you
could live without working—which was wrong. (It was the medieval notion that prayers and fighters were "working" at the jobs
for which they were fitted.) To answer that your money was working for you would only have angered Churchmen. They would have
replied that money was barren, it could not produce anything. To
take interest was definitely wrong—said the Church.

That's what it said. But what it *said* and what it *did* were two
different things. Though bishops and kings stormed and made laws
against the taking of interest, they were among the first to break

their own laws. They themselves raised and granted loans at interest —at the very moment when they were tracking down other usurers! The Jews, who in general were small money-lenders charging enormous rates of interest because their risks were great, were hated and hounded and everywhere despised as usurers; Italian bankers were great money-lenders doing a tremendous volume of business— and yet often, when the interest on their loans was not paid, it was the pope himself who collected it by threatening the debtors with spiritual punishment! But despite the fact that it was itself one of the biggest sinners, the Church continued to cry out against usurers.

You can readily see that the doctrine of the sinfulness of usury was going to cramp the style of the new merchant group that wanted to do business in commercially expanding Europe. It became a real handicap when money began to play a more and more important part in economic life.

The rising middle class did not keep its money in strong-boxes. (That habit belonged to the feudal period when there were few places to invest money.) This new merchant group could use all the money it could lay its hands on—and more. To support whatever business he was in, and to extend his field of operations so he could increase his profits, the merchant wanted more money. Where could he get it? He could go to the money-lenders, the Jews, as Antonio, the Merchant of Venice, went to Shylock, the Jew. Or he could go to the greater merchants—some of whom had left merchanting in goods to merchant in money—the great bankers of the period. But it wasn't easy. Standing in the way was this Church law forbidding money-lenders or bankers to lend money at interest.

What happened when Church doctrine, designed to fit an old economy, collided with the historical force represented by the rising merchant class? It was the doctrine that gave way. Not all at once, of course. Slowly, bit by bit, by new rulings which said as before, "Usury is a sin—*but,* under the circumstances . . ." and other rulings which said, "While it is a sin to exact usury, *nevertheless,* in special cases . . ."

The special cases which whittled away the usury doctrine are illuminating. If banker B loaned money to merchant M, it was wrong for him to charge interest for the loan. That had been the Church's position. But, said the Church, since merchant M was going to use the money he borrowed from banker B in a trading venture in which all the money might be lost, then it was only fair that M return to B not only what he had borrowed, but an extra bit as well—to pay B for the risk he had taken.

Or since, if banker B had kept the money, he could have used it himself to make a profit, therefore it was only fair for him to ask merchant M to return an extra bit to pay him for not using the money himself.

In these and in other ways the bothersome usury doctrine was modified to meet changing conditions. It is significant that Charles Dumoulin, a French lawyer writing in the sixteenth century, advances "everyday commercial practice" as part of a plea for the legalization of "moderate and acceptable usury." Here is his argument: "Everyday commercial practice shows that the utility of the use of a considerable sum of money is not slight . . . nor does it avail to say that money by itself does not fructify: for even fields do not fructify by themselves, without expense, labour, and the industry of men; money, likewise, even when it has to be returned after a time, yields meanwhile a considerable product through the industry of man. . . . And sometimes it deprives the creditor of as much as it brings to the debtor. . . . Therefore, all . . . hating, condemning, and punishing of usury should be understood as applying to excessive and unreasonable, not to moderate and acceptable, usury."

And so, gradually, the Church usury doctrine went out, and "everyday commercial practice" came in. Beliefs, laws, ways of living together, personal relationships—all were modified as society entered a new stage of development.

V

The Peasant Bursts His Bonds

ONE of the most important changes came in the position of the peasant. So long as feudal society remained static, with the relationship between master and serf fixed by tradition, it was practically impossible for the peasant to improve his condition. He was trussed up in an economic straitjacket. But the growth of trade, the introduction of a money economy, and the rise of cities brought to him the means of cutting the bonds which held him so closely tied.

When towns arise in which the inhabitants give all or most of their time to trade and industry, they have to get the major part of their food supplies from the country. Thus there is a division of labour between town and country. One concentrates on making industrial products and trading, and the other concentrates on producing more agricultural goods to supply the growing market represented by those who no longer produce their own foodstuffs. Throughout history the extension of the market has always been a tremendous incentive to the increase in production. But how can agricultural production be increased? There are two ways. One is through intensive development, which means getting more out of your old land through wider use of manures, better methods of ploughing, harder and more scientific work in general. The other is through extensive development, which means simply opening up new areas which have not been farmed before. Both methods were employed at this time.

Just as the pioneers in our own country, looking about for a way of bettering their position, cast their eyes on the virgin lands to the west, so the ambitious peasantry in twelfth-century western Europe looked to the unreclaimed land all about them as a means of escaping oppression. A German writer at the end of the century told about this: "The poor and the peasants are oppressed by the avarice and rapine of the powerful and are dragged off for unjust trials. This scourge of sin forces many to sell their patrimony and to migrate to distant lands."

But in our country the pioneers had open for settlement practically an entire continent. Where could this oppressed peasantry in twelfth-century Europe find land? It is a startling but true fact that at this time only about one-half the land of France, one-third the land of Germany, and one-fifth the land of England were under cultivation. The rest was forest, swamp, and waste. All round the edge of the small cultivated region was this larger uncultivated area open for colonization. Twelfth-century Europe had its beckoning frontier just as seventeenth-century America had. And the challenge of waste, swamp, and forest was accepted by a hard-working peasantry, "lured on by the bait of freedom and property . . . thousands of pioneers . . . came to prepare the way for the work of plough and hoe, by burning away brushwood, thickets, and parasitic vegetation, clearing forests with the axe, and uprooting trunks with the pick." Thus Europe had its "westward movement" five centuries before we had ours. When American pioneers cracked their axes against the trees of our West in the seventeenth to nineteenth centuries, the sounds they heard were echoes of those their ancestors in Europe had heard five hundred years before in similar circumstances. Just as the American pioneers transformed a wilderness into a country of farms, so the European pioneers drained the swamps, built dykes against the theft of land by the sea, cleared the forests, and turned the lands thus reclaimed into fields of growing grain. For the pioneers of the twelfth century, as for those of the seventeenth, the struggle was long and hard, but victory meant freedom and a chance to own, or at least partly own, a piece of land for themselves, exempt from the payment of the annoying labour services they had always known. No wonder many of the peasants seized the opportunity. No wonder they "earnestly begged" for the grant of lands, as the Bishop of Hamburg, in a charter given in 1106 informs us:

"1. We wish to make known to all the agreement which certain people living this side of the Rhine, who are called Hollanders, have made with us.

"2. These men came to us and earnestly begged us to grant them certain lands in our bishopric, which are uncultivated, swampy, and useless to our people. We have consulted our subjects about this and, considering that this would be profitable to us and to our successors, have granted their request.

"3. The agreement was made that they should pay us every year one denarius for every hide of land. . . . We also grant them the streams which flow through this land.

"4. They agreed to give the tithe according to our decree. That is, every eleventh sheaf of grain, every tenth lamb, every tenth pig, every tenth goat, every tenth goose, and a tenth of the honey and of the flax. . . .

"5. They promised to obey me in all ecclesiastical matters. . . .

"6. They agreed to pay every year two marks for every 100 hides for the privilege of holding their own courts for the settlement of all their differences about secular matters. . . ."

The Bishop of Hamburg made this agreement with the Hollanders because he saw that it "would be profitable to us and to our successors." Other lords of the land, both Church and lay, also saw that, having their unproductive land converted into productive land by pioneers, who then paid an annual rent for the privilege of farming it, was indeed profitable. Many of them did not sit back and wait until willing workers came and "earnestly begged" for grants of land, but rather set about to make it known far and wide that their land was to be leased to any and all who would clear it— and pay rent for it. Some more enterprising lords were very successful at this business of renting what had formerly been waste land; some succeeded in establishing whole villages on their virgin soil—at a profit. This growing movement of colonization brought thousands and thousands of acres of unused land under cultivation. So by 1350 in Silesia there were 1,500 new settlements farmed by 150,000 to 200,000 colonists. This extensive development was important. And of equal importance was the fact that serfs could now find land which was *free*, land which carried not the objectionable labour services, but a money rental. This new type of freedom was sure to spread until it affected the serfs on the old manors. It did.

For years the peasant had accepted his unhappy lot. Born into a system with the social divisions clearly marked, taught to believe that his was the kingdom of Heaven only if he performed satisfactorily and willingly his allotted task in a society consisting of prayers, fighters, and workers, he did his job without question. With the chance to rise above his station practically non-existent, there was small incentive for him to do more than what was required to exist. He performed his routine jobs according to custom. There was no particular point in his experimenting with seeds or with new ways of producing crops, because there was a limited market for what he had to sell, and anyway it was quite likely that the lord would claim the lion's share of the increase.

But now all that was changed. The market had grown so that any crops beyond what he needed and the lord took could be sold. In return he could get money. He was not yet entirely at home in the use of money but was getting more and more familiar with it, and he did know that there had come into existence a new class of people, the merchants, who did not fit into the old scheme of things. But they were prospering, and their city near by was a wonderful place where serfs like himself had occasionally wandered and done well. Now in this changing world there was a real chance for people like him. Now if he worked harder than ever before, grew more crops than he needed himself, he might collect a little store of money with which—perhaps—he could buy off some of his labour services to his lord. If his lord would not lighten his burdens, then he, too, would be off to the city or to the uncultivated area, where serfs like himself were clearing the forest, and receiving as payment bits of land exempt from bothersome dues.

But the lord was quite willing to commute his serf's labour services for money. He, too, had become familiar with money and what it could do in this changing world. He was in great need of money to pay for those beautiful cloths from the East that he had bought at the fair just a few months ago. Also there was that old bill he still owed the armourer for that handsome coat of mail he had bought for his latest warring expedition. The lord had a great many uses for any money his serf could scrape together. He was quite willing to agree that henceforward John Jones, his serf, was to pay fourpence per acre rent per year, instead of working two or three days a week as before. The lord really had no choice, because if he didn't lighten his serfs' burdens it was quite possible that some of them would run away, which meant he'd be left without money or labour, and then he would be in the soup. No, it was better to let the serf pay a rent instead of giving labour services as of old.

Besides, it had long since become plain to the lord that free labour was more productive than unfree labour; he had learned that a peasant called off his own piece of land to farm the lord's strip was an unwilling worker who would not give his best. It was better to get rid of the traditional labour services and hire the help he needed, to work for wages.

So it was that in the records of many villages throughout western Europe in the thirteenth and fourteenth centuries an increasing number of items like this one from Stevenage, in England, began to appear: "It is conceded by the lord that S. G. should have and should hold the aforementioned land by paying 13 solidi 4 denarii instead of all services and customs."

Other records of the same period show that large numbers of serfs, in addition to buying the freedom of their land from the obligation of labour services, also bought their personal freedom. The following quotation from the court rolls of Woolston refers to a villein, who "in order to be able to leave his domain and be considered a free man pays a fine of 10 solidi."

But you mustn't suppose that *all* the lords saw that it was wise to grant the serfs their freedom, any more than *all* the lords were wise enough to give up their feudal exactions over the growing towns. No, there are always in every period of history some people who cannot or will not understand that what has been, won't be any longer; some people who in the face of necessary change hang on tighter than ever before to what once was. So there were some lords who would not give liberty to their serfs.

You might expect that the Church would be the leader in a movement to free the serfs. On the contrary. The chief opponent of emancipation in both town and country was not the nobility, but the Church. At a time when most of the lords had come to realize that it was better for their own pocketbooks to give the serf his liberty and hire free labourers for cash wages by the day, the Church still held out against emancipation. The Statutes of the Cluniac, a religious Order, are an example of the length to which this attitude was carried: "[We excommunicate] those who, holding sway over serfs or bondmen, bondwomen or women of [servile] condition pertaining to the monasteries of our Order, grant to such persons letters and privileges of manumission and freedom."

That was in 1320. One hundred and thirty-eight years later, in 1458, the Cluniac still order that "those Abbots, Priors, Deans and other administrators of the Order, who have serfs and bondmen . . . must swear expressly that they will not manumit such serfs or their possessions." And two famous English historians after searching the records carefully, arrive at this conclusion: ". . . there is plenty of evidence that of all landlords the religious houses were the most severe—not the most oppressive, but the most tenacious of their rights; they were bent on the maintenance of pure villein tenure and personal villeinage. The immortal but soulless corporation with her wealth of accurate records would yield no inch, would enfranchise no serf, would enfranchise no tenement. In practice the secular lord was more humane, because he was more human, because he was careless, because he wanted ready money, because he would die . . . we find that it is against them [the religious] that the peasants make their loudest complaints."

The peasants did not stop with merely making loud complaints. Occasionally they marched on church property, threw stones at the windows, burnt down the doors, and beat up the monks. Often they were aided in their fight by the burgesses (bourgeoisie) of the towns, who themselves were usually at strife with the overlords, whether Church or lay.

Freedom was in the air and the peasants stopped at nothing to gain it. Where it was not granted willingly they tried to take it by force. In vain did obstinate overlords and the Church fight against emancipation. The pressure of economic forces was too great to resist. Freedom had to come in the end.

The Black Death was a great factor in bringing that freedom. We who live in civilized countries where medicine has made such tremendous advances, and hygiene is preached and practised, know nothing of such plagues as swept across whole continents in the Middle Ages. The nearest we come to it is an occasional epidemic of scarlet fever or influenza which horrifies us if the number of deaths reaches the hundreds. But the Black Death killed off more than twice as many people in fourteenth-century Europe as did the World War, our four years of organized slaughter with the twentieth century's most ingenious death-dealing devices. A few years after it happened, Boccaccio, a famous Italian writer, described it in this fashion: "In the year . . . of our Lord 1348, there happened at Florence, the finest city in all Italy, a most terrible plague; which, whether owing to the influence of the planets, or that it was sent from God as a just punishment for our sins, had broken out some years before in the Levant, and after passing from place to place, and making incredible havoc all the way, had now reached the west. There, spite of all the means that art and human foresight could suggest, such as keeping the city clear from filth, the exclusion of all suspected persons, and the publication of copious instructions for the preservation of health; and notwithstanding manifold humble supplications offered to God in processions and otherwise;

it began to show itself in the spring of the aforesaid year, in a sad and wonderful manner. . . . To the cure of this malady, neither medical knowledge nor the power of drugs was any effect . . . whichever was the reason, few escaped; but nearly all died the third day from the first appearance of the symptoms. . . . What gave the more virulence to this plague was that, by being communicated from the sick to the hale, it spread daily, like fire when it comes in contact with large masses of combustibles. . . . Such, I say, was the quality of the pestilential matter, as to pass not only from man to man, but what is more strange . . . anything belonging to the infected, if touched by any other creature, would certainly infect, and even kill that creature in a short space of time. One instance of this kind I took particular notice of: the rags of a poor man just dead had been thrown into the street; two hogs came up, and after rooting amongst the rags and shaking them about in their mouths, in less than an hour they both turned round and died on the spot."

That hog story may or may not be true, but there is no doubt that people were everywhere dying like flies. Florence, the city Boccaccio mentions, lost 100,000; London lost about 200 a day and Paris 800; in France, England, the Low Countries, and Germany, between one-third and one-half of the entire population were wiped out! Though the pestilence went through all the European countries from 1348 to 1350, to some it returned again and again in the following decades, attacking those people who were fortunate enough to escape before. So vast was the slaughter that this unusual note of despair crept into the writing of an Irish monk of the time: "In order that what I have written shall not perish together with the writer, and this work shall not be destroyed . . . I leave my parchment to be continued, *in the event that some one of Adam's race may survive the death* and wish to continue the work I have begun."

What would be the effect of a plague that killed so many people that there was some doubt in the mind of a learned man of the time whether anyone would be left alive? What effect did the plague have on the position of the peasant in western Europe?

With so many people dead, it was obvious that a greater value would be put on the services of those who remained alive. Labourers could ask and receive more for their labour than ever before. The land still remained untouched by the scourge—but it was of value only in relation to its productivity, and the essential factor in making it productive was labour. As the supply of labour diminished, the relative demand for it increased. The peasant's work was worth more than ever before—and he knew it.

The lord also knew it. Those lords who had refused to commute the labour services of their serfs were now more than ever determined to keep things as they were. Those lords who had commuted their serfs' labour services and had taken rents in money in exchange, now found that the wages of day labourers had risen, so these money rents would buy less labour. The price of hired labour shot up fifty per cent more than it had been before the Black Death. This meant that a lord whose money rents had enabled him to pay thirty hired labourers could now pay only twenty. In vain were proclamations issued putting a penalty on landlords who paid more, or ploughmen, shepherds, or swineherds who demanded more than the wages customary before the Black Death. The march of economic forces could not be blocked by governmental laws of that period.

A clash had to come between the lords of the land and the workers on the land. These workers had tested the advantages of freedom and it had given them an appetite for more. In the past, hatred born of grinding oppression had given rise to violent serf outbreaks. But these were brief local flare-ups—easily smothered in spite of their fury. The Peasant Revolts of the fourteenth century were different. The shortage of labour had put the agricultural workers in a strong position and had given them a sense of their power. In a series of uprisings all over western Europe, the peasants used that power in an attempt to gain by force what concessions they could not win—or keep—any other way.

Historians disagree about the causes of the Peasant Revolts. One school says that the landlords wanted to force the peasants to go back to the labour services of the past; another school says that the landlords refused to grant commutation in this period when the peasant sensed his power and struck out for it. Probably both are right. At any rate, we know from the documents that there were violent acts performed by both sides; burning of records and of property; murders of peasants and of their oppressors; and "legal" killings of the revolutionary peasants who were unfortunate enough to be caught. Such a peasant was Adam Clymme, according to the Assize Roll of Ely in England:

"Pleas in the Isles of Ely before the justices appointed in the county of Cambridge to punish and chastise insurgents and their misdeeds, on Thursday next before the feast of St. Margaret the Virgin [July 20] 5 Richard II.

"Adam Clymme was taken as an insurgent traitorously against his allegiance and because . . . he traitorously with others made insurrection at Ely, feloniously broke and entered the close of Thomas Somenour and there took and carried away divers rolls, estreats of the green wax of the lord the King and the Bishop of Ely . . . and forthwith caused them to be burnt there to the prejudice of the crown of the lord the King.

"Further that the same Adam on Sunday and Monday next following caused to be proclaimed there that no man of law or other officer in the execution of duty should escape without beheading.

"Further that the same Adam the day and year aforesaid at the time of the insurrection was always wandering armed with arms displayed, bearing a standard, to assemble insurgents, commanding that no man of whatsoever condition he were, free or bond, should obey his lord to do any services or customs, under pain of beheading. . . . And so he traitorously took upon him royal power. And he came, brought by the sheriff, and was charged. . . . And he says that he is not guilty of the premises imputed to him or of any of the premises, . . . And forthwith a jury is made thereon for the lord the King by twelve [good and lawful men] etc.; who being chosen hereto, tried and sworn, say on their oath that the aforesaid Adam is guilty of all the articles. By the discretion of the justices the same Adam is drawn and hanged, etc. And it was found that the same Adam has in the town aforesaid chattels to the value of 32s., which Ralph atte Wyk, escheator of the lord the King, seized forthwith and made further execution for the lord the King, etc."

Adam Clymme was hanged. Thousands of other peasants were hanged also. The Peasant Revolts were put down. But try as they might, the feudal overlords could not reverse the process of agrarian development. The old feudal organization was broken up by the pressure of economic forces that could not be withstood. By the middle of the fifteenth century over the greater part of western Europe money rents had been substituted for labour dues, and, in addition, many peasants had won complete emancipation. (In the more remote areas, away from the highways of trade and the liberating influence of the cities, serfdom remained.) The agricultural labourer was now more than just a workhorse. He could begin to hold his head up with an air of dignity.

Transactions which had been uncommon to feudal society became the order of the day. Where formerly land was granted or acquired only on the understanding of mutual service, now there arose a new conception of landed property. Large numbers of peasants were free to move about, and to sell or bequeath their land, although they had to make a certain payment for doing so. The Stevenage Court Rolls for 1385 record that a villein who "held a messuage and half a virgate of land for the length of his life, and paying for all other services due, 10 solidi, came into the court and disposed of and conceded the aforementioned land [to another] for the length of his life and he gives the lord a fee of 6 denarii for registering this on the court rolls."

The fact that land was thus bought, sold, and exchanged freely like any commodity spelled the end of the old feudal world. Forces making for change had swept over western Europe and given it a new face.

VI

"And No Stranger Shall Work . . ."

INDUSTRY, too, was changed. Whatever industry existed formerly had been carried on in the peasant's own house. Did his family need furniture? Then there was no calling in the carpenter to make it or no purchasing it at the furniture store on Main Street. Not at all. The peasant's own family chopped and cut and carved until it had whatever furniture it needed. Did the members of the family need clothing? Then the members of the family spun, and wove, and stitched, and sewed—their own. Industry was carried on in the home, and the purpose of production was simply to satisfy the needs of the household. Among the lord's domestic serfs there were some who did only this sort of work while the others farmed. In the ecclesiastical houses, also, there were some craftsmen who specialized in one craft and so became quite skilled at their jobs of weaving or working in wood or iron. But this, too, was not commercial industry supplying a market—it was simply serving the requirements of the household. The market had to grow before craftsmen as such could exist in their separate professions.

The rise of towns and the use of money gave craftsmen a chance to give up farming and make a living by their craft. The butcher, the baker, and the candlestick-maker then went to town and set up shop. They went into the business of butchering, baking, and candlestick-making not to satisfy only the needs of their own household, but to meet the demands of others. They were in business to supply a small but growing market.

Not much capital was required. A room of the house in which he lived would serve the craftsman as a workshop. All he needed was skill in his craft and customers to buy what he made. If he was a good workman and became well known among the townsmen so his wares were in demand, then he could increase his output by taking on a helper or two.

There were two kinds of helpers, apprentices and journeymen. Apprentices were youngsters who lived and worked with the master craftsman, and learned the trade. The length of apprenticeship varied according to the trade. It might be as little as one year or as many as twelve. The usual length of time spent as apprentice was from two to seven years. Becoming an apprentice was a serious affair. It meant an agreement on the part of the child and his parents with the master craftsman, that in return for a small fee (in food or money) and the promise to be hardworking and obedient, the apprentice was to be taught the secrets of the trade and be lodged and boarded with the master for the term of the agreement.

After he had served his term as learner the apprentice, if he passed his examination and had the means, might set up shop as a master himself. If he lacked sufficient funds to start his own business, then he became a journeyman and continued to work for the same master for wages, or else tried to get employment with another master. By hard work and careful saving of his wages, he was often able after a few years to open his own shop. In those days not much capital was required to set up a business and start production. The typical industrial unit of the Middle Ages was this small workshop in which the master was a small-scale employer working side by side with his helpers. And not only did this master craftsman produce the wares he had to sell, but usually he sold them himself as well. In one wall of the workshop there might be a window, looking out on the town street, in which the goods were displayed for sale and actually sold over the counter.

It is important to understand this new stage in industrial organization. Where formerly goods were made not to be sold commercially, but merely to supply the needs of the household, now goods were made to be sold in an outside market. They were made by professional craftsmen who owned both the raw material and the tools with which they worked, and sold the finished product. (Today workers in industry own neither the raw material nor the tools. They sell not the finished product, but their labour-power.)

These craftsmen followed the example set by the merchants before them, and formed gilds of their own. All the workers engaged in the same craft in a particular town formed an association called a craft gild. Nowadays when a politician or industrialist makes a speech about the "partnership of Capital and Labour" the old experienced worker in his audience is apt to shrug his shoulders and say, "T'aint so." He won't believe it. He has learned that there is a wide gap between the man who pays and the man who is paid. He knows that their interests are not the same and that all the talk in the world about their being partners won't change the situation any. It is for this reason that he is suspicious of company unions. He doesn't want, if he can help it, to be a member of a labour organization, in which his employer has too big a finger in the pie.

But the craft gilds of the Middle Ages were different. Everyone doing the same work—apprentices, journeymen, and master craftsmen—belonged to the same gild. Both masters and helpers could belong to the same organization and fight for the same things. This was possible because the distance between worker and boss was not too great. The journeyman lived with the master, ate the same food, was educated in the same way, believed the same things, and had the same ideas. It was the rule, not the exception, for apprentice or journeyman to become a master on his own. So long as this was true, the employer and the employee could be members of the same gild. Later, when abuses crept in and it was no longer true, then we find the journeyman forming gilds exclusively their own. But in the early stages of gild organizations, the harness-makers' gild included all harness-makers, the sword-polishers' gild included all sword-polishers, etc. Every apprentice had the same rights as every other apprentice, every journeyman the same as every other journeyman, and every master craftsman the same as every other master craftsman. There were ranks in the craft gilds, but within these ranks there was equality. And the steps up the ladder from lowly apprentice to master craftsman were not out of reach for many of the workers.

Did you ever hear of a tawyer? It's an out-of-date word now, probably because it pertains to an out-of-date profession. It means a person who dresses white leather. In the fourteenth century in London, this was a big business and a gild of tawyers had been organized. From that gild's ordinances, dated 1346, we can learn a few things about craft gilds:

"[1] . . . if by chance any one of the said trade shall fall into poverty whether thru old age, or because he cannot labour or work . . . he shall have every week . . . 7d. for his support if he be a man of good repute.

"[2] And that no stranger shall work in the said trade . . . if he be not an apprentice, or a man admitted to the franchise of the said city.

"[3] And that no one shall take the serving-man of another to work with him, during his term, unless it be with the permission of his master. And if any one of the said trade shall have work in his house that he cannot complete . . . those of the said trade shall aid him, that so the said work be not lost.

"[4] And if any serving-man shall conduct himself in any other manner than properly towards his master, and act rebelliously towards him, no one of the said trade shall set him to work, until he shall have made amends before the Mayor and Aldermen.

"[5] Also, that the good folks of the same trade shall once in the year . . . choose two men . . . to be overseers of work and all other things touching the trade for that year, which persons shall be presented to the Mayor and Aldermen . . . and sworn before them diligently to enquire and make search, and loyally to present to the said Mayor and Aldermen such defaults as they shall find touching the said trade without sparing any one for friendship or for hatred.

"Also, that all skins falsely and deceitfully wrought shall be forfeited.

"[6] Also that no one who has not been an apprentice and has not finished his term of apprenticeship in the said trade shall be made free of the same trade."

It is from the study of thousands of such documents that historians are able to reconstruct, hundreds of years later, the story of the craft gilds.

Rule number 1 shows that the gilds had the welfare of their members in mind. They were a kind of friendly brotherhood that took care of down-and-out members. Many gilds probably started for just that reason so that gildsmen could help one another in time of trouble. Incidentally, it is an interesting fact that unemployment insurance and old-age pensions so much in the news today were provided by craft gilds for their members almost six hundred years ago!

Rule number 3 is further proof of the fact that gilds were regulated so that the spirit of friendship, not of competition between gildsmen, was to exist. Look particularly at this provision that other tawyers were to aid a fellow tawyer who was behind in an order, so he should not lose the business. Evidently, the trade interests of the members of the gild was one of their major considerations.

Gildsmen were obviously banded together to keep the direct control of their industry in their own hands. Read rule number 2 again. It is important because it shows that the craft gilds, like the merchant gilds before them, wanted and obtained a monopoly of all their type of work in the town. In order to practise any trade in the town, you had to be a member of the craft gild. Nobody outside the gild was allowed to exercise that trade without permission from the gild. Even the beggars in Basle and Frankfort had their gilds which didn't allow beggars from the outside to beg in the towns except on two days a year! The gilds tolerated no interference with their monopoly. It was to their advantage to have it, and they fought to maintain it. Even the Church, powerful as it was, had to conform to gild regulations. In 1498 the heads of the Church of St. Johann in a German town wanted to have bread made of the wheat and rye that grew in their fields. They had to have the approval of the bakers' gild. Permission was graciously granted them—for a consideration. "The masters of the bakers' gild and all the gild members . . . have permitted with good intent that the deacons and canons . . . may take and keep a baker out of the gild so that he can bake the bread for them out of their barley, wheat, and rye . . . [and because the gild brothers will now no longer sell bread to the church, which is a loss to them, the church has] . . . handed over 16 marks."

The gildsmen fought to keep the monopoly of their craft in their town. And they would not allow outsiders to intrude on their town market. When you read in medieval history books about the fierce wars carried on between one city and another, remember that they were often fought simply because gildsmen would not stand for competition from outsiders.

Nowadays an inventor of a new or better method of making things can have his idea patented and no one else may use it. But in the Middle Ages there were no patent laws, and gildsmen, anxious to maintain their monopoly, would, of course, be quite concerned about concealing their trade secrets from others. Yet how could they prevent these secrets from becoming known? How could they prevent others from learning the tricks of their trade? A Venetian law of 1454 gives us a clue to at least one method: "If a workman carry into another country any art or craft to the detriment of the Republic, he will be ordered to return; if he disobeys, his nearest relatives will be imprisoned, in order that the solidarity of the family may persuade him to return; if he persists in his disobedience, secret measures will be taken to have him killed wherever he may be."

While the gilds made certain that outsiders were not to encroach on their monopoly, they were equally careful that among them-selves there must be no unfair practices that would lead to one member hurting the business of another. No cut-throat methods among friends is what the first sentence of the tawyers' rule 3 really comes to. A gildsman couldn't entice a journeyman or apprentice away from his master. Also taboo was the business practice fairly common today, of treating a customer or bribing him one way or another to get his business. In 1443 the bakers' gild of Corbie, France, ruled that "nobody shall give drinks or extend any other courtesy in order to sell his bread, on pain of paying a fine of 60 sols."

Read rules 5 and 6 again. They make it clear that in return for their monopoly, the gilds gave good service—they were concerned about the quality of their members' work. By enforcing the rule that every gildsman must have served his apprenticeship they were making certain that he knew his trade; then by carefully supervising his work they were insuring the customer against the purchase of inferior goods. The gild prided itself on its good name, and with every sale of a craftsman's goods went the official guarantee of the gild that the product was up to standard. The gilds had a thousand and one rules and regulations for the prevention of bad work and for the maintenance of a high quality standard, and violations of these rules brought severe penalties. The regulations made by the armourers of London in 1322, read: "And if there shall be found in any house . . . armour on sale of any kind whatsoever, which is not of proper quality . . . such armour shall be immediately taken and brought before the Mayor and Aldermen, and by them adjudged upon as being good or bad, at their discretion."

Gild supervisors made regular tours of inspection in which they examined the weights and measures used by members, the kinds of raw materials, and the character of the finished product. Every article was carefully scrutinized and stamped. This strict supervision of the quality of the product was deemed necessary by gildsmen so the gild's honour would not be soiled and its business spoiled as a result. The town authorities, too, demanded it as a protection for the public. For the further protection of the public some gilds stamped their products with their "just price."

To understand what was meant by the "just price" of an article you must recall the medieval notion concerning the doctrine of usury, and how much more the idea of right and wrong entered economic thought at that time than it does today. In the barter of the old natural economy, trading was carried on not to make a profit, but to benefit both buyer and seller. Neither party in an exchange of goods was expected to benefit more than the other. My overcoat was exchanged for your five gallons of wine evenly, because the cost of the wool and the days of labour I had spent on it were equal to the cost of your grapes and the time you had spent. Now when money was introduced there were still to be only these factors involved. The craftsman knew what his material and labour cost him, and they were to determine the price of the finished product which he sold. The goods the craftsman made and sold had their just price, honestly arrived at on the basis of actual cost, and they were to be sold for exactly that sum of money and not a penny more. St. Thomas Aquinas was emphatic on this point: "Now what has been instituted for the common advantage [i.e., trading] ought not to be more burdensome to the one than to the other. . . . Hence, whether the price exceeds the value of a thing, or conversely, the equality required by justice is lacking. Consequently, to sell dearer or to buy cheaper than a thing is worth is in itself unjust and unlawful."

What happened to the chiselers who tried to sell goods for more than their just price? What could medieval citizens do to protect themselves against the get-rich-quick trader? One case tells us much: "So when the price of bread rises, or when the London fruiterers, persuaded by one bold spirit that they are 'all poor . . . on account of their own simplicity, and if they would act on his advice they would be rich and powerful,' form a combine, to the great loss and hardship of the people, burgesses and peasants do not console themselves with the larger hope that the laws of supply and demand may bring them down again. Strong in the approval of all good Christians, they stand the miller in the pillory, and reason with the fruiterers in the court of the mayor. And the parish priest delivers a sermon on the Sixth Commandment, choosing as his text the words of the Book of Proverbs: 'Give me neither riches nor poverty, but enough for my sustenance.'"

That these protesting citizens brought the grasping fruiterers to the mayor's court proves that it wasn't left to the good conscience of the gildsmen alone to see that the just price was observed. In spite of the fact that the Church condemned the lust for gain, the "bold spirit" who promised to enrich the fruiterers was not one, but many. Traders were not wholly trusted. It is significant that the German word for "exchange"—"*tauschen*"—has the same root as the word for "deceive"—"*täuschen.*" So it became the general custom of the time for the town authorities to have it as one of their major duties to see that goods were not sold at unfair prices. The bailiff of Carlisle, for example, when taking office, had to swear the following oath: "Ye shall see that all manner of victuals coming to this market be good and wholesome and sold at a reasonable price." Where any gild used its monopoly of its own goods, not to maintain the just price but to make excess profits, then the town authorities had the right to abolish the privileges of that gild.

The idea of a just price for goods was a natural one before trade became extensive or towns large. The growth of the market, however, and the consequent large-scale production, brought a change in economic ideas, and just price gave way to market price. Remember how economic forces changed ideas about usury? So it was with the idea of the just price. It too was swept away by new economic forces.

In the early medieval period the market was a local one, catering to the townsmen and the immediate surrounding countryside. It was quite unaffected by happenings in distant parts of the country or in far-off towns, and therefore prices were determined by local conditions alone. But even in this local market conditions did change, and prices changed with them. If there had been a disease attacking the vines in the neighbourhood, there would be much less wine that year than usual, perhaps not enough to go round. In that case the wine would be sold to those people willing and able to pay the higher price for it, necessitated by the shortage. This was, of course, quite different from a rise in price due to the fact that some group in an effort to make extra profits, cornered the supply and raised the price. There was a difference between a rise in price due to unforeseen and uncontrollable conditions, and a rise in price due to the greed of some trader. It was generally understood that prices would go up in times of famine, but this was looked on as "unnatural" and due entirely to abnormal conditions. It didn't interfere with the just price which was a "natural" price, and it did not justify excess profits. It was legitimate for the peasant in a year of bad harvest to get more for his grain than in a good year, because he had fewer sacks of grain to sell. The idea of the just price fitted the economy of the small, local, stable market.

But it did not fit the economy of the large, outside, unstable market. The change in economic conditions brought a change in economic ideas. When the market came to consist not only of buyers and sellers of goods made in the town, and of produce from the immediate neighbourhood; when traders from outside, and goods from distant places, and buyers and sellers from a wider area brought new influences into the market, the stability of local conditions was shaken. This happened at the fairs where regulations as to just price were not in force. As trade extended, the conditions affecting the market were much more variable and just price was no longer practical. It gave way in the end to market price. But although this was actually going on, it took people a long time to realize it and a still longer time to admit it. Ideas and customs have a way of lingering on long after the conditions out of which they grew have disappeared. When people used to be carried round in sedan chairs, porters' suits were made with special straps to support the frame of the chair. But even when the last sedan chair had vanished from the streets, such suits continued to be made. The straps had come to be thought of as a necessary part of the porter's equipment, and the tailors went on making them even when their usefulness had entirely disappeared.

That's how it is with ideas, and that's how it was with the idea of just price. That idea had grown up in the old stable conditions, when everything that affected price originated in and was well known to the local community, and the idea persisted even when various distant and unknown influences penetrated the local market. In time, of course, the new conditions brought a new attitude. This new attitude is reflected in the writing of Jehan Buridan, rector of the University of Paris in the fourteenth century: "The value of a thing should not be measured by its intrinsic worth . . . it is necessary to take into account the needs of man, and to value things according to their relation to this need."

Buridan was here talking supply and demand. He argued that goods have no fixed value irrespective of conditions. So just price was thrown overboard and market price was substituted.

Just as change came in the conception of price, so change came in the set-up of the gilds. In fact, history is a record of change. So it is that this chapter begins with a description of how the gild system worked and it ends with the story of how that system fell to pieces.

Two fundamental characteristics of the gild system had been the equality between masters, and the ease with which workers could become masters. In general this prevailed until the thirteenth and fourteenth centuries, the heyday of the gild system—after that, inevitable changes occurred.

The equality between masters became, in some gilds, a thing of the past. Certain masters prospered, took more power to themselves, began to look down on their less fortunate brothers, and ended by forming exclusive gilds of their own. "Greater" and "lesser" gilds made their appearance, and masters in the inferior gilds even worked as wage-earners for the ruling masters of the greater gilds! The gild merchant of the earlier days, which, you remember, had had a monopoly of the trade of the town, had been supplanted by the craft gilds, each of which traded in its own goods. But in some cases the gild merchant gave up trading in general, dealt in one particular article, and instead of dying, now flourished as a great merchant gild. In other cases, the wealthy members of the craft gild gave up producing, and concentrated on trade, becoming exclusive corporations which shut out the working artisans, such as the twelve livery companies of London, the six Corps de Métier in Paris, and the Arti Maggiori in Florence. They were the select, powerful, richer gilds—and they ruled the roost. Where formerly the officers of a gild might be any of the masters, rich or poor, now discrimination set in. "Thus among the old-clothes dealers of Florence no one who cried his goods in the streets, and among the bakers no one who carried bread from house to house on his back or on his head could be elected rector."

From control of their own gilds to exclusive control of the municipal government was a short step and the members of the greater gilds took it. They became the real rulers of the town and almost everywhere the wealthiest and most influential were more or less identified with the town council. On the land the aristocracy of birth formed the ruling class; in the towns the aristocracy of money reigned supreme. "In the fifteenth century in Dordrecht and everywhere in the towns of Holland the municipal government became a pure money aristocracy and family oligarchy . . . power in the city lay with the so-called Rijkheit and Vroedschap, wealth and wisdom, just as if the two were always joined together, a corporation consisting of a small, fixed number of members, who had the right to nominate city officials, elect the mayor and through these means control the administration of the town."

And what was true "everywhere in the towns of Holland" was also true in Germany. In Lübeck "merchants and wealthy burgesses alone ruled the town . . . the Council controlled legislation, the highest court of justice, and the taxation of the townsmen; it ruled the town with unlimited powers."

Another cause of the breakdown of the gild system was the widening of the gap between masters and journeymen. Apprentice-journeymen-master had been the rule. Now it became apprentice-journeyman, and there it stopped. It became increasingly difficult to rise from worker to boss. As more and more people flocked to the town, the old masters hastened to preserve their monopoly by making the steps upward harder to climb—except for a privileged few. The masters' test was made more strict, and the amount you had to pay on becoming a master was raised—except for a privileged few. For the rank and file, the obligations were increased, making it more difficult to become masters; for the privileged few, favors were granted, making it easier to become masters. So in the town of Amiens the statutes of the painters' and sculptors' gild for the year 1400 required that an ordinary apprentice had to be apprenticed three years, present his *chef d'œuvre* and pay 25 livres, but "if the sons of masters wish to begin and carry on their craft in the said town, they may do so if they are experienced, and shall pay only the sum of 10 livres." This closing of the ranks was carried to its ultimate conclusion in the Statutes of the napery weavers of Paris which read that "no one may be master weaver except the son of a master."

How did the journeymen feel when they saw their chances of improving their position by becoming masters fade away? Naturally they resented it. It became increasingly clear to them that their rights and interests were opposed to those of the masters. What could they do about it? They formed their own journeymen's unions. "They attempted to secure a monopoly of work, just as the masters attempted to secure the monopoly of this or that manufacture. Thus amongst the nail-makers of Paris it was forbidden to hire a compagnon [journeyman] from elsewhere as long as one belonging to the district was left in the market . . . the working bakers of Toulouse, the working shoemakers of Paris, set up their brotherhoods in opposition to the corresponding societies of masters. . . ."

These journeymen's unions, like the trade unions today, tried to get higher wages for their members. And like the trade unions today, they were opposed in this effort by the masters. The masters complained to the town authorities, who obligingly declared the journeymen's unions illegal. This happened in London in 1396 according to an old document which tells of a dispute between the master saddlers and their journeymen: "and that under a certain feigned colour of sanctity, many of the serving-men in the trade had influenced the journeymen among them [they'd be called "Reds" today] and had formed covins [associations] thereon, with the object of raising their wages greatly in excess . . . it was determined [by the Mayor and Alderman] that the serving-men in the trade aforesaid should in future be under the governance and rule of the masters of such trade; the same as the serving-men in other trades in the same city are wont, and of right are bound to be; and that in future they should have no fraternity, meeting, or covins, or other unlawful things under a penalty," etc.

In France the same thing happened. In 1541, the Consuls, Aldermen, and inhabitants of Lyon complained to Francis I that "in the last three years certain serving-men, bad living journeymen printers, have . . . made mutinous the greater part of the other journeymen, and have banded themselves together to compel the master printers to pay them higher wages and give them richer food than they have ever had by the ancient customs . . . as a result of which the said art of printing today has entirely ceased in the said town of Lyon. . . ." The enraged petitioners not only complained, but suggested a remedy, which Francis graciously made law. It provided that "the said journeymen and apprentices of the estate of printing shall make no oath, monopolies, nor have among themselves any captain, lieutenant . . . nor any banner or badge, nor shall they assemble outside the houses and kitchens of their masters, nor anywhere to a greater number than five, unless with the consent and authority of the court, on pain of being imprisoned, banished, and punished as monopolists. . . .

"The said journeymen must finish any work begun, and shall not leave it incomplete, and shall not go on strike."

As you would expect, the dispute about higher wages was particularly fierce immediately following the Black Death. With labour so much in demand, wages were bound to shoot upwards. And just as laws had been passed in the villages to keep wages down to what they had been before the Plague, so similar laws with the same purpose were passed in the towns. In England, the Ordinance of Labourers in 1349 provided that "no man shall pay or promise to pay to any man more wages, liveries, hire, or salaries than is accustomed . . . nor shall any man in any wise demand or receive the same, under penalty of the double of that which shall be so paid . . . saddlers, skinners, tawyers, shoemakers, tailors, smiths, carpenters, masons, tilers, boatmen, carters, and other artificers and workmen whosoever shall not take for their labour and craft more than used to be paid."

And in France a similar law was passed in 1351: "Those who picked grapes in years gone by must take care of the vines and shall have and take for this work one-third more than they were given before the Plague, and not more, even if greater sums had been promised them. . . . And whoever shall give them more for a day's labour than is here set down, and whoever shall take more . . . the receiver and the giver shall each pay sixty sols . . . and if they have not with which to pay the fine in money, they shall be imprisoned for four days on bread and water. . . ." Notice that while the law in this case was seemingly fair, it was certain that the prison sentence following the non-payment of the fine was more apt to be meted out to the moneyless worker than to the master. Notice too that throwing men into prison was not going to relieve the shortage of labour.

These regulations were not successful. Masters paid more and workers demanded and received more. Though workmen's associations were dissolved and their members fined or imprisoned, other associations sprang up and strikes for better wages and conditions continued. The journeymen, in fact, were better off than many other workmen who were not allowed to join these unions; workmen who had no rights at all in any gild and who were at the mercy of the richer industrialists for whom they worked under miserable conditions and at starvation wages. These people lived in wretched unsanitary hovels; they owned neither the raw materials on which they worked nor the tools with which they worked; they were the forerunners of the modern proletariat, owning nothing but their labour and dependent for their living on an employer and favourable market conditions. The cities, then, had both extremes, the down-and-outs (the city of Florence in its great days is said to have had over 20,000 beggars) and at the top, the very wealthy living in true luxury.

In the fight for the freedom of the towns from their feudal overlords, all the townsmen rich and poor, merchants, masters, and workers, had joined forces. But the fruits of victory went to the upper classes. The lower classes found that they had simply changed masters; where formerly government was in the hands of a feudal overlord, now it was in the hands of the richest burgesses. The discontent of the poor allied with the resentment and jealousy of the small crafts toward these powerful rulers gave rise to a series of uprisings in the latter half of the fourteenth century, which, like the Peasant Revolts, swept over Western Europe. It was a class struggle—the poor vs. the rich, the unprivileged vs. the privileged. In some places the poor won the fight, and for a few brief years had possession of a town and introduced some much-needed reforms before they were overthrown; in other places, though victory was theirs, quarrels among themselves led to their immediate downfall; in most places, victory from the beginning went to the rich—though not before they had spent some anxious moments in genuine fear of the might of the combined oppressed classes.

After this period of disorder the gilds entered their declining years. The power of the free towns was weakened. Once again they were controlled from without—this time by a stronger duke or prince or king than any they had known before—one who was welding together the unorganized sections into a national state.

VII

Here Comes the King!

IF A book like this had been written in the tenth or eleventh century it would have been a lot easier for the author. Much of the material here set down is based on a study of the writings of long ago. These writings are often in a foreign language—either Latin, old or modern French, or old or modern German. But the history-writer of the early Middle Ages, thumbing through the documents of the past, would have found them all written in the language he knew best—Latin. It would have made no difference if he lived in London or Paris or Hamburg or Amsterdam or Rome. Latin was the universal language of all the scholars. Children in the schools of the period did not study English, French, German, Dutch, or Italian. They studied Latin. People talked English, French, German, etc., but these languages were not written until later. The Spanish monk reading his Bible in Spain, read the same Latin words as did the monk in an English monastery.

If you went to a university of the period you would find there students from all over western Europe talking and studying together without any difficulty. Universities were truly international institutions.

Religion, too, was universal. Everybody who called himself a Christian was born into the Catholic Church. There was no other. And whether you wanted to or not, you paid taxes to that Church, and you were subject to its rules and regulations. Church services in Southampton were very much the same as they were in Genoa. There were no state boundary lines to religion.

Many people today think that babies are born with an instinct of national patriotism. Of course this is not true. National patriotism comes largely from constant reading and hearing about the great deeds performed by national heroes. The children in the tenth century did not find in their schoolbooks any pictures of the ships of their country sinking those of an enemy country. For a very good reason. There were no countries as we know them today.

Industry, you will recall from the preceding chapter, left the household and moved into the town. It was local, not national. To the gildsman of Chester, England, London goods which might interfere with his monopoly were just as "foreign" as those coming from Paris. The merchant in wholesale goods felt that the whole world was his province—he tried just as hard to get a foothold in one part of the world as in another.

But by the end of the Middle Ages, along about the fifteenth century, all this is changed. Nations come into being; national divisions become marked; national literatures spring up; national rules for industry take the place of local regulations; national laws, national tongues, even national churches come into existence. People begin to think of themselves not as citizens of Madrid, or of Kent, or of Burgundy, but of Spain or of England or of France. They feel that they owe allegiance not to this city or that feudal lord, but to their king, who is the monarch of a whole nation.

How did this rise of the national state come about? There were many reasons—political, social, religious, economic. Whole books have been written about this interesting subject. We have space for only a few of the causes—primarily the economic.

The rise of the middle classes is the important development of this period from the tenth to the fifteenth century. Changes in ways of living fostered the growth of this new class, and the coming of that class brought further changes in society's ways of living. Old institutions which had served a purpose in the old order now decayed and died; new institutions arose to take their place. This is a law of history.

It's the man with a lot of money who worries the most about whether there are enough policemen on his block. The people who use the highways to send their goods or money to other places are the ones who shout the loudest about keeping those highways free of robbers and toll gates. Confusion and insecurity are bad for business. The middle class wanted order and security.

To whom could they turn? Who in the feudal set-up could guarantee order and security? Protection in the past had come from the nobility, the feudal overlords. But it was against the exactions of these very overlords that the towns had fought. It was the feudal armies that pillaged and destroyed and stole. The soldiers of the nobles, not receiving regular pay for being soldiers, sacked every town and stole everything they could lay their hands on. The strife between warring overlords frequently meant disaster to the local population, no matter which side won. It was the presence of different overlords in different places along the highways of business that made trade so difficult. What was needed was a central authority, a national state. A supreme power that would be able to bring order out of feudal chaos. The old overlords could no longer fulfil their social function. Their day was done. The time was ripe for a strong central power.

In the Middle Ages the authority of the king existed in theory, but in fact it was weak. The greater feudal barons were practically independent. Their power had to be broken and it was.

The steps by which a central authority became able to exercise national power were slow and irregular. It was not like a staircase with one step on top of another leading steadily in a definite direction; it was a rough road with many backslidings. It did not take one year, or two years, or fifty years or a hundred years. It took centuries—but finally it came.

The lords had been growing weaker because they had lost a great deal of their possessions in land and in serfs. Their power had been challenged and partly broken by the towns. In some places in

their constant warfare among themselves they were obligingly ex-
terminating each other.

The king had been a strong ally of the towns in their fight against
the overlords. Whatever lessened the power of the barons strength-
ened his. In return for his help the townspeople were willing to
aid him with loans of money. This was important because with
money he could dispense with the military help of his vassals. He
could hire and pay for a trained army always at his service, not
dependent on the loyalty of a lord. It would be a better army, too,
because its only business would be to fight. Feudal troops had no
training, no regular organization which enabled them to work together smoothly. An army paid for fighting, well-trained and well-
disciplined, and always on hand when needed, was a great improvement.

Moreover, technical improvements in military weapons also called
for a new kind of army. Gunpowder and cannon were coming in
and effective use of these arms required trained cooperation. And
while a feudal warrior could bring his own armour, he couldn't
easily bring cannon and powder.

The king was thankful to the commercial and industrial groups
that made it possible for him to hire and pay for a permanent
soldiery well equipped with the latest weapons. Time and again the
king appealed to the rising class of money men for loans and gifts.
Here is an example from the fourteenth century when the king of
England asked help of the city of London: "Sir Robert de Asheby,
Clerk of our Lord the King, came to the Guildhall of London, and
on the King's behalf brought word to Andrew Aubri, the Mayor,
that he and all the aldermen in the City . . . were to appear before
our Lord the King and his Council. . . . And the King then orally
made mention of the expenses incurred by him in his war in the
parts beyond sea, and still to be incurred therein, and he requested
them to lend him £20,000 sterling. . . . They unanimously agreed
to lend him 5,000 marks; which sum they said they could not
exceed . . . whereupon, our Lord the King altogether rejected it,
and commanded the Mayor, aldermen, and commonalty, upon the

fealty and allegiance in which they were bound to him, to take better counsel as to the matters aforesaid . . . and although it was a hard thing, and difficult to do, they agreed to lend £5,000 to our Lord the King . . . which offer the King accepted . . . twelve persons were chosen and sworn to assess all men in the City aforesaid, and in the suburbs thereof, every one according to the requirement of his condition, for levying the said sum of £5,000 and lending the same to our Lord the King."

Don't think for a minute that the people with money enjoyed parting with it. They didn't. They made this and other loans to the kings because they received definite benefits in return. For example, it was a decided advantage to business to have laws, such as the following, passed by a central authority (1389): "It is ordained and accepted, That one Measure and one Weight be through all the Realm of England . . . and everyone that shall be convict that he hath or useth any other Measure or Weight shall have Imprisonment of Half a Year."

Besides, to be free from the marauding troops of a petty feudal baron was worth money to them. They were willing to pay for the support of an authority which freed them from the irritating demands and petty tyrannies of numerous feudal superiors. In the end it was economical to link up with a strong leader who in return could make and enforce laws like the following, passed in France in 1439:

"To obviate and remedy and put an end to the great excesses and pillagings done and committed by the armed bands, who have for long lived and are still living on the people. . . .

"The King prohibits all, on pain of being charged with lèse-Majesté . . . and deprived forever, he and his posterity, of all public honours and offices, and of the rights and prerogatives of the nobility, and the confiscation of his person and possessions, that no one of whatever estate he may be, may . . . raise, conduct, lead or receive a company of men at arms . . . without leave, licence, and consent and Ordonnance of the King. . . .

"On the same penalty, the king prohibits all Captains and men of war, that they shall not take merchants, workmen, cattle, nor horses, nor other beasts of burden, whether in the fields or in carriages, and shall not trouble them, nor the carriages, goods, and merchandise which they are carrying, and shall not hold them to ransom in any manner; but shall suffer them to labour, and to come and go, and carry their goods and merchandise in peace and safety, without asking anything of them, or hindering or disturbing them in any way."

Formerly the income of the sovereign had consisted of the revenues from his own domains. There was no national system of taxation. In 1439, in France, the king was able to introduce the *taille*, a regular money tax. In the past, you remember, the services of vassals had been secured by grants of land. Now with the growth of a money economy this was no longer necessary. Taxes could be raised in money, all over the kingdom, by officers of the king who were paid not in land, but in money. Salaried officeholders planted in every part of the country could carry on the work of governing for the king—a work which in feudal times had had to be done by the nobility, paid in land. This was important.

It was quite plain to the sovereigns that their power depended on their finances. It became increasingly plain, too, that money poured into their treasuries only as commerce and industry prospered. So the kings concerned themselves with the progress of trade and industry. It soon became obvious that those gild regulations designed to create and maintain a monopoly for a small group in each particular city, were fetters on expanding trade and industry.

To anyone thinking in terms of the nation as a whole the excessive and conflicting local regulations would have to be set aside, and the jealousy among towns ended. It was ridiculous, for example, that "it needed an ordinance of the Prince in 1443 to open the Frankfurt Leather Fair to the Berlin Shoemakers." With the increasing power of the national monarchy, the kings began to crack down on local monopolists, in the interest of the whole nation. One of the Statutes of the Realm for England in 1436 reads: "Whereas the Masters, Wardens and People of [the] Guilds, Fraternities, and other Companies incorporate . . . make themselves many unlawful and unreasonable Ordinances . . . whereof the Cognisance, Punishment and Correction all only pertaineth to the King. . . . The same our Lord the King, by the Advice and Assent of the Lords Spiritual and Temporal, and at the Prayer of the Commons aforesaid, hath ordained by Authority of the same Parliament, that the Masters, Wardens and People of every such Guild, Fraternity or Company incorporate . . . shall bring . . . all their Letters Patent and Charters to be registered of Record before the Justices of Peace . . . and moreover hath ordained and defended, by the Authority aforesaid, that from henceforth no such Masters, Wardens, nor People make nor use no Ordinance . . . if it be not first discussed and approved for good and reasonable . . . by the Justices of Peace."

And a much more far-reaching law passed by the king of France is real proof of the growing power of the monarch in that country: "Charles by the Grace of God King of France . . . after long deliberation of our Great Council . . . have ordained and ordain . . . that, in our said town of Paris, there shall from henceforth be no masters of métiers or communalties whatever. . . . But we wish and ordain that in every metier there shall be chosen by our said Provost . . . certain elders of the said metier . . . and from henceforth they are forbidden to hold any assembly as a craft fraternity or otherwise . . . unless it be with our consent, leave and licence . . . or the consent of our Provost . . . on pain of being treated as rebels, and disobedient to us and to our crown of France, and to lose person and possessions."

It was no small achievement to curb the monopolistic power of mighty cities. Where the cities had been strongest, in Germany, and Italy, it was not until centuries later that a central authority arose powerful enough to make them submit. This was one of the reasons why these mightiest and wealthiest communities of the Middle Ages were the last to attain that unification which was necessary to cope with changing economic conditions. In the other territories, though some cities resisted this check on their powers even to the point of fighting, jealousy and hatred kept them from combining against the national forces and—fortunately for them—they were beaten. In England, France, the Netherlands, Spain, the state replaced the city as the unit of economic life.

It was true that many towns and gilds tried hard to retain their exclusive privileges. In so far as they did so it was under the supervision of the royal authority. The national state came out on top because the advantages offered by a strong central government and by a wider field for economic activities were in the interests of the middle classes as a whole. The kings relied on the money they obtained from the bourgeoisie, and more and more they grew to depend on it for advice and help in running their growing kingdoms. Their justices, ministers, and civil servants in general came from this class. In fifteenth-century France, Jacques Cœur, a Lyons banker and one of the richest men of the time, became the king's counsellor; in Tudor England, Thomas Cromwell, a lawyer, and Thomas Gresham, a mercer, became ministers to the Crown. "A tacit pact is concluded between it [royalty] and the industrial bourgeoisie of entrepreneurs and employers. They placed at the service of the monarchical state their political and social influence, the resources of their intelligence, and their wealth. In return the state multiplied in their favour economic and social privileges. It subordinated to them . . . the common wage workers, held down to that position and bound to strict obedience."

It was a perfect example of "You scratch my back and I'll scratch yours."

One interesting sign of the times, in England, was the ousting of the Venetians, and the German merchants of the Hanseatic League, which had a "station" in London called the Steelyard. Foreigners had always controlled the import and export trade of the country. Their money-making trading privileges they had bought from successive kings. Now in the fifteenth and sixteenth centuries English merchants began to show their heads. The Merchant Adventurers particularly, was a live wide-awake company of men who wanted to crash into this profitable trade in the hands of foreigners. At first they couldn't make much headway, because the king wanted the money he received in return for the concessions, and because harsh measures might mean trouble with other powers. But the English Merchant Adventurers persisted, and in 1534 the Venetians lost their privileges, and six years later the Hanse complained to the king: "Albeit it hath been granted time out of mind to the merchants of Hanse, and the same grant . . . renewed and promised of your most excellent majesty, that no manner of exaction, pension, or undue payment should be set upon the persons, goods or wares of the said merchants . . . yet all this notwithstanding, in the Favour of the Fullers and Shearmen of London . . . it is ordained and now so used that no merchant of Hanse shall dare to lade or carry out of the Realm of England any cloths Raw and Unshorn under pain of loss of the same."

Since the Hanse bought English wool to be made up into cloth *in Flanders and Germany*, the growing English cloth-making industry came to the support of the English Merchant Adventurers. Together English cloth-makers and English Merchant Adventurers (with the aid of Gresham, mercer, happily placed in the position of minister to the Crown) won their point. The privileges of the German Hanse were gradually cut down, and in 1597, the Steelyard, London home of the once powerful Hanse, was finally closed.

The peasant who wanted to till his fields, the artisan who wanted to pursue his craft, and the merchant who wanted to engage in trade—peacefully—welcomed the formation of a strong central government that would be powerful enough to substitute one comprehensive regulation for dozens of local ones, unity for disunity. Out of the various causes making for *nation*-ality, there grew up a sentiment of nationality. This is well shown in the life, struggles, and death of Joan of Arc. In France the feudal lords were particularly strong, and during the Hundred Years' War with England, the most powerful, the Duke of Burgundy, allied with the English, and inflicted serious defeats on the French king. Joan, who wanted Burgundy to be part of France, wrote to the duke, "Jeanne the Maid desires you . . . to make a long, good, and assured peace with the King of France . . . in all humility, I pray, implore, and beseech you to make war no more on the holy kingdom of France."

It was in this matter of inspiring the French army with heart and confidence, with a belief in the sentiment of being *Frenchmen*, with making the king's cause the cause of *all* Frenchmen, that Joan rendered her service, inciting many to be as fanatical in the cause of France as she was. A soldier in the service of a feudal lord who heard Joan make such statements as "I never see French blood spilt but my hair rises for horror" was apt to look beyond his overlord and think of his allegiance to France, My Country. So localism was supplanted by nationalism, and the era of a powerful sovereign at the head of a united kingdom began.

Bernard Shaw in *Saint Joan*, his excellent play about The Maid, has an important passage on the effects of this rising spirit of nationalism. An English churchman and an English feudal lord are discussing the military ability of a French lord:

"*The Chaplain:* He is only a Frenchman, my lord.

"*The Nobleman:* A Frenchman! Where did you pick up that expression? Are these Burgundians and Bretons and Picards and Gascons beginning to call themselves Frenchmen, just as our fellows are beginning to call themselves Englishmen? They actually talk of France and England as their countries. Theirs, if you please! What is to become of me and you if that way of thinking comes into fashion?

"*The Chaplain:* Why, my lord? Can it hurt us?

"*The Nobleman:* Men cannot serve two masters. If this cant of serving their country once takes hold of them, good-bye to the authority of their feudal lords, and good-bye to the authority of the Church."

This far-seeing noble was of course correct. The one powerful rival left to the sovereigns was the Church and it was inevitable that the two should clash. In the minds of the national monarchs there was no room for two heads of a state. And the power assumed by the pope made him much more dangerous than any of the feudal lords. Pope and king quarrelled again and again. There was, for example, the question of who should have the right to appoint bishops and abbots whenever a vacancy occurred. It was of great importance because these jobs paid well—the money, of course, coming from the great mass of people who paid taxes to the Church. It was a lot of money and both king and pope wanted their own followers to get it. Kings naturally looked with greedy eyes on these money-making jobs—they disputed the right of the popes to make these appointments.

The Church was tremendously wealthy. It has been estimated that it owned between one-third to one-half of all the land—yet it refused to pay taxes to the national government. The kings needed money, they felt that Church wealth, already enormous and ever on the increase, ought to be taxed to help pay the cost of running the state.

Another reason for the quarrel was the fact that certain cases were tried in Church courts, not in the regular courts. Oftentimes a Church-court decision was contrary to the decision of the king's court. Equally important was whether State or Church would get the money collected in fines and bribes.

Then, too, there was the difficulty caused by the right assumed by the pope, that he could interfere even in the internal national affairs of a country. The Church was thus a political rival of the sovereign.

Here, then, was a super-national power, dividing the allegiance of the king's subjects, fabulously wealthy in land and money; the income from that property instead of finding its way to the king's treasury, left the country as tribute to Rome. The king was not alone in his opposition to the Church. Pope Boniface VIII himself wrote in 1296 "That the laity are bitterly hostile to the clergy is a matter of ancient tradition which is also plainly confirmed by the experience of modern times."

The many abuses of the Church could not pass unnoticed. The difference between Church preaching and Church practice was wide enough for even the most stupid to see. The concentration on money-getting by every method, no matter how foul, was common talk. Aeneas Silvius, who later became Pope Pius II, wrote, "Nothing is to be had at Rome without money." And Pierre Berchoire, living in Chaucer's time, wrote, "It is not upon the poor that church moneys are spent, but upon the cleric's own favourite nephews and kinsfolk."

A troubadour's song of the fourteenth century showed the popular feeling toward all classes of the clergy, from top to bottom:

I see the pope his sacred trust betray,
For while the rich his grace can gain alway,
   His favours from the poor are aye withholden.
He strives to gather wealth as best he may,
Forcing Christ's people blindly to obey,
   So that he may repose in garments golden. . . .

No better is each honoured cardinal.
   From early morning's dawn to evening's fall,
Their time is passed in eagerly contriving
   To drive some bargain foul with each and all. . . .

Our bishops, too, are plunged in similar sin,
For pitilessly they flay the very skin
   From all their priests who chance to have fat livings.
For gold their seal official you can win.
To any writ, no matter what's therein.
   Sure God alone can make them stop their thievings . . .

Then as for all the priests and minor clerks,
There are, God knows, too many of them whose works
   And daily life belie their daily teaching . . .
For, learned or ignorant, they're ever bent
To make a traffic of each sacrament,
   The mass's holy sacrifice included. . . .

'Tis true the monks and friars make ample show
Of rules austere which they all undergo,
   But this the vainest is of all pretences.
In sooth, they live full twice as well we know,

As e'er they did at home, despite their vow
And all their mock parade of abstinences. . . .

The many scandals and abuses of the Church had become matters of general knowledge centuries before Martin Luther nailed his "Ninety-five Theses" to the church door in Wittenberg in 1517. There had been religious reformers before the Protestant Reformation. Why, then, did the split in the western Catholic Church, and the establishment of national churches in place of the one universal Church, come at this time and not before?

The earlier religious reformers, unlike Luther, Calvin, and Knox, made the mistake of trying to reform more than religion. Wycliffe in England had been the spiritual leader of the Peasants' Revolt, and Hus in Bohemia not only protested against Rome, but also inspired a communistic peasants' movement threatening the power and privilege of the nobility. This meant, of course, that these movements were opposed not only by the Church, but also by the secular authorities, and so they were crushed. Luther and the religious reformers who followed him did not lose the support of the ruling class by preaching dangerous equalitarian doctrines. Luther was no radical. He did not spoil his chances of success by siding with the oppressed. On the contrary, when, shortly after he began his reformation, a widespread peasants' revolt broke out in Germany, partly under the influence of his teaching, he helped to suppress it. This rebel against the Church could say, "I shall always side with those who condemn rebellion and against those who cause it." This reformer, so indignant at the governing body of the Church, could write, "God would prefer to suffer the government to exist, no matter how evil, rather than allow the rabble to riot, no matter how justified." While the revolting peasants in 1525 shouted, "Christ has made all men free," Luther urged the nobles to annihilate them with these encouraging words: "He who slays a rioter . . . does what is right. . . . Therefore, whoever can should smite, strangle or stab, secretly or publicly. . . . If you are killed in this struggle, you are indeed to be felicitated, as no nobler death could befall anyone."

One reason, then, for Luther's success, was that he did not make the mistake of trying to unseat the privileged. Another important reason for the Reformation coming when it did lay in the fact that the appeals which Luther, Calvin, and Knox made to their followers were appeals to their nationalist spirit, in a period of growing nationalism. Because this religious opposition to Rome coincided with the interests of the growing national state, it had a chance to succeed.

At this time, when the struggle of the national state against papal authority was becoming more and more acute, Luther's "Address to the German Nobility" contained this cheering advice for the princes: "Forasmuch as the temporal power has been ordained by God for the punishment of the bad and the protection of the good, therefore we must let it do its duty throughout the whole Christian body, without respect of persons, whether it strikes popes, bishops, priests, monks, nuns or whoever it may be." And part of that duty, it is shrewdly suggested, is to get rid of the control by foreigners, and—it is hinted—take over the lands and treasures of the Church. Important, that last point. "Some think more than three hundred thousand guilders are sent from Germany to Rome every year, for nothing whatever. . . . Long ago the emperors and princes of Germany allowed the pope to claim the *annates* from all German benefices; that is half of the first year's income from every benefice . . . and since the *annates* are so shamefully abused . . . they [the princes] should not suffer their lands and people to be so piteously and unrighteously flayed and ruined; but by an imperial or a national law they should either retain the *annates* in the country, or abolish them altogether."

Tell a group of people that it is not only their right but their duty to get rid of the powerful foreigner who has been challenging their authority in their own country; dangle before the eyes of that group of people the extensive wealth of that foreigner, as a prize to be taken when he is kicked out—and there will be fireworks. But the Church would have lost its power if the Protestant Reformation had not come when it did. In fact, the Church had already lost its power in the sense that its great usefulness was being lessened.

Where formerly the Church had been strong enough to bring to society a measure of relief from feudal wars by enforcing its Truce of God, now the king was better able to stop these pesky wars; where formerly the Church had complete control of education, now independent schools founded by merchants had been started; where formerly Church law had been supreme, now the old Roman law better suited to the needs of a commercial society had been revived; where formerly the Church alone provided the educated men who could help carry on affairs of the state, now the sovereign could rely on a new class of people trained in commercial practice and wise to the needs of the nation's commerce and industry.

This new group of people, the rising middle class, sensed that standing in the way of its further development, was the outmoded feudal system. The rising middle class realized that its own further progress was blocked by the Catholic Church, which was the stronghold of that system. The Church defended the feudal order from attack; it was itself a powerful part of the feudal structure; it owned, as a feudal lord, about one-third of the land, and drained from the country a great part of its wealth. Before the rising middle class could wipe out feudalism in each separate country, it had first to attack the central organization—the Church. It did so.

That struggle took on a religious disguise. It was called the Protestant Reformation. It was, in essence, the first decisive battle of the rising middle class against feudalism.

VIII

"Rich Man . . .

WHEN the President of the United States, at 3:10 o'clock on the afternoon of January 31, 1934, signed a proclamation decreeing that the number of gold grains in a dollar should be reduced from 25 8/10 to 15 5/21, he was following an old Spanish custom. It was an old English, French, and German custom as well. Debasement of the currency is a practice that is centuries old. Kings of the Middle Ages who wanted the golden touch of Midas, but didn't have it, turned to debasing the currency as a convenient substitute for getting money.

When President Roosevelt lowered the gold content of the dollar, his primary object was to raise prices. It was an incidental fact that this debasement of the currency brought to the United States Treasury a profit of some $2,790,000,000. With the kings of the Middle Ages, however, the primary object was the getting of a profit. They did not want to raise prices, but prices rose in spite of them because of the devaluation.

What does debasement of the coinage mean, and how does it bring about an immediate profit to the sovereign and a rise in the price level?

Debasement means simply reducing the amount of gold or silver in coins. When the king made the silver formerly in one coin spread over two, by adding worthless or base metals to the silver, he had two coins in place of the old one. Nominally the value was the same, the coin was still called a crown, or a livre, but actually it was only half as valuable as before. Now if twelve eggs usually exchanged for a loaf of bread, you wouldn't expect to go on getting the same size loaf if you offered only six eggs—even if you still called them a dozen. In the same way, you couldn't get as much for your debased money as you could for the old good money. You were offering less silver, so the loaf you could get for it was smaller. The value of the coins in circulation depended on the value of their metallic content, so the less silver or gold there was in a coin, the less it was worth, despite the fact that it went by the same name. To say that a coin is worth less is to say, simply, that it will buy less. In other words, prices rise.

Of course all that the kings saw was that there was an immediate profit for them in currency debasement. The fact that when money changes in value quickly, trade is hurt; the fact that when prices rise, poor people and those with fixed incomes suffer—this may have been of small importance to the king, but it was of great importance to some of his subjects. Most people, including the king very often, did not see the tie-up between the debasement of the currency and the rise in prices, but there were some who did. After there had been seventeen changes in the value of silver money in as many months in France, from October, 1358, to March, 1360, a Parisian wrote: "As a result of the excessive rate of gold and silver money, foodstuffs, commodities, and merchandise which everyone needs for his consumption have become so dear that the common people cannot find the means to exist."

Nicholas Oresme, bishop of Lisieux in 1377, wrote a famous book on money, in which he pointed out that debasement of the currency which temporarily profited the king, was in a sense cheating the people: "Measures for wheat, wine, and other less important things are often marked with the public stamp of the King, and if anyone is found guilty of practising fraud upon them, he is considered an infamous falsifier. In the same way the inscription placed upon a coin indicates the correctness of its weight and quality. Who, then, would trust a prince who should diminish the weight or fineness of money bearing his own stamp? . . . There are three ways, in my opinion, in which one may make profit from money, aside from its natural use. The first of these is the art of exchange, the custody of or trafficking in money, the second is usury, and the third is the altering of money. The first is base, the second is bad, and the third is even worse."

Richard Cantillon, an Englishman, writing nearly four hundred years later, neatly summed up the effect on prices of the debasement of the coinage: "The history of all times shows that when Princes have debased their money, keeping it at the same nominal value, all raw produce and manufactures have gone up in price in proportion to the debasement of the coinage."

You probably know the name of Copernicus as the great scientist who first put forth the theory, in 1530, that the earth travels round the sun. But Copernicus was also a student of money. He advocated that the monetary system of his country, Poland, be changed. He saw that many different currencies were an obstacle to commerce, so he urged one unified system of coinage, instead of allowing the various petty barons to mint coins; and, most strongly of all, he advocated that there be no debasement of currency: "However innumerable the scourges which usually lead to the decadence of kingdoms, principalities and republics, the following four are, in my opinion, the most formidable: strife, plague, an unfruitful earth, and the deterioration of money." Some of the chief reasons for the opposition of these students to the debasement of the currency were those given by Oresme: "It is scandalous and disgraceful for a prince to allow the money of his Realm to have no fixed value, but to fluctuate from day to day. . . . As a result of these alterations, people are often unable to tell how much a coin of gold or silver is worth, so that they have to bargain as much about their Money as about their wares, which is contrary to its nature; and that which ought to be very certain is quite uncertain and confused . . . the amount of gold and silver in a Realm decreases as a result of such alterations and debasements, and despite the precautions they are carried out to places where they are rated higher. . . . Hence the supply of the

money material decreases in countries where debasement is practised.
. . . Again, as a result of alterations and debasements, merchants
cease coming from foreign countries with their good merchandise
. . . to countries where they know such bad money is current. . . .
Moreover, in the country itself where such alterations take place,
traffic in merchandise is so disturbed that merchants and artisans
do not know how to deal with each other."

The king's advisers were worried about these results of the debasement of the currency. They wanted trade to prosper, and they
did not want the inadequate supply of metal to grow even smaller
through the export of gold and silver to other countries by the
merchants and bankers. While the poor man is usually a victim
of fluctuations in prices, because he is so busy working that he has
neither the time nor the means to protect himself, the men in the
know, the money-dealers, take care of their wealth and even make
a profit in such times. In several countries laws were passed again
and again to forbid the export of gold and silver, so necessary at
that time to the growth of commerce. In 1477 such a law was passed
in England: "And Whereas by the Statute made in the Second Year
of . . . the late King Henry the Sixth, it was ordained amongst
other, that no Gold nor Silver should be carried out of this Realm
. . . Contrary to which Statute and Ordinance, and divers other
Ordinances touching the same . . . the Money of Gold and Silver,
and Vessel and Plate of Gold and Silver of this Land, as Merchandise is carried and sent out of this Realm, to the great impoverishing
of the same Realm, and final Destruction of the Treasure of the
same Realm, if hasty Remedy be not provided: It is ordained by the
Authority aforesaid, That no Person shall carry nor make to be carried out of this Realm . . . any manner of Money of the Coin of
this Realm, nor of the Coin of any other Realms, Lands, or Seign-
iories, nor no Plate, Vessel, . . . Bullion, nor Jewels of Gold . . . or
of Silver, without the King's Licence."

Not only did the kings try hard to keep in the country whatever
gold and silver there was, but they also tried to increase the amount,
by giving special privileges to the miners: "All and every miner,

master and workman, who works continually at mines opened and to be opened in our kingdom . . . have our permission, at their own cost, and not otherwise, to open and to work the mines freely and without charge, and nobody may disturb or molest or interfere with them in any way, neither the lords spiritual nor temporal, nor merchants, nor our own officers, who say that they have rights in the said mines."

At this time, when gold and silver were so necessary to the further expansion of trade, the expansion of trade itself led to the discovery of huge stores of these metals, which in turn led to a still further expansion of trade. Today, with our four-hundred-year perspective, we can appreciate the true worth of Columbus's discovery; but to the people of the fifteenth century Columbus, since he had not succeeded in finding the Indies, was a failure. It was only in the sixteenth century with the flow of silver from the mines of Mexico and Peru to Spain, that his discovery was appreciated.

If goods are sent thousands of miles over mountains and deserts, on camels, horses, and mules; if part of the way they are carried on the backs of men; if along the way there is constant danger from attack by villainous tribesmen; if on the ocean route there is danger from destructive storms and murderous pirates; if here and there along either route high toll charges are demanded by the various governments in power; if at the last port of call the goods are sold to a group of merchants who have a monopoly of the trade at that end and so can tack on a stiff profit to the already high price—then the cost of those goods will be prohibitive. That is what happened to the much-sought-after goods from the East in the fifteenth century. By the time Eastern spices, precious stones, drugs, perfumes, and silks reached those ports where Venetian boats waited to load, they cost a lot of money; after the Venetians had resold them to the merchants of the South German towns who were the principal distributors throughout Europe, their price had shot skyward.

Merchants of other countries were not content to see the huge profits of the Eastern trade go to the Venetians alone—they wanted a share. They knew that there was money to be made on Eastern goods, but they could not break the monopoly of Venice. The eastern Mediterranean was a Venetian lake and there was nothing they could do about it—there.

But they could try to reach the Indies by another route not controlled by Venice. Now that the compass, first used by Italian sailors in the thirteenth century, had been mounted on a compass card; now that it had become possible to determine latitude by the use of the astrolabe; now that Italian seamen had begun to make maps based on actual observation, instead of relying on those which had been made from hearsay and imagination; now at last it was no longer necessary to hug the shore closely. Perhaps, if men were daring enough, a new route to the East, that treasure-house of spices and gold and precious stones, could be found.

Ships sailed forth bravely in every direction. Columbus's voyage west was only one of a number of similar voyages. Other daring sailors turned their course north to the Arctic Sea in the hope of finding a northeast passage. Still others made their way south along the coast of Africa. Finally, in 1497, Vasco da Gama, on this southeast passage, rounded the continent of Africa, and in 1498 he dropped anchor in the harbor of Calicut, India. An all-water route to the Indies had been found.

Did that mean that the search in other directions was stopped? Not at all. Columbus tried again and again—he made other voyages in an effort to get past the barrier which was the American continent. Others on the westward route confronted with the same barrier, sailed north, still others sailed south, searching . . . searching. . . . As late as 1609 Henry Hudson was still searching a way to the East.

And well they might. There was money—lots of it—in a route to the East. On Vasco da Gama's first voyage to India the profits had been 6000 per cent! Small wonder that other ships made the same perilous—but profitable—journey. The trade grew by leaps and bounds. Where Venice had bought 420,000 pounds of pepper every year from the Sultan of Egypt, now *one* boat on its journey homeward to Portugal had 200,000 pounds in its hold! It no longer mattered that the old route to the East had been captured by the Turks; it no longer mattered that the Venetians charged exorbitant prices; the route to the East via the Cape of Good Hope made the merchants independent of Turkish goodwill and broke the Venetian monopoly.

Now the direction of the currents of commerce was changed. Where formerly the geographical position of Venice and the South German cities had given them an advantage over the countries lying farther west, now those countries on the Atlantic seaboard had the advantage. Venice and the cities which had been tied to it commercially were now off the main road of commerce. What had been the highway of trade now became the byway. The Atlantic became the new highway, and Portugal, Spain, Holland, England, and France rose to commercial prominence.

With good reason is this period of history called the "Commercial Revolution." Commerce, which, as we have seen, had been growing steadily, now took giant strides. Not only the old world of Europe and parts of Asia were open to enterprising traders, but whole new worlds in America and Africa. No longer was trade confined to rivers and land-locked seas like the Mediterranean and the Baltic. Where formerly the term "international trade" meant a European trade with a section of Asia, now the term applied to a much larger area, embracing four continents, with ocean routes as highways. The discoveries opened up a period of magnificent expansion in the entire economic life of Western Europe. The extension of the market has always been one of the strongest spurs to economic activity. The extension of the market at this time was greater than anything that had ever happened before. New places with which to trade, new markets for the goods of your own country, new goods to bring back home—it was all very infectious and stimulating and ushered in a period of intense commercial activity, of further discovery, exploration, and expansion.

Companies of merchants were formed to seize the dangerous but exciting—and highly lucrative—opportunities. Just look at the name of one of the earliest and most famous of the new training companies, "Mysterie and Companie of the Merchant Adventurers for the discoverie of regions, dominions, islands and places unknown." Now that alone is quite a bit to chew off. But that name doesn't tell even half the story. Because once the "discoverie" was made, then forts had to be erected, a garrison of men set up at the "station," arrangements effected with the natives, actual trading carried on, methods found for keeping outsiders out of the trade—to say nothing of the long and expensive preliminaries, such as buying or building ships, hiring crews, and furnishing food and equipment for the uncertain and perilous journey.

All that would take money—lots of it. It would take more money than any individual would have or would care to risk on so dangerous a venture.

The customary forms of trading associations which had grown up to deal with old established trades and routes were not suited to the new conditions. Trading to a considerable distance in unknown lands, with strange people, under unfamiliar conditions, necessitated a new type of trading association—and, as always happens, that new type arose to meet the need.

What one or two or three separate individuals could not do, many individuals united into a single body acting as a unit with a single management, could do. The Joint Stock Company was the answer of the merchants in the sixteenth and seventeenth centuries to the problem of how to raise the huge sums of money needed for such vast undertakings as trading with America, Africa, and Asia represented. The first English Joint Stock Company was the Merchant Adventurers. It had 240 shareholders who put up £25 each—a large total sum in those days. It was by the sale of shares of stock to many individuals that the considerable capital necessary for the great trading, privateering, and colonizing expeditions was mobilized. These joint stock companies were the forerunners of the great corporations of today. Then, as now, anyone—with money—could become a partner in a joint stock company by the purchase of stock. Even piratical expeditions were organized on joint stock lines. On one of Drake's expeditions against the Spaniards, Queen Elizabeth herself held shares, in return for the loan of some ships. The profits on this one occasion were 4700 per cent, of which Good Queen Bess received some £250,000 as her share!

That the secret partnership of the Queen in these plundering expeditions was not so secret after all is shown by a Fugger News Letter from Seville, dated December 7, 1569. "And the most annoying part of this affair is that this Hawkins could not have fitted out so numerous and so well-equipped a fleet without the aid and secret consent of the Queen. This conflicts with the agreement for the sake of which the King sent an envoy extraordinary to the Queen of England. It is the nature and habit of this nation not to keep faith, so the Queen pretends that all has been done without her knowledge and desire."

The names of some of these companies organized in the sixteenth and seventeenth centuries, show us where they carried on their business of trading, or colonizing, or both. There were seven "East India" companies, the most famous being those of the British and the Dutch; there were four "West India" companies, organized in Holland, France, Sweden, and Denmark; "Levant" companies and "African" companies were also popular; particularly interesting to us in America, were the "Plymouth" company and the "Virginia" company organized in England.

You can readily guess that any company set up to carry on these expensive and risky ventures, would make certain that it received from its government as many privileges concerning the trade as was possible. One of the most important, of course, was the right to a monopoly of the trade. The company wanted no outside traders to crash in on its particular territory. It used to be thought that the great expansion of trade was in large measure due to the daring pioneering of these trading companies. Now, some historians question that. They argue that the existence of so many merchants outside the companies who tried to break into the trade is proof that but for these restrictive monopolies the volume of trade might have been even greater than it was.

At any rate, we know that the companies were in business primarily to make profits for their shareholders. Where that could be done by increasing production and selling more widely, they did that; where profits could be made by limiting production, they did that. Our "ploughing-under" program of the AAA seems to be old stuff in the light of the following: The Dutch "paid pensions of about £3,300 to native rulers to exterminate the clove and nutmeg in other islands, and concentrated the cultivation in Amboyna, where they were able to control it themselves. So far as their East Indian trade was concerned, they were not eager to develop it, but preferred to keep it within such limits that they might secure a high rate of profit."

Despite the fact that in this particular instance "a high rate of profit" could be secured by limiting rather than developing trade, in the main there were high profits in trade development. This was the golden age of commerce, when the fortunes were made— the capital accumulated—which was to provide the basis for the great industrial expansion of the seventeenth and eighteenth centuries.

History books go on at great length about the ambitions, conquests, and wars of this or that great king. Their emphasis is all wrong. The pages they devote to the stories of these kings would be much better devoted to the real powers behind the thrones— the rich merchants and financiers of this period. They were the powers behind the thrones because the kings at every turn needed their financial help. For the two hundred years of the sixteenth and seventeenth centuries wars were almost continuous. Wars have to be paid for. They were financed by the men with money—the merchants and bankers.

The question of whether Charles V of Spain or Francis I of France was to wear the crown of the Holy Roman Empire was settled by a little German banker, Jacob Fugger, head of the great banking-house of the Fugger. The crown cost Charles 850,000 florins, of which 543,000 were lent by the Fugger. We can get an idea of the influence of Jacob Fugger, the man behind the scenes, from the tone of a letter which he wrote to Charles, when the latter was slow in paying back what he owed. Only because Jacob Fugger's money gave him such tremendous power did he have the nerve to write such a letter: ". . . We have, moreover, advanced to Your Majesty's Agents a Great Sum of Money, of which we ourselves have had to raise a large part from our Friends. It is well known that Your Imperial Majesty could not have gained the Roman Crown save with mine aid, and I can prove the same by the writings of Your Majesty's Agents given by their own hands. In this matter I have not studied mine own Profit. [Don't you believe that!] For had I left the House of Austria and had been minded to further France, I had obtained much money and property, such as was then offered to me. How grave a Disadvantage had in this case accrued to Your Majesty and the House of Austria, Your Majesty's Royal Mind well knoweth."

Very little of importance went on in the sixteenth century without the shadow of the Fuggers lying across it in some way. They began business in the fifteenth century as a merchant house dealing in wool and spices. But it was as bankers that they made their fortune. They loaned money to other merchants, to kings and princes, and in return they received revenues from mines, from trading ventures, from crown lands, from practically every kind of enterprise that yielded a revenue. When loans were not paid, they became the owners of the estates, the mines, the lands—whatever had been pledged as security. Even the pope owed money to the Fuggers. They had branches and agents everywhere. The Fugger balance sheet of 1546 shows debts from the German emperor, the city of Antwerp, the kings of England and Portugal, and the queen of the Netherlands. Their capital in that year was five million gulden. The history time-line which dates this period, not as the reign of King So-and-so, but as the Age of the Fuggers, is much nearer the truth.

Though the Fuggers were the most important financial house of the time, there were many others nearly as big. The Welser, another German banking-house, had helped Charles V to the tune of 143,000 florins; they too had large investments in trading enterprises, in

mines, and in lands. The Hochstetter, the Haug, and the Imhof
carried on much the same kind of merchant-banking-managing
business. Among the Italian financiers in this period the Frescobaldi,
the Gualterotti, and the Strozzi were becoming great. One or two
centuries before, the Peruzzi and the Medici had been the outstanding names. One of the best gauges of the tremendous increase in
the scale of financial and commercial activity is a comparison of
the fortunes of these great banking families with that of the Fuggers:

> "1300—the Peruzzis $ 800,000
> 1440—the Medicis   7,500,000
> 1546—the Fuggers   40,000,000"

The centre of all this financial and commercial activity was
Antwerp. When the current of trade shifted from the Mediterranean
to the Atlantic, the once great Italian cities went into a decline and
Antwerp took their place. It was not its size that made it great—
it had only about 100,000 people. It was rather its freedom from
restrictions of all kinds. Where the other cities in the Middle Ages
made it difficult for foreign merchants to do business within their
gates, Antwerp welcomed them with open arms. It was a really
free international business centre—anybody could trade there and
everybody did trade there. Its hall where merchants, brokers, and
bankers met to do business had engraved on its walls this motto,
"For the use of merchants of any nationality and language." That
invitation was accepted by merchants from every part of the world.
The English cloth business was centred in Antwerp, and it was the
most important market for spices from the East. When the Venetians lost their monopoly of the spice trade, they lost it to the
Portuguese, and the Portuguese did practically all of their business
through Antwerp. A practice of tremendous importance grew up
there—one that proves what giant strides trade and industry had
taken. This was the sale, by sample, of standard and recognized
goods. Instead of having on hand all the goods to be turned over
to the buyer, the modern type of broker and commission agent
made his appearance. He sold his goods merely by showing a stand-

ard sample. Fairs, which had owed their importance largely to temporary suspension of the usual restrictions on trading, received their death blow from a market which was always free. The old market had been displaced by the modern exchange.

Because Antwerp was of such great commercial importance it became the chief financial centre as well. Here the great German and Italian banking-houses had their key depot, and dealings in money came to be even more important than actual trade. It was at this time in Antwerp that the modern instruments of finance came into daily use. The bankers of the period devised ways and means for making payment for the exchange of goods easy and quick. When a merchant of one country, say England, buys goods from a merchant of a distant country, say Italy, how is he to pay for them? Shall the Englishman send gold or silver to the Italian? That's dangerous and expensive. Some credit system had to be devised which would make such shipments of gold unnecessary. So it was agreed that the Englishman, in payment of his debt to the Italian, would give him a slip of paper saying he owed him so much for the goods. Then, on another deal, perhaps another Italian merchant owed money to an English merchant for goods for which he likewise sent the Englishman a slip of paper acknowledging the debt. Then with a central clearing-house, the two debts could be cancelled—without any money having been sent over the long distance from England to Italy and from Italy to England. Such a system was devised centuries ago. It is described by a writer of the sixteenth century: "As to the payments of the said countries among the merchants of Lyons [a financial centre like Antwerp] and other countries and towns, the greater part are done on paper, that is to say: You owe me on one side and I owe you on the other; we cancel it all out and compensate each other; and scarcely any money is used for the said payments."

And this miracle of doing business without the actual transfer of money is explained by Cantillon, too: "If England owes France 100,000 ounces of silver for the balance of trade, if France owes 100,000 ounces to Holland, and Holland 100,000 to England, all these three amounts may be set off by bills of exchange between the respective Bankers of these three States without any need of sending silver on either side."

All this is not important information by itself. It is important only because it shows that the financial machinery to meet the needs of expanding commerce had been worked out in the sixteenth century by the merchants and bankers. Of course new and better methods have been added since to meet changing conditions, but the foundation was there hundreds of years ago.

With new lands opened up for exploitation, with trade leaping forward and merchants and bankers growing wealthy, you would expect that this Age of the Fuggers would go down in history as a golden age of prosperity and happiness for mankind. You would be wrong.

IX

. . . *Poor Man, Beggar Man, Thief"*

THE Age of Fuggers was also the Age of Beggars. The figures for the number of beggars in the sixteenth and seventeenth centuries are astounding. One-fourth of the population of Paris in the 1630's were beggars, and in the country districts their number was as great; in England conditions were equally bad; Holland teemed with beggars; and in Switzerland in the sixteenth century "when there was no other means of getting rid of the beggars who besieged their houses or wandered in bands about the roads and forests, the wealthy even organized hunting parties against these wretched *heimatlosen* (homeless ones)."

What is the explanation of this widespread distress for the masses in a period of great prosperity for the few? War, as always, was one cause. The World War, 1914-1918, is thought by many to have touched a new high in bringing disaster and misery to the sections of Europe where the fighting raged. But the wars of this period were even more devastating—probably nothing quite so terrible as the Thirty Years' War in Germany (1618-1648) has ever been experienced. "About two-thirds of the total population had disappeared, the misery of those that survived was piteous in the extreme. Five-sixths of the villages in the empire had been destroyed. We read of one in the Palatinate that in two years had been plundered twenty-eight times. In Saxony, packs of wolves roamed about, for in the north quite one-third of the land had gone out of cultivation."

War, then, was one cause of the intense misery and suffering of the people. There was another. America. The New World played an indirect but important part in creating the Age of Beggars. How?

While the merchants of England, Holland, and France were piling up huge fortunes in commerce, the Spaniards had found a simpler way to increase the sums of money in their treasury. Though their explorers had failed to discover a route to the Indies which was to bring them trading profits, they had stumbled on the conti-nents of North and South America. And in Mexico and Peru there were gold and silver mines of great value—theirs for the stealing. In Spanish galleons the holds were loaded not with goods to be sold at a profit, but with gold and silver—especially silver. The mines in Saxony and Austria had been turning out large quantities of silver, but they were very small indeed compared with the wealth that poured into Spain from its possessions in the New World. In the fifty-five years from 1545 to 1600 it is estimated that each year about £2,000,000 was added from American mines. And it seemed that just as the limit of one supply was in sight, a discovery of a new mine would continue the flow. The Spanish mint turned out only 45,000 kilograms of silver in the period from 1500 to 1520; but for the fifteen-year period from 1545 to 1560 its production increased six times, to 270,000 kilograms; and the twenty-year period from 1580 to 1600 saw production leap to 340,000 kilograms, almost eight times what it had been in 1520!

Year	Spanish mint's output of silver
1500–1520	——
1545–1560	————————————————
1580–1600	————————————————————

Did this huge supply of silver which was brought from America to Spain stay in Spain? Not at all. It circulated all over Europe as fast as it poured in. The kings of Spain fought one series of stupid wars after another—they paid in money for supplies and soldiers. The Spaniards bought more goods than they sold—they couldn't eat the silver—and their money filtered through their hands into the pockets of the merchants who sold to them.

What was the effect of this unprecedented influx of silver into Europe? It brought about a sensational rise in prices. Not just a penny or two on this article or that, but a spectacular increase in the price of everything. There was a real revolution in prices such as has occurred only three or four times in the last thousand years of world history. The prices of goods in 1600 were more than twice what they had been in 1500, and by 1700 they were still higher— more than three and one-half times what they had been when the price revolution started.

We have seen how a debased coinage lowers the value of money, or, looking at it from another angle, raises prices. The increase in the amount of money in circulation has the same effect. Money is just like anything else which people want, and of which there is not an unlimited supply. We all want air, but the supply is so large that it has no economic value—we don't have to pay anything for it. We don't think of buying and selling water, but in a dry, hot country, in desert areas, water is sold because the supply is so limited in relation to the demand. If, when barter was used as a method of exchange, the wine harvest had been good, and the wheat harvest bad, we would understand that a man would have to give more wine than formerly in order to obtain the same amount of wheat. With money the same principle applies. If it becomes more plentiful in relation to the things for which it is exchanged, its value will fall in terms of those things—that is to say, prices will rise. A fall in the value of money means a rise in prices, and a rise in the value of money means a fall in prices. This change is brought about by the relative plenty or scarcity of money in circulation.

So it was that, following the influx of precious metals into Europe, prices soared—and how!—until the favorite topic of conversation of people was, "I remember the good old days when you could get butter for one-fourth of what you have to pay now, and eggs—why, they practically gave them away!"

American treasure came to Spain first, and it was there that the jump in prices was first evident. Nicolas Cleynaerts, a Dutchman travelling in Spain and Portugal in 1536, had his breath taken away by the high prices there. The cost of a shave was so steep that it prompted him to write home this amusing note: "Was it not necessary at Salamanca, to pay a demi-real to get a shave, which will prevent one being astonished at the greater number of bearded men in Spain than in Flanders."

After American silver spread from Spain throughout Europe, the high prices which so surprised this tourist from Flanders were evident in every country. The average person did not understand the reason. He did not know that the price revolution was international, not merely confined to his particular section of the country. He grumbled, and looking about for the cause, blamed it on the wickedness of this or that grasping person. So, in *A Discourse of the Common Weal of this Realm of England*, written in the sixteenth century, the author shows how the farmer charges that high prices are caused by the exorbitant rents demanded by the landowning class, while the knight argues that the high rents are due to the exorbitant prices asked for farm produce:

"*Husbandman:* I think it is long of you gentlemen that this dearth is, by reason you enhance your lands to such an height, as men that live thereon must needs sell dear . . . or else they were not able to make the rent again.

"*Knight:* And I say it is long of you husbandmen, that we are forced to raise our rents, by reason we must buy all things so dear that we have of you; as corn, cattle, goose, pig, capon, chicken, butter, and eggs. What thing is there of all these things, but you sell it dearer now by the one-half than you did within these VIII years? Can not your neighbours in this town Remember that within these VIII years you could buy the best pig or goose that I could lay my hands on for IV d. which now cost me VIII d.; and a good Capon for III d. or IV d.; a chicken for a penny, a hen for II d., which now will cost me double the money; and it is likewise of great ware, as of mutton and beef."

There were, of course, some thinkers of the period who gave up the medieval habit of dealing with economic matters in terms of the sinfulness of man alone. Men like Jean Bodin and Cantillon were on to the fact that behind the rise in prices was the force of an impersonal law, not influenced by "good" or "bad" people. Bodin wrote in the latter half of the sixteenth century: "I consider that the dearness which we observe comes from three causes. The chief and almost the sole cause (which nobody so far has touched upon) is the abundance of gold and silver, which is in this kingdom today greater than it has been in the last 400 years . . ."

That there was a tie-up between higher prices and the influx of gold and silver, began to percolate into the minds of others, shortly after Bodin wrote his great works. In *A Treatise of the Canker of England's Commonwealth*, written in 1601 by Gerrard De Malynes, merchant, there is the following passage: ". . . plenty of money maketh generally things dear, and scarcity of money maketh likewise generally things good cheap. . . . According to the plenty or scarcity of the money then, generally things became dearer or good cheap, whereunto the great store or abundance of money and bullion, which of late years is come from the west Indies into Christendom, hath made every thing dearer."

What was hotly disputed in the sixteenth and seventeenth centuries was quite plain to everybody in the eighteenth, according to Cantillon: "If mines of gold or silver be found . . . and considerable quantities of minerals drawn from them . . . all this money, whether lent or spent, will enter into circulation and will not fail to raise the price of products and merchandise in all the channels of circulation which it enters. . . . Everybody agrees that the abundance of money . . . raises the price of everything. The quantity of money brought from America to Europe for the last two centuries justifies this truth by experience."

What are the results of such a rise in prices? Who benefits and who suffers? The people who gained were the merchants. While their expenses went up, the returns from their business showed a greater increase. They paid more for what they bought, but they charged much more than ever before for what they sold. Another group that gained were those whose expenses remained fixed but whose products increased in price—those people who had a long lease on the land at an old-established rent, who were now able to sell their butter, eggs, wheat, barley, etc., at the greatly increased prices.

On the other hand, there were several groups that were badly hit by the price revolution. Governments, for example, found it increasingly difficult to make ends meet. Their income was fixed, while their expenses were ever on the increase. This was a period of change when the national state was emerging—and the government's financial organization was out-of-date, not yet suited to the new conditions. It was being changed slowly, but meanwhile it creaked badly in places, and the revolution in prices added to its difficulties. Money troubles threw the kings more and more into the hands of the rising class of money men, and many concessions were wrung from the kings at this time. The revolutions of this period which brought increasing political power to the bourgeoisie were thus closely connected with the revolution in prices.

Wage workers also suffered. A period of rising prices is almost always a period of rising wages also, so you would expect that everything would come out all right in the end. But no, there's an important catch to that argument. The catch is that wages never rise to the same extent as prices. Wage increases usually have to be fought for. They are generally obtained by deliberate mass action which meets with resistance, whereas prices are raised by the operations of the market. The workman was up against it. Whereas at the end of the fifteenth century the wages for a day of a workman in France would buy 4.3 kilograms of meat, a century later, they would buy only 1.8 kilograms; a hectolitre of grain which cost him four francs in the first period, could not be bought under twenty francs in the second. Rogers estimates that in England a peasant in 1495 could earn enough in fifteen weeks to provision his household for a year, but by 1610 he could not earn the same amount of provisions even if he worked every single week of the year! And "in 1610 . . . a Rutland [England] artisan . . . would have to work forty-three weeks in order to earn that which an artisan obtained in 1495 with ten weeks' labour." For the workingman this meant either tightening his belt or fighting for higher wages to meet the higher costs, or becoming a beggar. All three happened—as a result of the price revolution.

Another group that suffered were those who had a fixed money income, the *rentier* class, who lived on annuities, pensions, or the income from securities bearing a fixed rate of interest. Here, for example, is the case of a Miss Reynerses, who at the end of the fourteenth century invested her money in obtaining an annuity for life:

"We the Council, mayor, and gild masters of the city of Halberstadt hereby make known that we have sold to the pious virgin Alheyde Reynerses a yearly rent of half a lodighe marks . . . for the sum of five lodighe marks which has been truly paid to us."

Perhaps Miss Reynerses had counted on this annual return to keep her in comfort in her old age. Well and good. But if she had lived in this period of rising prices she would have had the unfortunate experience of going hungry, because, while her income remained the same, (one-half a lodighe mark in this case) the things she could buy with that income had become much dearer, so she could buy less of them. Her nominal income was what it always had been, but her *real* income would have declined. This always happens to people with a fixed income in a period of rising prices.

Similarly, the people with fixed incomes from the land were hard hit. You remember how the payment of rents in money for the use of land had taken the place of customary services. That worked well for the landed gentry until the price revolution came. Then they found themselves receiving the old low rents while they had to pay the new high prices. They were in a hole. What could they do about it? What could those lords and rich men who had either been given or had bought the church lands that the kings had confiscated do about the fact that prices were rising while rents remained the same? They felt they had to get more money out of their land. But how?

There were two ways—enclosure and rack-renting.

Enclosure went on to some extent throughout Europe, but particularly in England. You remember the open-field system of agriculture which was described in the first chapter. It was a bad system because it was wasteful. It was bad, too, because the progressive, wide-awake, enterprising farmer could not go his own pace or try out new experiments, but had to fit into the tempo of the others who held strips next to his. A few stupid unintelligent farmers could keep a whole village from progressing. There had grown up, therefore, in some places, a practice of strip-swapping, which enabled the various farmers to change their holdings from thirty acres of strips scattered in and out of other people's land, to four or five compact holdings of six or seven acres each. A lucky or bright strip-swapper might succeed in "untangling" all of his strips and getting them into one compact piece. The next step was to put a fence around your holding or holdings. What was once open field now became enclosed—that is, fenced in. If you have ever travelled in New England you will remember the stone walls which enclose each farmer's field; in old England, where they had stone easily available, they also built their enclosures of stone; and where there was no stone they enclosed their fields with hedges. Enclosure of this type, where farming on the land continued, hurt no one and led to an improvement in production. No one objected to this, and the poor farmer as well as the rich did it and benefited from it.

But there was enclosure of another sort that worked great hardship on thousands of people. This was enclosure for sheep-raising. Because the price of wool had been going up (wool was England's chief export), many lords saw a chance to get a bigger money return from their land by converting it from farm land to sheep pasture. This had happened before the price revolution, but now higher prices acted as a spur to the movement, and more lords enclosed their land for the purpose of raising sheep. While this did mean more money for the lord, it also meant the loss of a job and of a living for those farmers who had been on the enclosed land. Fewer people are needed to tend sheep than to run a farm—the

extra number were now down and out. Often the lord found that
in order to get a good-sized holding together into a compact piece,
he had to turn off those tenants whose holdings stood in the way.
He did so—and more poor people lost their means of earning a
living. From the bitter outcry of the pamphleteers of the period
we learn what great hardship enclosure for pasture brought to the
poor farmer.

Sometimes the lord merely enclosed the common. This meant,
of course, that the poor tenant's cattle had no place to pasture,
which in turn meant ruin. Had the tenants no rights in the matter?
Couldn't they go to law about it? Yes, they could. But going to
law has always been easier for the rich man who can pay the costs,
so even in those cases where the tenants might have won they
seldom had the means to continue the fight. The lord who had the
money could afford to keep the case going until the tenants had
to give up—and then he could buy their land and add it to his piece
to be enclosed. That is the story contained in the following petition
to the House of Commons from farmers from Wootton Bassett
"for Restoration of Rights of Common":

"That whereas the Mayor and Free Tenants of the said Borough
. . . had and did hold unto them free common of pasture for the
feeding of all sorts of other beasts . . . one Sir Francis Englefield
. . . did enclose the said park . . . and this did continue so long, he
being too powerful for them, that the said free tenants were not
able to wage law any longer; for one John Rous, one of the free
tenants, was thereby enforced to sell all his land (to the value of
£500) with following the suits in law, and many others were
thereby impoverished. . . . We are put out of all the common that
ever we had and have not so much as one foot of common left
unto us. . . . We are hereby grown so in poverty, unless it please
God to move the hearts of the Honourable House to commiserate
our cause, and to enact something for us, that we may enjoy our
right again. . . .

[Here follow twenty-three signatures]

"Divers hands more we might have had, but that many of them doth rent bargains of the lord of the manor, and they are fearful that they shall be put forth of their bargains, and then they shall not tell how to live . . . otherwise they would have set to their hands."

Not all enclosure was for sheep pasture. Because a large farm was easier and cheaper to run than a lot of little farms, manorial lords often enclosed for better crop-raising. Those unfortunate tenants who held strips of land that the lord wanted were soon among the growing ranks of landless and homeless people.

Though most of us know more about enclosure than we do about the rack-renting of this period, it was the latter that was more important. Rents of land and the fines paid when a new tenant took over a holding had been practically stationary. They had been fixed by custom—and in the past custom had had the force of law. But now that the revolution in prices necessitated a greater return from his land, the lord disregarded custom which had been the peasant's protection in the past. When a tenant's lease expired, instead of renewing at the same terms as the old lease, according to custom, the lord jacked up the rent so high that the tenant often found it impossible to pay and had to give up his land. That's what happened to leaseholders. But though holding land on a lease was to become important later, at this time most of the peasants were copyholders. This meant that they held their land according to the custom of the manor "by will of the lord in the copy of the roll." Unfortunately for many copyholders, the custom of the manor was taken by the lord to mean what he wanted at that particular moment, and what he wanted above all else was either more money from the land, or the land itself to be rented to some one else who would pay more money. Every possible trick was used to force the tenant out. When a copyhold changed hands—say at the death of the head of the family—then the son who expected to take over the holding on payment of the usual small fine according to custom, found that the fine was no longer small. The lord jumped the fine upward to so high a figure that the peasant could not pay and had to give up his old rights. Then the lord either sold the land or leased it to some one able and willing to pay the new scale of rents.

A petition of 1553 from the inhabitants of Whitby shows how rents and fines increased:

	The old rent	The new rent	And the fine
"From Henry Russell	42 s. 11½ d.	4 £. 7 s. 3 d.	3 £. 6 s. 8 d.
From Thomas Robynson	12 s. 11½ d.	40 s. 7 d.	33 s. 4 d.
From Thomas Coward	14 s. 9 d.	31 s.	2 s. 6 d.
From William Walker	7 s. 3 d.	17 s.	5 s.
From Robert Barker	14 s. 6 d.	30 s.	2 s. 8 d."

In a sermon preached before the courtiers of Edward VI, Bishop Latimer had the courage to call a spade a spade: "You landlords, you rent-raisers . . . you unnatural lords, you have for your posses-sions yearly too much. For that here before went for twenty or forty pound by year (which is an honest portion to be had *gratis* in one Lordship, of another man's sweat and labour) now is it let for fifty or a hundred pound by year."

Latimer was not alone in denouncing grasping landlords. Other speakers and writers of the period also came out strong against enclosure, rack-renting, higher fines, and landlords who by their evictions were adding to the huge army of tramps and beggars. In *The Prayer for Landlords* offered up at this same time, we find the following: "We heartily pray that they (who possess the grounds, pastures, and dwelling-places of the earth) may not rack and stretch out the rents of their houses and lands, nor yet take unreasonable fines and incomes . . . give them grace also that they may be content with that that is sufficient, and not join house to house nor couple land to land to the impoverishment of others." . . .

But in spite of prayers, the lords continued their practice of en-closure and rack-renting. Whole villages were left derelict, with the evicted inhabitants starving, stealing, or begging on the road. More than prayers were tried. Laws were passed. The Crown was really worried. It wanted to stop the depopulation of villages. It was frightened because the army was recruited largely from the peasant and small-holding class. Then, too, these peasants whose means of livelihood was being snatched from them had paid their taxes and had been a good source of revenue for the Crown. Also, these wandering groups of beggars constituted a real danger—there had been burnings, pulling down of enclosures, risings. So laws were passed against enclosure. The first in 1489, and others right on through the sixteenth century. But their very frequency shows that they were to a large extent disregarded, otherwise there would have been no need for re-enactment. Though some of the worst abuses were modified, it was a cinch that where the local landlords were also the local justices, the laws would not be strictly enforced. It is interesting to remember that when the peasants rose against the enclosures, *they* were not the lawbreakers—the landlords were breaking the law. Which did not mean, however, that these peasant uprisings were not dealt with severely. They were. They always are.

Notice an important change in this period. The old idea that land was important according to the amount of labour on it had disappeared; the development of commerce and industry, and the revolution in prices, had made money more important than men, and land was now regarded as a source of income. People had learned to treat it as they did property in general—it became the plaything of speculators who bought and sold it on the chance of making money.

The enclosure movement caused a great deal of suffering, but it did extend the possibilities of improving agriculture. And when capitalist industry had need of workers, it found part of its labour supply in those dispossessed landless unfortunates who now had only their labour power with which to earn a living.

X

Help Wanted—Two-year-olds May Apply

THE expansion of the market. Roll that phrase over and over on your tongue. Stamp it indelibly on your mind. It is an important key to an understanding of the forces which brought about capitalist industry as we know it.

It's one thing to produce goods for a small and stable market, for a market in which the producer turns out an article for a customer who comes into his place of business and gives him an order. It's quite another thing to produce goods for a market which has grown from the limits of a town to the broad expanse of a nation, and beyond. The gild set-up was designed to fit a local small market; when the market became national and international, the gild set-up no longer fitted. The local craftsman could understand and handle the trade of a town, but world trade was quite a different matter. The widening market threw up a middleman who made it his job to see to it that the goods made by the workers reached the consumer, who might be hundreds or thousands of miles away.

The gild master craftsman had been more than just a maker of goods. He had four other functions. He was five people in one. In so far as he had to seek out and bargain for the raw material he used, he was a merchant; because he had journeymen and apprentices working under him he was an employer; because he supervised their work he was a foreman; since he sold his finished product over the counter to the consumer, he was a shopkeeper.

Enter the middleman. Now the five functions of the master crafts-man are reduced to three—worker, employer, foreman. The mer-chanting and the shopkeeping are no longer his concern. The middleman brings him the raw material and collects the finished product. The middleman now stands between him and the cus-tomer. It has become the master craftsman's job simply to turn out finished goods as fast as raw material is brought to him.

This method whereby a middleman employs a number of artisans to work on his material in their own homes is called the "domestic" or "putting-out" system. Notice that as far as the technique of pro-duction is concerned, the putting-out system did not differ from the gild system. It left the master craftsman and his helpers in the home working with the same tools. But while the method of production remained the same, the marketing of the goods was organized on a new basis, by the middleman, acting as merchant.

Though the middleman did not affect the technique of produc-tion, he did reorganise it to increase the output of goods. He soon saw the advantages of specialization. William Petty, a famous seven-teenth-century economist, put into words what the middleman was putting into action. "Cloth must be cheaper made when one cards, another spins, another weaves, another draws, another dresses, an-other presses and packs, than when all the operations above men-tioned were clumsily performed by the same hand." When you employ a large number of people to make a certain product, you can divide the labour among them. Each workman has one par-ticular job to do. He does it over and over again, and as a result he becomes quite expert at it. This saves time and so speeds up production. Still other changes would have to be made to meet the needs of an expanding market. That's what the enterprising middle-men thought.

But the gildsmen thought otherwise. You remember how jealous the gilds were of their monopoly on the manufacture and sale of their particular product. So watchful were they of their "rights" that it is even reported of the Glasgow Corporation of Mechanics that it tried to prohibit James Watt from carrying on his work on the model of a steam-engine—because he was not a member of the Corporation! It is quite clear that gildsmen long accustomed to believing that the manufacture of this or that product was their exclusive privilege were going to howl hard and long when middle-men dared to introduce changes in the old way of doing things. Tradition ruled the gilds. The old methods, the old market, the old monopoly, Business As Usual—that suited most of the gilds-men. But it did not suit the enterprising wide-awake middleman. He had no time for tradition in a period of increased demand. He wanted to change the old methods, cater to the new market, and fight the old gild monopoly. The gild set-up with its innumer-able rules and regulations was old-fashioned, out of date, and stood in the way of further development of industry. It had to be over-thrown. It was overthrown.

Not all at once, and not too openly. (Gilds were not legally abolished in France until the Revolution; in England it was not until the early nineteenth century that the gilds lost their last privileges.) The middlemen often worked within the framework of the gild system, apparently accepting its form but actually under-mining it. Sometimes wealthy masters of a gild became employers of other masters in their own gilds; sometimes one gild in an industry gradually took over the trading function and "put out" work to other gilds in the same industry. Gone was the old equality among masters which had been fundamental to the gild system.

Wherever necessary the middleman beat the hampering gild rules and regulations by moving his industry outside the gild prov-ince, out of the towns into the country districts, where work could be carried on by whatever methods were suitable without worrying about gild restrictions as to wages, number of apprentices, etc. Thus Ambrose Crowley, an ironmonger in Greenwich, England, moved to Durham and organized the large-scale production of hardware, on the putting-out system. "In what had previously been a small village Crowley planted a thriving industrial town of 1,500 inhabi-tants, and proceeded to organize the manufacture of nails, locks, bolts, chisels, spades, and other steel tools. The houses were apparently owned by Crowley, and the materials and the tools were advanced to the workmen by him, after the former had deposited 'a bond for a considerable amount.' This deposit gave the right to hold a workshop and be a master workman, labouring with his own family and employing in turn a hired journeyman or two and an apprentice. The place of work was the master workman's shop, and payment was made to him by the piece for the work done. . . . Knighted in 1706, Sir Ambrose Crowley later became M.P. [member of Parliament] for Andover, and by that time he possessed a fortune of £200,000."

Naturally gildsmen objected to this change in the organization of industry. They fought to retain their old monopolies. But the heyday of the gilds was over. They were fighting a losing battle. The expansion of the market had made their system antiquated, unable to cope with the increasing demand for goods. "In a complaint dated 4 February, 1646, objections are made about the growth of ribbon manufacture in the countryside. . . . The 'putters out' thereupon replied that the position had changed completely since 1612. Trade had increased a great deal . . . the number of gildsmen was too small to provide even one 'putter out' with enough goods for the whole year."

Middlemen engaged in the selling of cloth were particularly eager to speed up production because for a long time cloth was Europe's chief export to the East. More and more workers were needed to supply the increasing demand, so the middlemen brought their raw materials not only to those gildsmen in the towns who were willing to work on them, but also to the men, women, and children in the villages.

To those peasants who had suffered from the enclosures, this spread of industry to the countryside gave an opportunity to add a few shillings to their diminished income. Many who would otherwise have had to leave the village were enabled to hang on because the merchant brought them work to do. Daniel Defoe, whom you remember as the author of *Robinson Crusoe*, wrote another famous book, in 1724, called *A Tour Through Great Britain*. He describes some of these villagers at the task set them by the middlemen. "Among the Manufacturers Houses are likewise scattered an infinite Number of Cottages or Small Dwellings, in which dwell the work-men which are employed, the Women and Children of whom, are always busy Carding, Spinning etc., so that no Hands being un-employ'd all can gain their Bread even from the youngest to the ancient; hardly any thing above four Years old, but its Hands are sufficient to itself. This is the reason also why we saw so few People without Doors; but if we knock'd at the door of any of the Master Manufacturers, we presently saw a House full of lusty Fellows, some at the Dye-fat, some dressing the Cloths, some at the Loom . . . all hard at work, and full employed upon the Manufacture, and all seeming to have sufficient business. . . ."

And just as Crowley, the hardware manufacturer, grew wealthy by successfully managing to supply the expanding market with goods that it was calling for, so middlemen in the cloth business grew rich also. Defoe informs his readers further:

"They told me at *Bradford*, that it was no extraordinary thing to have Clothiers in that Country worth, from ten thousand, to Forty thousand Pounds a Man, and many of the great Families . . . have been originally raised from, and built up by this truly noble Manu-facture. . . . But to go back to *Newbery*, the famous *Jack* of *Newberry*, who was so great a Clothier, that when King *James* met his Waggons loaden with Cloths going to London, and inquiring whose they were, was answered by them all, They were *Jack* of *Newbery's*, the King returned, if the Story be true, That this *Jack* of *Newbery* was richer than he."

This famous Jack of Newbury was an important figure because, unlike most of the other middlemen who brought the raw mate-rial to the craftsmen to be worked on in their own houses, he set up his own building containing over two hundred looms on which some six hundred men, women, and children laboured. This was early in the sixteenth century. It was the forerunner of the factory system of three centuries later.

Newbury and the middlemen who brought the raw materials to the craftsmen to be combed, spun, woven, in their own homes were capitalists. They owned the cloth; they marketed it; they kept the profits. The master craftsmen and the journeymen under them were wage earners. They worked in their own houses; they arranged their own time. They owned their own tools (though this was not always true). But they were no longer independent; they no longer owned the raw materials—these were brought to them by the middlemen, the entrepreneurs (there were exceptions to this also—some did their own raw materials). They were now merely piece-work makers of goods, no longer trading directly with the consumer; their trading function had been taken over by capitalist entrepreneurs and they had become merely manufacturers in the real sense of the word (*manu*, by hand + *factura*, a making = a making by hand).

In the gild system, which had risen with the town economy, capital played only a small part; in the putting-out system which arose with the national economy, capital played an important part. It took lots of money to buy the raw materials for many workers; it took lots of money to organize the distribution of those raw materials and their sale as finished products later. It was the man with money, the capitalist, who became the directing head of the putting-out system.

Increased demand meant the reorganization on a capitalist basis of those heavy industries which needed an expensive plant. A good example of this was coal mining in the sixteenth century in England. The surface seams of coal were used up and deep mining was necessary. This meant the investment of large sums of money. It meant the entrance upon the scene of the capitalist.

Similarly in the mining of metals, large sums of money were invested to meet the demand for iron, brass, copper, etc., needed in industry, as well as for supplying the warring armies. So huge was the outlay of capital necessary in the metal industries that combinations of capitalists formed joint-stock companies to amass the sums required. This had been done before in trading ventures—now it began in manufacturing.

With the discovery of hitherto unknown lands, it was natural that completely new industries such as sugar-refining, tobacco, etc., should make their appearance. The governments granted monopolies to those people who dared to risk their money in these new ventures. The new industries were organized from the start on a capitalist basis.

From the sixteenth to the eighteenth century, the independent craftsmen of the Middle Ages tend to disappear and in their place comes a wage-earning class growing more and more dependent on the capitalist-merchant-middleman-entrepreneur.

It might be helpful to go over an outline of the successive stages of industrial organization:

I. *Household* or *family* system: The members of the household produced goods for their own use, not for sale. Work was not carried on to supply an outside market. Early Middle Ages.

II. *Gild* system: Production carried on by independent masters, employing two or three men, for a small, stable, outside market. The workers owned both the raw materials on which they worked and the tools with which they worked. They sold not their labour, but the product of their labour. Throughout Middle Ages.

III. *Putting-out* system: Production carried on in the home for growing outside market, by master craftsmen with helpers, as in the gild system. With this important difference—that masters were no longer independent; they still owned their tools but were dependent for their materials on an entrepreneur who had come between them and the consumer; they were now simply piece-work wage-earners. Sixteenth to eighteenth century.

IV. *Factory* system: Production for increasingly wider and more fluctuating market carried on outside the home, in employer's buildings and under strict supervision. Workers have completely lost their independence; they own neither the raw material as they did under the gild system, nor their tools as they did under the putting-out system. Skill not so important as formerly because of increasing use of machinery. Capital more important than ever before. Nineteenth century to present day.

A word of warning.

> Stop
>> Look
>>> and
>>>> Listen.

The outline above is offered as a guide, not as gospel. It's dangerous to accept it as the whole truth. It isn't. Taken with reservations it may be helpful. Taken by itself it will lead you up many wrong trails.

It's a mistake, for example, to believe, as the outline suggests, that all industry passed through the four successive stages. That was true only of some, by no means of all. New industries arose which began in the third stage. Other industries skipped several stages.

The time periods indicated are only rough approximations. Always when one stage was widely prevalent, signs of its decay were already there, and the seeds of the next stage were pushing upward. Thus in the thirteenth century when the gilds were at their height, instances of the putting-out system had already appeared in northern Italy. Similarly, examples of the factory system almost as we know it today, were already in evidence in the period which the outline calls the putting-out system. Remember Jack of Newbury in the sixteenth century.

The reverse is also true. The wide prevalence of any stage of industrial development does not mean the total disappearance of the preceding stage. The gild system persisted long after the outline indicates that the putting-out system had come in. Perhaps the best proof that one stage continues long into the next is furnished by the following quotation on "homework"—i.e., the putting-out system. "A survey of homework in the fabricated-metal industry. . . . The products include hooks and eyes, snap fasteners, safety pins, bobby pins, and metal buttons. Attaching strings or wires to tags is another operation which is performed by some of the homeworkers studied. . . .

Distribution of homeworkers according to average hourly earnings	Number of families
1 cent and under 2 cents	5
2 cents " " 3 "	9
3 " " " 4 "	15
4 " " " 5 "	9
5 " " " 6 "	14
6 " " " 7 "	8
7 " " " 8 "	5
8 " " " 9 "	15
9 " " " 10 "	14
10 " " " 11 "	13
11 " " " 12 "	5
12 " " " 13 "	2
13 " " " 14 "	5
14 " " " 15 "	3
15 " " over	7
Total.....	129

". . . The average family, then, works a total of thirty-five man-hours a week, for which it receives $1.75. . . .

"Crowded, unsanitary and dilapidated houses, worn-out clothing, and frequent complaints about the inadequacy of food, both as to amount and quality, characterized the homes investigated. . . .

"Children under sixteen were working in 96 of the 129 families studied. . . . Half of these children were less than twelve years of age. Thirty-four of them were eight years old and under, twelve were less than five years old. . . .

"Distribution of employed children according to age:

Age	Number of children employed
2– 3 years	2
3– 4 "	2
4– 5 "	8
5– 6 "	2
6– 7 "	7
7– 8 "	13
8– 9 "	15
9–10 "	19
10–11 "	23
11–12 "	21
12–13 "	40
13–14 "	26
14–15 "	29
15–16 "	35
Unknown	4
Total.....	246

Shocking, isn't it? Think of two- and three-year-old children at work! Is that a report of the putting-out system in the sixteenth to eighteenth centuries? Indeed no. What is the time and place of the conditions described in this quotation?

> Time: August, 1934
> Place: Connecticut, U.S.A.

XI

"Gold, Greatness, and Glory"

WHAT makes a country rich? Got any suggestions? Just for the fun of it, make a list of your ideas and see how they compare with those of the smart men of the seventeenth and eighteenth centuries. They were keenly interested in the subject because thinking in terms of a national state, of a whole country instead of a city, presented new problems to them. They had now to consider not what was best for the city of Southampton or the city of Lyons or the city of Amsterdam, but rather what was best for the country of England or the country of France or the country of Holland. They were concerned with transferring to the national field those principles which had made the towns wealthy and important. Having achieved the political state, they turned their attention to the economic state. The things they wrote and the laws they advocated were all in terms of the whole country. Governments passed laws which they thought would bring wealth and power to the whole nation; in the pursuit of that end they kept their eye on every facet of day-to-day life and deliberately changed and moulded and regulated all the activities of their subjects. The theories that were expressed and the laws that were passed have been neatly classified by historians as the "mercantile system." But, in truth, they were not a system at all. Mercantilism was not a system in our sense of the word, but rather a number of prevailing economic theories applied by the state at one time and another in its effort to attain wealth and power. Statesmen were interested in this problem not because they liked to sit and think about this, that, or the other thing, but because their governments were all up against it—always broke and in great need of money. What makes a country wealthy, then, was no idle question. It was real. And it had to be answered.

The country of Spain in the sixteenth century was perhaps the richest and most powerful in the world. When the smart men of other countries asked themselves the reason for that, they thought they had found the answer in the treasure that was pouring into Spain from its colonies. Gold and silver. The more there was of it in the country the richer that country would be—that seemed to hold good for nations as it did for individuals. What made the wheels of industry and commerce turn faster and faster? Gold and silver. What enabled a monarch to hire an army to fight his country's enemies? Gold and silver. What bought the stout timber that went into the making of ships, or the corn that went into hungry mouths, or the woollen cloth that covered people's backs? Gold and silver. What made a country strong enough to conquer an enemy country—what were the "sinews of war"? Gold and silver. The possession of gold and silver, then, the amount of bullion in the country, was the index to its wealth and power.

Most writers of the period harped on the idea that "a rich country, in the same manner as a rich man, is supposed to be a country abounding in money; and to keep up gold and silver in any country is supposed to be the readiest way to enrich it."

As late as 1757, Joseph Harris, in *An Essay Upon Money and Coins*, wrote: "Gold and silver, for many reasons, are the fittest metals hitherto known for hoarding: they are durable; convertible without damage into any form; of great value in proportion to their bulk; and being the money of the world, they are the readiest exchange for all things, and what most readily and surely command all kinds of services."

If governments believed this theory that the more gold and silver in a country the richer it would be, then their next step was obvious. Pass laws forbidding people to take these metals out of the country.

One government after another did just that, and "Acts Against the Exportation of Gold and Silver" became common. Here is one from England: "It was ordained by the authority of . . . Parliament, that no person should carry or make to be carried out of this Realm or Wales from no part of the same, any manner of Money of the Coin of this Realm, nor Money of the Coin of other Realms, Lands or Lordships, nor Plate Vessel Bullion or Jewel of Gold garnished or ungarnished, or of Silver, without the King's licence."

The news reports of the Fuggers' agents to their central banking-house might be compared to the Associated Press of today. At every important spot correspondents were stationed who dispatched the story of big happenings as soon as they learned of them. Here are a few "flashes" from the Fugger News Letters:

"Venice, 13th December, 1596. The King of Spain has sternly commanded that no gold or silver should be exported from the kingdom, or used for the purposes of trade."

"Rome, 29th January, 1600. The Pope's chamberlain . . . has had all the local and foreign silver coins valued anew and has made a decree that no one in future should take away from here more than five crowns."

Such measures might keep within a country whatever gold and silver it already had. And countries which had mines within their own boundaries, or other countries, like Spain, which were lucky enough to own colonies whose mines were rich in gold and silver, could constantly add to their stock of metals. But what of those countries which had neither? How could they become wealthy—assuming, as some mercantilists did, that money meant wealth?

For these countries the mercantilists offered a happy solution. A "favorable balance of trade" was their way out. What was meant by a favorable balance of trade?

In *Policies to Reduce this Realm of England unto a Prosperous Wealth and Estate*, written in 1549, we find the answer: "The only means to cause much Bullion to be brought out of other realms into the king's mints is to provide that a great quantity of our wares may be carried yearly into beyond the Seas and less quantity of their

wares be brought hither again. . . . If such means may be found as
I ensure your grace, it is neither impossible, nor unlikely, to send
over the Seas yearly in wares the value of eleven hundred Thousand
pounds, and to receive again in all kinds of wares but the value of
six hundred Thousand pounds: Must it not follow of necessity that
we should then receive for the other five hundred Thousand pounds,
either so much Bullion or English coin."

Countries could increase their supply of bullion, argued the mercantilists, by engaging in foreign trade—always being careful to see
that they sold more to other countries than they bought from them.
The difference in the value of their exports over their imports would
have to be paid to them in metal.

The English East India Company had a clause in its charter
which gave it the right to export bullion. When in the seventeenth
century, many pamphleteers attacked this company for sending
wealth out of England, Thomas Mun, one of the directors, defended
the company in a famous book called *England's Treasure by Foreign
Trade*. The title of the book indicates the nature of his defence.
Mun argued that while the East India Company did send gold and
silver to the East to buy goods there, those goods were either re-
exported from England to other countries, or worked up in England,
and later resold to other countries. In both cases more money poured
back into England, which justified the previous export of the precious metals. Mun argued that the really important way to increase
the wealth of the state was for it to sell to foreign countries more
than it bought from them to keep a favorable balance of trade. "The
ordinary means, therefore, to increase our wealth and treasure is by
Foreign Trade, wherein we must ever observe this rule: to sell more
to strangers yearly than we consume of theirs in value . . . because
that part of our stock which is not returned to us in wares must
necessarily be brought home in treasure . . . Whatsoever courses
we take to force money into the Kingdom, yet so much only will
remain with us as we shall gain by the balance of our trade."

The trick, then, was to export valuable goods, import only what
you needed, and get the balance in hard cash. This meant encour-

aging industry in every possible way, because the products of industry were more valuable than those of agriculture and so would sell for more in the foreign markets. Also, what was equally important, having your own industry in your own country, making the things your own people needed, meant that you would have to buy less from foreigners. This was a step in the direction of attaining that favourable balance of trade as well as in making your country self-sufficient, independent of other countries.

One country after another, then, concerned itself with the important problem of how best to help its old industries to prosper and new ones to begin. In the Bavaria of Maximilian I, in 1616, a special Brain Trust was appointed to consider the question: "Be it resolved, that special persons be appointed, who on fixed days each week shall meet together and diligently discuss and deliberate . . . the means by which more trades and crafts shall be exercised in the country and how they may usefully be continued."

What were some of the ways these Brain-Trusters and others like them in other countries hit upon as the means of building up industry? They thought of quite a number.

There was, for example, the bounty given by the government on manufactured goods for export. If you were a manufacturer of knives and you received from your government a sum of money for every dozen knives you exported, you'd probably try to make more and more knives. And the makers of hats, woollens, munitions, linens, etc., would probably feel the same way. Government bounties on production were designed to stimulate manufacturing.

So was the protective tariff. Because you and I are more familiar with American history than with any other, we are inclined to make the mistake of believing that the idea of a protective tariff on imported goods originated with our own Alexander Hamilton. That's not true. The protective tariff to encourage "infant" industries was a device at least as old as the mercantilists, and probably older. Here is a plea for help for an infant industry, written in England before Hamilton was born: "I have now, I think, shewn, Sir, that the linen manufacture . . . is but in its infancy in Britain

and Ireland, that therefore it is impossible for our people to sell so
cheap . . . as those who have had this manufacture long established
among them, and that for this Reason, we cannot propose to make
any great or quick progress in this manufacture, without some
public encouragement."

The public encouragement this manufacturer wanted came in the
form of protection against foreign competition, by high duties on
imported manufactured goods. In some cases governments even
forbade the importation of certain articles under any circumstances.

Not only was industry to be fostered by bounties and high tariffs,
but skilled foreign workmen who could introduce new trades or
new methods were to be encouraged by every means possible to
settle in the country. Foreign craftsmen were attracted by tempting
privileges such as tax-exemption, free dwellings, a monopoly for a
certain number of years on the manufacture of their product, or
loans of capital with which to set up their necessary equipment.
When they could not be induced to come out of their own free
will, then occasionally governments resorted to kidnapping them.
Colbert, who was the Mussolini of his time in that he held so many
Cabinet posts in seventeenth-century France, was particularly eager
to get foreign craftsmen to live and work in France. He stationed
agents in other countries whose sole job it was to recruit labourers—
by whatever means possible. On the 28th of June, 1669, he wrote
to M. Chassan, French minister at Dresden: "Please continue to
help him [the recruiting agent] in every way that you can to make
his commission successful, and rest assured that the good treatment
which will be accorded to the ironworkers whom he has already
brought to France will enable him to engage others for our manufacturers."

Strict precautions were taken against their returning home, just
as precautions were taken against native artisans going to other
countries and giving away or selling their trade secrets. One dra-
matic cross-current, however, was the expulsion for religious reasons,
of whole groups of people who were industrious, capable, skilled
craftsmen and tradesmen. On the one hand, France was bending

every effort to bring into France skilled workmen, yet, on the other hand, in the expulsion of the Huguenots in the seventeenth century it was driving out by force many of its own best craftsmen.

Interesting proof of the fact that governments really concerned themselves about the welfare of foreign craftsmen is shown in a letter of Queen Elizabeth's written in 1566 to the Justices of Cumberland and Westmoreland. In a period when branding, chopping off of ears, legs, or arms, and hanging were common punishments for ordinary offences—in a period when life was cheap, see how concerned the Queen becomes because of the murder of a single German: "Whereas certain Almaynes privileged by our letters patent under our great seal of england, with their great travail, skill and expense of money, have of late to their great commendation recovered out of the mountains and Rocks within our counties of Westmoreland and Cumberland great quantity of minerals, with their full intention to have further proceded about the same, have of late been . . . assaulted, Riotously and contrary to our peace and laws, by a great number of disordered people of our said counties, whereupon manslaughter and murder of one of the said Almaynes hath ensued, to the likely discouragement of all their said company. We . . . therefore . . . charge and command you to apprehend and safely to retain in ward so many as were occasions of the said tumult or murder. . . . But also vigilantly and carefully to foresee, that the said Almaynes at all times hereafter may friendly and quietly be treated . . . fail you not hereof, as you tender our pleasure, and will answer the contrary at your peril."

Just as the foreigners whose skill would benefit industry were to be protected, so inventors of new processes were also to be aided by the government. When Jehan de Bras de fer in 1611 invented a new kind of mill, the government granted him a monopoly which ran for twenty years, similar to our government patents of today: "We have . . . permitted that he and his associates . . . build and construct mills according to his said invention . . . in all the towns and cities of our kingdom. . . . We forbid all, of whatever quality or condition they may be, to build mills after the said invention . . .

whether in whole or in part . . . without his express permission and consent, on pain of paying a fine of 10,000 livres and having the said mills confiscated."

Not only were grants of monopoly given to inventors, but in some countries prizes were also held out as bait to those who would put their minds to work on the problem of building up home industry through the invention of new and better methods. In France, Colbert established state institutes for technical education, as well as industrial works run by the state itself. In Bavaria, at the end of the seventeenth century, the state cloth works employed 2,000 hands. These state works were to act as models, as inspiration, as laboratory. It was in these large-scale undertakings not subject to gild restrictions of any kind, that experiment and progress could go on freely, which was often difficult for single enterprising craftsmen.

But though it was difficult, it was not impossible. And the state was ever willing to encourage industry by direct subsidy, as well as in the other ways mentioned. The French textile industries, while Colbert was in charge, received some eight million livres in subsidies of one kind or another. To a group of men who were to set up a plant for the manufacture of silk and of cloth of gold and silver in seventeenth-century France, the government gave many valuable privileges as well as direct aid in money: "One of the principal means of attaining this end [common good of our subjects] is the establishment of arts and manufactures, both for the hope which they give of enriching and improving this kingdom, that we may no longer have to go to our neighbours like beggars . . . seeking afar what we do not ourselves possess, and also because it is an easy and good means of cleansing our kingdom of the vices produced by idleness, and the only way by which we may no longer have to send out of the kingdom gold and silver to enrich our neighbours . . . [then names the men, for twelve years] . . . during which time no other may, in the said town . . . of Paris, set up or have set up silk mills . . . unless with their permission and consent . . . and in order to assist them in the great outlay necessary for this establishment, we grant to the said entrepreneurs . . .

the sum of 180,000 livres, which will be assigned them . . . without any delay, which sum they shall retain for twelve years without payment of interest, and at the end of the said time, they shall be called upon to return us only 150,000 livres, and the 30,000 remaining we shall give them as a gift in consideration of the extraordinary expenses which we realise to be necessary and which they have to make to their own loss in order to set up the said establishment."

This edict introduces another advantage the mercantilists emphasized in their reasons for wanting to build up industry. They continually pointed out that the growth of industry not only meant an increase in exports, which in turn helped toward a favourable balance of trade, but also brought about an increase in employment. Mr. T. Manley, writing in 1677, argued that "a pound of wool Manufactured and Exported, is of more worth to us by employing our people, than ten pounds exported raw at double the present rate." In a period when beggars and unemployed were causing trouble, as well as costing considerable sums of money in poor relief, such an argument carried considerable weight. To the monarch who was concerned with the welfare of his people, to mercantilist thinkers who, above all, were interested in securing national power and national wealth, the necessity of keeping the men of their country—the cannon fodder—in good condition, was obvious. So industry which brought employment to workers was to be encouraged. And considerable attention, too, was paid to the production of corn, to ensure enough food to the people, so they would be sturdy—when war came. Since it was clear to all that an adequate food supply was of paramount importance in case of war, bounties were given in England to stimulate the production of corn. A nation self-sufficient in food in war time, composed of strong, well-fed fighting-men, was one of the chief reasons for the various corn laws that were passed in the different countries.

Fighting-men. War time. People who were thinking in these terms would naturally concern themselves with the number and quality of their ships. Both for defending the home country and attacking the enemy country, ships would be needed. And just as the mercantilists thought of encouraging industry as a vital step in bringing about a favorable balance of trade, so they looked upon the building up of a merchant marine as essential for the same reason. To the extent that governments were interested in foreign trade, they emphasized the importance of adequate shipping facilities to carry their industrial products to other countries. They turned their attention, therefore, to the encouragement of shipping with much the same zeal that they showed for the fostering of industry. And the methods used were somewhat the same. The shipbuilder was given government bounties; the products necessary in the shipping industry, tar, pitch, stout timber, etc., were sought out and admitted duty free to the home country; men were forced into the navy—in France the judges were encouraged to sentence criminals to the galleys whenever possible; in England the fishing industry was fostered because it was a training-school for seamen; people were asked to eat more fish, and, no doubt, the propaganda machinery of that day went to work trying to persuade people that fish contained some elements that were not only good for their health, but absolutely necessary to ensure a ripe old age.

With the decline of Spain at the end of the sixteenth century, the little country of Holland rose to first place as the leading power of the time. Holland was small, but it was rich and strong, and one of the chief reasons was its concentration on shipping. The inhabitants of Holland, like those of Venice, were forced by their geographical set-up to learn all about boats; the North Sea, with its wonderful treasure of fish, continually beckoned to the Hollander; the stream of northern products going to the Mediterranean, and vice versa, found Holland almost in the exact centre—of course the enterprising Dutchmen seized their opportunity. They took to the sea and became the carriers of the growing world's goods. Dutch boats scurried everywhere—carrying everybody else's goods to every place else.

But England and France were not content to see English or French goods being carried away in Dutch boats. Part of their plan for self-sufficiency was the building up of their own fleets. They didn't like the idea of paying out good money to Dutch seamen for acting as carriers of their goods. The English Navigation Acts so famous in American history had for one of their major purposes the wresting away from the Dutch of their command of the carry-ing service on the sea. That intent is plain in one of the Acts, dated 1660, which reads: "For the increase of shipping and encourage-ment of the navigation of this nation . . . be it enacted . . . that from and after the first day of December one thousand six hundred and sixty . . . no goods or commodities whatsoever shall be im-ported into or exported out of any lands, islands, plantations or territories to his Majesty belonging or in his possession . . . in Asia, Africa or America, in any other ship or ships, vessel or vessels whatsoever, but in such ships or vessels as do truly and without fraud belong only to the people of England or Ireland, [or] domin-ion of Wales or . . . built of and belonging to any of the said lands, islands, plantations or territories, as the right owners thereof, and whereof the master and three-fourths of the mariners at least are English."

Dutch ships · · · → | Empire wall—Keep out!

In this the mother country and the colonies were to act as one, united in a common fight against the foreign intruder. It was a great advantage to the American colonists to have this defence against the stronger Dutch shipping interests. This part of the Navi-gation Acts helped the Americans to build up their own merchant marine, so that Yankee boats were soon a familiar sight in every port of the world. To have part of the monopoly of the shipping of the growing British Empire brought wealth to Yankee ship-builders, shipowners and sailors.

But you know that there were other parts of the Navigation Acts which were not so advantageous to the colonies. It was part of the mercantilist idea to regard colonies as another source of revenue *for the mother country.*

So it was that laws were passed prohibiting the colonists from turning to any industry which might compete with the industry of the mother country. The colonists were forbidden to manufacture caps, hats, woollen or iron goods. All the raw materials for these things were on hand in America; yet the colonists were expected to send these raw materials to England to be manufactured, then buy them back in the form of manufactured goods.

> Colonial raw materials · · · → to England, manufactured there · · · → sent back to America
> *instead of* colonial raw materials · · · → manufactured in America.

This was England's attitude not only to America, but to all her colonies. Ireland, for example, was a colony of England. When the Irish took their wool and made it into cloth, laws were passed squashing their cloth industry. Could the Irish then export their raw wool freely? No, it must be sold to England only, and England would use what it could, and re-export the rest. Because England could thus dictate the price, large numbers of Irishmen were impoverished. Thus mercantilist policy played its part in the Irish struggle for independence from British domination just as it did in the American.

Similarly, certain American products, such as tobacco, rice, indigo, masts, turpentine, tar, pitch, beaver-skins, pig-iron, (the list increased with time) had to be sent to England only. The English wanted these things for themselves, for their own manufacturing industries. And what they couldn't consume themselves, they would re-export—at a profit.

> Virginia tobacco → to English merchant → to French snuff-manufacturer, *instead of* Virginia tobacco directly → to French snuff-manufacturer.

The key to an understanding of the friction that arose between mother country and colonies was that, while the mother country thought that its colonies existed for her sake, the colonies thought they existed for their own sakes. Sir Francis Bernard, the royal governor of Massachusetts, made the mercantilist notion of the relation between mother country and colonies quite clear: "The two great

objects of Great Britain in regard to the American trade must be
(1) to oblige her American subjects to take from Great Britain
only, all the manufactures and European goods which she can
supply them with; (2) To regulate the foreign trade of the Americans so that *the profits thereof may finally centre in Great Britain*,
or be applied to the improvement of her empire."

Here was a plain statement of the fact that colonies existed solely
as an aid to the mother country in its struggle for national wealth
and power. This was true not only of England but of France, of
Spain, of every mother country of the mercantilist era. It's important to remember that.

It is also important to remember that "national wealth" and "national power" are loose phrases. It was an interesting coincidence
that what many writers suggested as the best way of making "our
country" wealthy, was also the best way of making themselves or
their class wealthy. Which doesn't mean that they were putting
something over. Not at all. It was natural for them to identify their
own interests with those of the whole country. At no time, perhaps,
has the connection between economic interest and national policy
been more obvious.

You remember what a lot of head-scratching the kings had to
go through in order to raise money. When there was no extensive
and well-developed system of taxation, they were never sure of
getting enough cash where they needed it when they needed it.
The treasury could not count on a steady flow of money. That was
why the king had farmed out his revenues to tax collectors who
paid him the money in advance (and screwed out every cent they
could get from the poor taxpayers). That was why the king had
sold offices to the highest bidder and granted monopolies for great
sums. That was why, much as he hated to do it, he had been forced
to sell Crown lands. That was why he had been compelled to turn
to the bankers and merchants for loans. It was because governments
were always so hard up that such great emphasis was laid on the
piling up of precious metals. And since it was also believed that
treasure was to be obtained by trade, it was natural to think of the

interests of the state and of the merchant class as identical. So it was that the state made it its chief business to support and encourage trade and everything pertaining to it.

It was through commerce that the state was accounted great and could get its share in the expansion of trade and territory. Mercantilism was merchant-ilism.

The mercantilists believed that, as far as trade was concerned, one country's loss was another country's gain—i.e., one country could only increase its trade at the expense of another. They did not think of trade as something conferring mutual benefit—an advantageous exchange—but as a fixed quantity in which each should try to grab the largest part. The eighteenth-century author of *The Dictionary of Trade and Commerce* put it this way: "There seems to be but a limited quantity of trade in Europe. Suppose that in the trade of the woollen manufacture . . . England is in the channel of exporting and supplying to the value of fifteen millions; if it should in any year supply twenty millions, it must be at the expense and diminution of the sales of the others."

And Colbert wrote to M. Pomponne, the French minister at The Hague in 1670, "Since commerce and manufacture cannot decrease in Holland without passing into the hands of some other country . . . there is nothing so important and necessary for the general welfare of the State, as that we should, at the same time as we see our commerce and manufacture increasing within the kingdom, also be assured of their real and effective diminution in the States of Holland."

You can see that belief in the idea that "there is nothing so important and necessary for the general welfare of the State" as to be certain that the commerce and manufacturing of a rival state be diminished, was bound to lead to only one thing. War. The fruit of mercantilist policy was war. The scramble for markets, the fierce competition for the trade of this country or that, the fight for more colonies—all these plunged the rival nations into one war after another. Some of these wars were openly labelled what they really were—trade wars. The purpose of the others was disguised by high-sounding names, as so often happens, even today. But we have the word of the Archbishop of Canterbury in 1690, that: "In all the Strugglings and Disputes, that have of late years befallen this corner of the World, I found, that although the pretence was fine and Spiritual, yet the ultimate end and true scope, was Gold, and Greatness, and Secular Glory."

Let us borrow the archbishop's last phrase. His three G's—Gold, Greatness, and Glory—sum up quite neatly exactly what the mercantilists were aiming at.

XII

Let Us Alone!

THE year 1776 was one of rebellion. It was a memorable year. To Americans it brings to mind the Declaration of Independence, our revolt against the mercantilist colonial policy of England; to economists of every country it brings to mind the publication of Adam Smith's *Wealth of Nations*, the summary of the rising revolt against the three R's of mercantilist policy—restriction, regulation, and restraint. There was a growing number of people in the eighteenth century who did not agree with mercantilist theory or practice. They did not agree with it because they suffered from it. Traders wanted a share in the huge profits of the privileged monopoly companies. When they tried to cut in they were excluded as "interlopers." Men with money wanted to use it, how, when, and where they liked. They wanted to take advantage of every opportunity which expanding trade and industry offered. They knew the power which capital gave them and they wanted to exercise it freely. They were tired of "you must do this, you may not do that." They were sick of "Acts against . . . Duties on . . . Bounties for. . . ." They wanted free trade.

The governments wanted to help industry. Well and good. But it seemed that they couldn't help one class of people without hurting another. And the class that was hurt didn't like it. It protested. In Prussia in the 1700's, wool-producers were not allowed to export their wool. The idea was to stimulate the manufacture of cloth by assuring the manufacturers enough raw material—at a cheap price. The manufacturers liked this prohibition on the export of wool. But the producers of wool objected to it. In 1721 they drafted a petition to the king asking that the law be abolished: ". . . on their own admission, the warehouses have great stocks of wool. . . . It is also obvious that this year's crop of wool . . . will not be even half sold. Your royal Majesty's gracious intention of seeing that there shall be no shortage of wool for the manufacturers, that the industry shall thereby be increased . . . has now been fully realized; on the other hand, however, the injury done to those who raise sheep is growing . . . for everything is overstocked, and they must now sell their wool at the price which suits the purchaser. . . . The country as a whole is suffering a great deal from this legal lowering of wool prices (which must fall even lower if the prohibition on export continues) . . . the sheep cost more than they bring in, and many sheep farmers might get the idea of letting their herds die out."

But King Frederick William I held fast to the policy of restriction. Here is his reply to the petition: "His Majesty the King of Prussia . . . considers it necessary to retain the prohibition on the export of wool . . . since experience shows that other powers, and particularly England, which also do not allow wool to leave the country, are doing well thereby, and their countries grow rich."

Maybe the King of Prussia was right about the fact that England was growing rich. But merchants of that country would have argued with him about the reason. We know that they too disliked mercantilist restrictions. They wanted changes made that would help them in their business. They borrowed the mercantilist way of putting their case—that is, they said they were arguing for what would best bring about wealth and prosperity *to the country*. An old and pardonable error—this coupling of their own interests with their country's. In the Journal of the House of Commons for May 8, 1820 we find their argument for free trade: "A petition of the . . . Merchants of the City of London, was presented, and read; setting forth, That foreign commerce is eminently conducive to the wealth and prosperity of a country, by enabling it to import the commodities, for the production of which the soil, climate, capital, and industry of other countries are best calculated, and to export in payment those articles for which its own situation is better adapted; that freedom from restraint is calculated to give the utmost extension to Foreign trade, and the best direction to the capital and industry of the country; that the maxim of buying in the cheapest market, and selling in the dearest, which regulates every merchant in his individual dealings, is strictly applicable, as the best rule for the trade of the whole nation; that a policy founded on these principles would render the commerce of the world an interchange of mutual advantages, and diffuse an increase of wealth and enjoyment among the inhabitants of each state . . . that the prevailing prejudices in favour of the protection or restrictive system may be traced to the erroneous supposition, that every importation of Foreign commodities occasions a diminution or discouragement of our own productions to the same extent—so that if the reasoning upon which these . . . regulations are founded were followed out consistently, it would not stop short of excluding us from all Foreign commerce whatsoever."

Adam Smith's *Inquiry into the Nature and Causes of the Wealth of Nations* was one of those books that captures the public imagination and sweeps through country after country. Unlike earlier writers who said a state must follow this or that policy to become powerful, Adam Smith concerned himself more with a study of the causes which influence the production and distribution of wealth. Where many of the mercantilists had an axe to grind but concealed it with the suggestion that the country would increase its power—by grinding that axe, Smith interested more in analysis than in special pleading approached the subject in a scientific manner. Part of his famous book was devoted to a study of mercantilist doctrine. He showed it up.

There had been others before him who showed it up, too. In the heyday of mercantilism there were some thinkers who attacked its principles. Every mercantilist practice had its critic.

Take the tax on and prohibition of the importation of foreign goods. As early as 1690 Nicholas Barbon, in *A Discourse of Trade*, had written: "The Prohibition of *trade*, is the Cause of its Decay; for all Foreign Wares are brought in by the Exchange of the Native [wares]: So that the Prohibiting of any Foreign Commodity, doth hinder the Making and Exportation of so much of the Native, as used to be Made and Exchanged for it. The Artificers and Merchants that Dealt in such Goods, lose their trades. . . ."

Or take the well-known "balance of trade" argument. Dudley North way back in 1691 hammered away at that in a famous book called *Discourses Upon Trade*: "It is not long since there was a great noise with Inquiries into the Balance of Exportation and Importation; and so into the Balance of Trade, as they called it. For it was fancyed that if we brought more Commodities in, than we carried out, we were on the High-way to Ruin. . . . Now it may appear strange to hear it said, that the whole World as to Trade, is but as one Nation or People, and therein Nations are as Persons . . . That there can be no Trade unprofitable to the Publick; for if any prove so, men leave it off. . . . That no Laws can set Prizes in Trade, the Rates of which, must and will make themselves. But when such Laws do happen to lay any hold, it is so much Impediment to Trade, and therefore prejudicial."

Similarly Joseph Tucker, in 1749, aimed a shot at the mercantilist policy of granting monopolies: "*Our Monopolies, publick Companies, and Corporate Charters* are the Bane and Destruction of a free Trade. . . . The whole Nation must suffer in its Commerce, and be debarred trading to more than three-fourths of the Globe to enrich a few rapacious Directors. *They* get wealthy the very same Way by which the *Publick* becomes poor."

Tucker also took a crack at mercantilist colonial policy: "Our ill judged Policy, and unnatural Jealousy in cramping the *Commerce and Manufactures* of Ireland, is another very great Bar to the extending our Trade. If *Ireland* gets rich, what is the Consequence? *England* will be rich too; and *France* will be the poorer. The Wool, which is now smuggled from *Ireland* into *France*, and manufactured there, and from there sent to Market to oppose our own Commodities, would be manufactured in Ireland. . . . The Rents of the *Irish* Gentlemen's Estates would rise; and then the Money would soon find its Way into England."

What about the mercantilist notion of the importance to a country of a stock of gold and silver? David Hume, a friend of Adam Smith's, exploded that one in 1742. He pointed out that greater treasure gives a country no lasting advantage. His theory was that through the workings of international trade each country with a metallic currency will get the amount of gold which makes its prices such that its imports will balance its exports. How?

You remember that it had long been recognized that prices rise and fall according to the quantity of money in circulation. Hume went on from that point. "If we consider any one kingdom by itself, it is evident, that the greater or less plenty of money is of no consequence; since the prices of commodities are always proportioned to the plenty of money."

Now what happens to the trade of a country if prices rise? Obviously, people in other countries will buy less of its goods because they have grown dearer. That means the country will export less. Therefore its exports will not balance its imports. It will be buying a greater quantity of goods from other countries than other countries are buying from it. But somehow or other the difference has to be paid. If its exports of goods don't pay for its imports of goods, it will have to make up the difference in cash. This means that there will be a drain of gold out of the country where prices have risen. But this drain will decrease the amount of money in circulation, and prices, therefore, will fall again; then the other countries find that they can again purchase the goods cheaply, so the exports go up until they once more balance the imports. The reverse, of course, is also true. If prices fall in a country owing to a decrease in circulating money, other countries will buy more goods from it, because they will be cheaper. The country then will be exporting more than it imports, and the difference will be paid to it in cash. This increase in the gold of the country will send prices up again.

It will lose the advantage in its export trade which low prices gave it. Exports will drop off and a balance will once more be established between the country's exports and imports.

This is, of course, only the bare outline of the case. Actually it doesn't work that smoothly, and it takes a fair amount of time—it is true only "in the long run." But Hume's explanation effectively disposed of the mercantilist emphasis on the necessity for a great amount of the precious metals.

One after the other the theories of mercantilism had been attacked by writers at the very moment they were being put into practice. The case for free trade, particularly, had been put by the Physiocrats in France.

You might have expected that opposition to mercantilist restriction and regimentation would have developed in France, because it was in that country that control of industry by the state reached its highest point. Industry in France was surrounded by such a network of "musts" and "must nots" with an army of meddling inspectors who enforced the troublesome regulations, that it is hard to understand how anything got done at all. Gild rules and regulations were bad enough. They continued in force, or in their place came government regulations even more minute. These regulations were designed to help and protect the industry of France. In some ways they did. But even when they were wise they were always annoying to the manufacturers. Could a manufacturer of cloth, for example, make any kind of cloth he pleased? He could not. Cloth had to be of such and such quality and exactly so long. Could a hat manufacturer cater to public demand by producing hats made of a mixture of beaver, fur, and wool? He could not. He could make either all-beaver or all-wool hats, but nothing else. Could a manufacturer use a new and perhaps better kind of tool in the production of his goods? He could not. Tools were to be a certain size and shape and the inspectors came around to see that they were just that.

The natural result of this going too far in one direction would be a movement going equally far in the other. Too much control of industry would breed a demand for no control of industry. One of the earliest movers in the direction of no control was a French business man named de Gournay. Of him, Turgot, a famous French minister of finance, wrote: "He was astonished to find that a citizen could neither make nor sell anything without having bought the right to do so by getting at great expense his admission into a corporation. . . . Nor had he imagined that in a kingdom where the order of succession was only established by custom . . . the Government would have condescended to regulate by express laws the length and breadth of each piece of cloth, and the number of threads of which it must be composed, and to consecrate with the seal of the legislature four quarto volumes full of these important details; and also to pass innumerable statutes dictated by the spirit of monopoly. . . . He was no less astonished to see the Government occupy itself with regulating the price of each commodity, proscribing one kind of industry in order by that to make another flourish . . . and fancying that it ensured abundance of corn by making the condition of the cultivator more uncertain and unhappy than that of all other citizens."

Gournay was more than astonished at this excessive regulation. He wanted France to get rid of it. He coined the phrase which has since become the rallying-cry of all those opposed to restrictions of any kind—"*Laissez-faire.*" A free translation of that famous phrase is "Let us alone."

Laissez-faire became the cry of the French Physiocrats who lived at the same time as Gournay. They are important because they were the first "school" of economists. They were a group of people who, beginning in 1757, met regularly under the leadership of François Quesnay to discuss economic problems. The members of the school wrote books and articles calling for freedom from restrictions, for free trade, for *laissez-faire*. When Mirabeau, a famous Physiocrat, was asked by Carl Friedrich, the ruler of Baden in 1770, for advice on how to manage his kingdom, he wrote: "Ah, Monseigneur, be the first to give to your states the advantage of a free port and a free fair, and let the first words read on setting foot in your territory be your loved and revered name, and beneath it these three noble words: *Freedom, Immunity, Liberty!* . . . Your states will rapidly become the privileged habitation of men, the natural *route* of trade, the meeting-place of the universe."

The Physiocrats arrived at their belief in free trade by an indirect route. They believed first and foremost in the sacredness of private property, particularly property in land. Because they believed in the right to property, they believed in liberty—the right of the individual to do with his property what he liked, so long as he did not injure others. Behind their argument for free trade was their belief that the agriculturist should be allowed to produce whatever he pleased, for sale wherever he pleased. At that time in France not only could grain not be sent outside of France without paying a duty, but even in moving from one part of the country to another it would be taxed. It was as though a New Jersey farmer could not send his vegetables to New York without paying a duty at the state line. The Physiocrats were against this. Mercier de la Rivière, who wrote the best account of the beliefs of the Physiocrats, pointed out that complete liberty was essential to the enjoyment of the rights of property: "There can be no great abundance of production without great liberty. . . . Is it not true, that a right which one has not the liberty to exercise is not a right? It is therefore impossible to think of property rights without liberty. . . . Man does not undertake anything unless he is spurred thereto by the desire to enjoy; now this desire to enjoy cannot affect us if it is separated from the liberty to enjoy."

The Physiocrats approached every problem from the standpoint of its effect on agriculture. They argued that land is the only source of wealth, and labour on the land is the only productive labour. In his correspondence with Carl Friedrich, Mirabeau said: "Our peasant, in his capacity as cultivator, devotes himself to productive labour and it is from that labor alone that we seek profit, expenses having been deducted; in his capacity as weaver he is doing sterile work; he plays a useful part in the totality of services, but he produces nothing."

It is agriculture alone, the Physiocrats argued, which furnishes the raw materials essential to industry and commerce. While it was true that craftsmen might do a useful job in changing raw material to its finished form, they were not adding to the stock of wealth. After craftsmen had worked on raw material it was worth more, but the increase in the value of the object was just equal to the amount spent to pay them for their work. No wealth was added. This, the Physiocrats argued, was not true of agriculture. Whereas industry was sterile, agriculture was fruitful. Over and above the cost of agricultural labour and the profit to the owner of the land, there was a net product—due to the bounty of Nature—which was a true increase in wealth. This agricultural surplus above expenses, this *produit net*, they argued, would vary from year to year. It was great or small according to the seasons.

Though economists today would disagree with much of Physiocratic theory, they give it due credit for pointing out that the wealth of a nation must not be considered as a fixed sum of accumulated goods, but rather as its income, not as a stock, but as a *flow*.

Adam Smith had this to say about the theories of the Physiocrats: "This system, however, with all its imperfections, is, perhaps, the nearest approximation to the truth that has yet been published upon the subject of political economy. . . . Though in representing the labour which is employed upon land as the only productive labour, the notions which it inculcates are perhaps too narrow and confined; yet in representing the wealth of nations as consisting, not in the unconsumable riches of money, but in the consumable goods annually reproduced by the labour of society; and in representing perfect liberty as the only effectual expedient for rendering the annual reproduction the greatest possible, its doctrine seems to be in every respect as just as it is generous and liberal."

Though the Physiocrats came ahead of Adam Smith in arguing for "perfect liberty," his influence was far greater. His "Wealth of Nations" went into one edition after another. He was widely read during and after his lifetime. In so far as mercantilist theory was knocked out at all, his were the knockout blows. He disposed of the bullionists in this fashion: "A country that has no mines of its own must undoubtedly draw its gold and silver from foreign countries, in the same manner as one that has no vineyards of its own must draw its wines. It does not seem necessary, however, that the attention of government should be more turned towards the one than towards the other object. A country that has wherewithal to buy wine, will always get the wine which it has occasion for; and a country that has wherewithal to buy gold and silver, will never be in want of these metals. They are to be bought for a certain price like all other commodities."

His point of view on the colonial policy of the mercantilists was summed up in this sentence: "The monopoly of the colony trade, therefore, like all the other mean and malignant expedients of the mercantile system, depresses the industry of all other countries, but chiefly that of the colonies, without in the last increasing, but on the contrary diminishing, that of the country in whose favour it is established."

The very first sentence of Smith's book begins the plea for free trade. First we are told that "the greatest improvement in the productive powers of labour . . . seems to have been the effects of the division of labour." And by division of labour, Smith meant, way back in 1776, what you and I mean by that term today. He meant specialization—keeping a worker at a single job until he became expert at it: "To take an example, therefore, from a very trifling manufacture; but one in which the division of labour has been very often taken notice of, the trade of the pin-maker; a workman not educated to this business . . . nor acquainted with the use of the machinery employed in it . . . could scarce, perhaps, with his utmost industry, make one pin in a day, and certainly could not make twenty. But in the way in which this business is now carried on, not only the whole work is a peculiar trade, but it is divided into a number of branches, of which the greater part are likewise peculiar trades. One man draws out the wire, another straights it, a third cuts it, a fourth points it, a fifth grinds it at the top for receiving the head; to make the head requires two or three distinct operations; to put it on, is a peculiar business, to whiten the pins is another; it is even a trade by itself to put them into the paper; and the important business of making a pin is, in this manner, divided into about eighteen distinct operations, which, in some manufactories, are all performed by distinct hands, though in others the same man will sometimes perform two or three of them. I have seen a small manufactory of this kind where ten men only were employed, and where some of them consequently performed two or three distinct operations. . . . They could, when they exerted themselves, make among them about twelve pounds of pins in a day. There are in a pound upwards of four thousand pins of a middling size. Those ten persons, therefore, could make among them upwards of forty-eight thousand pins in a day. Each person, therefore, making a tenth part of forty-eight thousand pins, might be considered as making four thousand eight hundred pins in a day. But if they had all wrought separately and independently, and without any of them having been educated to this particular business, they certainly could not each of them have made twenty, perhaps not one pin in a day; that is, certainly, not the two hundred and fortieth, perhaps not the four thousand eight hundredth part of what they are at present capable of performing, in consequence of a proper division and combination of their different operations."

So what? Suppose that we agree with Adam Smith that division of labour, because of greater skill, economy of time, and general efficiency, etc., does increase the productivity of labour. What of it? What has that to do with free trade?

A great deal. Because, said Adam Smith, the division of labour is determined by the extent of the market: "As it is the power of exchanging that gives occasion to the division of labour, so the extent of this division must always be limited by the extent of that power, or, in other words, by the extent of the market. When the market is very small, no person can have any encouragement to dedicate himself entirely to one employment, for want of the power to exchange all that surplus part of the produce of his own labour, which is over and above his own consumption, for such parts of the produce of other men's labour as he has occasion for."

If increased productivity comes about through the division of labour, and the division of labour is limited by the extent of the market, then the wider the market the greater the division of labour and the greater the increase in productivity—i.e., the greater the wealth of a nation. Since with free trade you have your markets as wide as possible, therefore you have division of labour as much as possible, therefore you increase productivity as far as possible. Therefore free trade is desirable.

That's quite involved. Here is a simple way of seeing it.

1. Increased productivity comes about through division of labour.
2. The division of labour grows or diminishes according to the extent of the market.
3. The market is extended to its widest limits by free trade. *Therefore*—free trade brings about increased productivity.

One further point. Free trade between countries is the division of labour carried to its highest degree. It has just the same advantages on a world scale as the division of labour within Adam Smith's pin-making factory. It enables each country to specialize in the goods it can produce most cheaply, and thus increases the total wealth of the world.

But it is as the rebel against mercantilist restriction, regulation, and restraint, that we introduced Adam Smith at the beginning of the chapter. What did he say about interference with industry? In the following quotation he damns government meddling and calls for freedom: "Every system which endeavours, either, by extraordinary encouragements, to draw towards a particular species of industry a greater share of the capital of the society than what would naturally go to it; or, by extraordinary restraints, to force from a particular species of industry some share of the capital which would otherwise be employed in it; is in reality subversive of the great purpose which it means to promote. It retards, instead of accelerating, the progress of the society towards real wealth and greatness; and diminishes, instead of increasing, the real value of the annual produce of its land and labour.

"All systems either of preference or of restraint, therefore, being thus completely taken away, the obvious and simple system of natural liberty establishes itself of its own accord. Every man, as long as he does not violate the laws of justice, is left perfectly free to pursue his own interest his own way, and to bring both his industry and capital into competition with those of any other man, or order of men."

Re-read that last sentence and you will readily see why *The Wealth of Nations* became the business man's Bible in a period when business was rarin' to go but was hampered at every turn by bothersome regulations.

XIII

"The Old Order Changeth . . ."

WHAT would you think of a government that taxes the poor and does not tax the rich? Plain crazy would be your first thought, and then, on reflection, it might occur to you that, to some degree, that is what the government of the United States is doing today. However, you would find plenty of people who would argue the point with you—people who would try to prove that the rich in the United States pay more than their fair share of the taxes. But about the fact that the government of France in the eighteenth century did tax the poor and not the rich, there could be no argument.

There could be none because the privileged classes themselves admitted that they were exempt from practically all of the taxes of the time. The clergy and the nobility felt that it would spell the end of France, if they, like the common people, had to pay taxes. When the government of France was in a bad way financially, as expenses piled up faster and faster, so income could not get within hailing distance of outgo, it occurred to some Frenchmen that the only way out of the difficulty was to tax the privileged as well as the unprivileged. Turgot, Minister of Finance in 1776, tried to put into practice some much-needed reforms in the tax system. But the privileged would have none of them. They rallied around the Parliament of Paris, which stated their position quite plainly in these words: "The first rule of justice is to preserve to everyone what belongs to him: this rule consists, not only in preserving the rights of property but still more in preserving those belonging to the person, which arise from the prerogative of birth and position. . . . From this rule of law and equity it follows that every system which under an appearance of humanity and beneficence, would tend to establish an equality of duties, and to destroy necessary distinctions would soon lead to disorder (the inevitable result of equality) and would bring about the overturn of civil society. The French monarchy, by its constitution, is composed of several distinct estates. The personal service of the clergy is to fulfil all the functions relative to instruction and worship. The nobles consecrate their blood to the defence of the State, and assist the sovereign with their advice. The lowest class of the nation, which cannot render to the King services so distinguished acquits itself toward him by its tributes, its industry, and bodily service. To abolish these distinctions is to overthrow the whole French Constitution."

The clergy and the nobility were the privileged classes. They were called the First Estate and the Second Estate, respectively. The clergy numbered about 130,000 and the nobility about 140,000. Though these were the privileged classes, that did not mean that they were all rich or that they all did nothing. There were poor clergymen and poor nobles. There were very rich bishops and very rich nobles. There were hard-working churchmen and hard-working nobles. There were idlers in the Church and among the nobility. And there were still others in between.

The common people were the unprivileged class. They were called the Third Estate. Of the 25,000,000 people of France they numbered well over 95 per cent. And just as there were differences in wealth and style of living among the privileged classes, so there were differences among the unprivileged. About 250,000 of them, the upper middle class or bourgeoisie, were, by comparison with the rest of the Third Estate, quite well off. Another group consisted of the artisans living in the towns and cities. They numbered about 2,500,-000. All the rest, some 22,000,000, were peasants working on the land. They paid taxes to the States, tithes to the clergy, and feudal dues to the nobility.

You and I so order our lives that our expenses are determined by our income. Governments, in the main, try to do the same. But the government of France in the eighteenth century worked it the other way around. It spent money foolishly, extravagantly, unsystematically, and corruptly. One example will prove that. The *Livre Rouge* was a Red Book containing the list of all those granted government pensions. On its rolls was the name of Ducrest, a barber. Why was he entitled to a pension of 1,700 livres annually? Because he had been the hairdresser to the daughter of the Comte d'Artois. The fact that this daughter had died at an early age before she had any hair to dress, made no difference. Ducrest received his pension.

That was one example of the mad way in which French finances were administered. There were thousands of others. Instead of income regulating outgo, outgo determined income. A loose, reckless way of spending meant that a larger amount of money had to be raised in taxes. And since the privileged classes would not bear their share (but rather inflicted taxes of their own on the unprivileged), and since the richer members of the Third Estate managed by devious ways to get themselves exempted from direct taxation, the whole burden fell on the poor. It was a hard burden. A true picture of the period would have shown the peasant bent way over, carrying on his back the king, the priest, and the noble.

A famous Frenchman, de Tocqueville, showed what this burden of taxation meant in the daily life of the hard-working peasant: "Picture to yourself a French peasant of the eighteenth century . . . so passionately enamoured of the soil, that he will spend all his savings to purchase it. . . . To complete this purchase he must first pay a tax. . . . He possesses it at last; his heart is buried in it with the seed he sows. . . . But again these neighbours call him from his furrow, and compel him to work for them without wages. He tries to defend his young crops from their game; again they prevent him. As he crosses the river they wait for his passage to levy a toll. He finds them at the market where they sell him the right of selling his own produce; and when, on his return home, he wants to use the remainder of his wheat for his own sustenance . . . he cannot touch it till he has ground it at the mill and baked it at the bake-house of these same men. A portion of the income of his little prop-erty is paid away in quit-rents to them also. . . . Whatever he does, these troublesome neighbours are everywhere in his path . . . and when these are dismissed, others in the black garb of the Church present themselves to carry off the clearest profit of his harvest. . . . The destruction of a part of the institutions of the Middle Ages rendered a hundred times more odious that portion which still survived."

But this reads like a description of the feudal system of the elev-enth century. Had there been no changes, then, in the seven cen-turies that followed? Yes, there had. Of the 22,000,000 peasants in France in the 1700's only 1,000,000 were serfs in the old sense. The others had gone up the scale from serfdom toward complete free-dom. But that did not mean that all the old feudal dues and services had been swept away. Some had, but many remained. They re-mained in spite of the fact that the original cause of their coming into being had long since been abolished. The nobles who had re-ceived feudal dues and services because they gave military protec-tion, no longer formed the king's army—their military function had gone. They did not help to govern as a group—only individually—they had no administrative political function. They did not farm the land, nor did they as a whole engage in business—they had no eco-nomic function. They took without giving. Too often they had be-come idlers, parasites, frittering their time away at court, far away from their estates. Nevertheless, they still demanded and still re-ceived payments and services from the peasants. It was a hangover which the peasants rightly resented. And as de Tocqueville points out in the last sentence of the above quotation, the very fact that some of the customary dues had been destroyed, meant that those still remaining were all the more hated.

Exactly how much of his income did the peasant pay in taxes? The answer will surprise you. It has been estimated that as much as eighty per cent of his earnings were paid out to the various tax-collectors! Out of the twenty per cent remaining he had to feed,

shelter, and clothe his family. Small wonder that the peasant grumbled. Small wonder that a bad harvest found him on the borderline
of starvation. Small wonder that at such a time a good many of his
neighbours tramped the roads as beggars, hungry for food.

The French Revolution broke out in 1789. But don't gather from
that that the peasant was worse off in the eighteenth century than
he had been in the seventeenth. He was not. He was perhaps better
off. As a matter of fact, the peasants had in one way or another
been able to save enough from the tiny bit remaining to them after
the many taxes had been collected, to buy the land. For a hundred
years or more before the Revolution the peasants had been steadily
buying the land, so that when 1789 rolled around, about one-third
of the land of France was in their hands. But this made them more
discontented than before. Why?

They were land-hungry. They had been able to satisfy their crav-
ing a little. What stood in the way of their further advancement?
The crushing burden imposed on them by the State and the privileged classes. Now they saw more clearly than ever before that with
this heavy burden off their backs they could stand straighter—rise
from the position of animals to that of men. The very fact that
their position had improved a little opened their eyes to what might
be if only . . .

Not that it hadn't occurred before to the peasants of France (and
of other western European countries) that feudal payments and
restrictions should be overthrown. It had. There had been Peasant
Revolts before. While these revolts had not succeeded in throwing
overboard the whole set of feudal regulations, they had improved
the lot of the peasant. But to clear the boards entirely the peasants
had to have help and leadership.

They found it in the rising middle class.

It was this rising middle class, the bourgeoisie, that brought on
the French Revolution and gained the most from it. The bourgeoisie
brought on the Revolution because it had to. If it had not succeeded
in throwing off its oppressors it would have been crushed itself. It
was in the same position as the young chicken living in its shell and

at last growing to such a degree that it must break through the
shell or die. To the growing bourgeoisie, the regulation, restriction,
and restraint on commerce and industry, the government grant of
monopoly and privilege to small groups, the continued blocking of
progress by stick-in-the-mud outworn gilds, the unequally distributed and constantly increasing tax burden, the existence of old
laws and the passing of new laws about which they had little or no
say, the swelling number of meddling government officers, and the
ever-mounting volume of the government debt—this whole decaying
and corrupt feudal society—was the shell which had to be broken.
Not wishing to be strangled to a painful death, this growing bourgeois middle class took very good care to see that that shell was
broken.

Who were the bourgeoisie? They were the writers, the doctors,
the teachers, the lawyers, the judges, the civil servants—the educated
class; they were the merchants, the manufacturers, the bankers—
the moneyed class, both in the money already and eager for more.
Above all else they wanted—or rather, they *needed*—to cast off the
rule of feudal law in a society which in actual fact was no longer
feudal. They needed to shake off their tight feudal doublet and re-
place it with a loose-fitting capitalist coat. They found the expression of their needs in the economic field in the writings of the
Physiocrats and Adam Smith; they found the expression of their
needs in the social field in the writings of Voltaire, Diderot, and
the Encyclopædists. *Laissez-faire* in commerce and industry had its
counterpart in the "rule of reason" in religion and science.

There's nothing more maddening than to see some fellow who
hasn't your ability or capacity for hard work, walk off with the
juicy plums merely because he has "pull" of some kind. The bourgeoisie were somewhat in that position. They had talent. They had
culture. They had money. But they did not have the legal position in
society which all these things should have brought them. "Barnave
became a revolutionary the day that his mother was turned out of
the box which she was occupying in the theatre at Grenoble by a
nobleman. Mme. Roland complains that when she was asked to

stay to dinner at the Château of Fontenay with her mother, it was served to them in the servants' quarters. How many enemies of the old regime were made by wounded self-esteem!"

The bourgeoisie owned little land, but they did have capital. They had loaned money to the State. They wanted it back. They knew enough about the affairs of government to see that the stupid and wasteful management of the public money was bound to lead to bankruptcy. They were alarmed for their savings.

The bourgeoisie wanted their political power to measure up with their economic power. They had property—they wanted privilege. They wanted to make certain that their property would be freed from the annoying restrictions to which it was subject in this decaying feudal society. They wanted to make certain that their loans to the government would be repaid. To make certain of these things they had to win for themselves not only a voice but *the* voice in government. Their chance came—and they seized it.

Their chance came because France was in such a mess that it was no longer possible to carry on in the old way. This was admitted by the Comte de Calonne, himself a member of the nobility. His position in the key office of Minister of Finance made him better able to see the handwriting on the wall. "France is a kingdom composed of separate states and countries with mixed administrations, the provinces of which know nothing of each other, where certain districts are completely free from burdens the whole weight of which is borne by others, where the richest class is the most lightly taxed, where privilege has upset all equilibrium, where it is impossible to have any constant rule or common will: necessarily it is a most imperfect kingdom, very full of abuses, and in its present condition, impossible to govern."

Note particularly those last three words. A member of the ruling class admits that it is *impossible to govern* any longer; add to that, the discontented masses; now let an intelligent rising class anxious to seize power stir up the mixture and a revolution will result. It came in 1789. It is called the French Revolution.

A brief simple statement of the purposes of the revolutionists was that given by one of their leaders, the Abbé Sieyès, in a popular pamphlet called *What is the Third Estate?* "We must put to ourselves three questions:

First: What is the Third Estate? Everything.

Second: What has it been hitherto in our political system? Nothing.

Third: What does it ask? To become something."

While it was true that all the members of the Third Estate, the artisans, the peasants, and the bourgeoisie, were trying "to become something," it was primarily the last group that got what it wanted. The bourgeoisie furnished the leadership, while the other groups did the actual fighting. And it was the bourgeoisie that gained the most. During the course of the Revolution the bourgeoisie found one opportunity after another to enrich and strengthen themselves. They speculated in the lands taken from the Church and the nobility, and reaped huge fortunes through fraudulent army contracts.

Marat, the spokesman for the poorer labouring class, described what was happening during the Revolution in these words: "At the moment of insurrection the people smashed their way through every obstacle by force of numbers; but however much power they attain at first, they are defeated at last by upper-class plotters, full of skill, craft, and cunning. The educated and subtle intriguers of the upper class at first opposed the despots: but only to turn against the people after they had wormed their way into its confidence and made use of its might, and to place themselves in the privileged position from which the despots had been ejected. Revolution is made and carried through by the lowest ranks of society, by workers, handicraftsmen, small shopkeepers, peasants, by the plebs, by the unfortunate, whom the shameless rich call the *canaille* and whom the Romans shamelessly called the proletariat. But what the upper classes constantly concealed was the fact that the Revolution had been turned solely to the profit of landowners, of lawyers and tricksters."

This is a fair statement of what happened. After the Revolution was over it was the bourgeoisie which had won political power in

France. The privilege of Birth was indeed overthrown, but the privilege of Business took its place. "Liberty, Equality, Fraternity" was a popular slogan shouted by *all* the revolutionists, but they came, in fact, primarily to the bourgeoisie.

A study of the Napoleonic Code makes that quite plain. It is obviously designed to protect property—not feudal, but bourgeois property. The Code has some 2,000 articles, of which only 7 deal with labour and close to 800 deal with property. Trade unions and strikes are prohibited, but employers' associations are O.K. In a court dispute concerning wages the Code says the employer's statement, not the workman's, is to be believed. The Code was made by the bourgeoisie for the bourgeoisie; it was made by the owners of property for the protection of property.

When the smoke of battle was cleared away, it was seen that the bourgeoisie had won the right to buy and sell what they pleased, how, when, and where they pleased. Feudalism was dead.

It was dead not only in France, but in every country which the armies of Napoleon conquered. Napoleon brought the free market (and the principles of the Code Napoleon) with him on his victorious marches. Small wonder that he was welcomed gladly by the bourgeoisie of the conquered nations! In these countries, serfdom was abolished, feudal dues and payments were swept away, and the right of peasant proprietors, merchants, and manufacturers to buy and sell without regulation, restriction, and restraint was definitely established.

An excellent summary of this phase of the French Revolution is that written in 1852 by Karl Marx in *The Eighteenth Brumaire of Louis Bonaparte*: "Desmoulins, Danton, Robespierre, Saint-Just, Napoleon, the heroes as well as the parties and masses of the great French Revolution . . . achieved the task of their day—which was to liberate the bourgeoisie and to establish modern bourgeois society. The Jacobins broke up the ground in which feudalism had been rooted, and struck off the heads of the feudal magnates who had grown there. Napoleon established throughout France the conditions which made it possible for free competition to develop, for landed property to be exploited after the partition of the great estates, and for the nation's powers of industrial production to be utilized to the full. Across the frontiers he everywhere made a clearance of feudal institutions. . . ."

Revolutions are bloody affairs. Many people were shocked at the violence and terror of the French model. It is an interesting fact that the most powerful opponents of the French Revolution were the English. It is especially interesting because the struggle of the English bourgeoisie to win political power to equal their economic power had taken place in England more than a century before the French Revolution, and the violence that accompanied it had been conveniently forgotten.

There was a difference, however. While Business in France had to give Birth a real knockout blow from which it never fully recovered, in England victory went to Business, but by a decision rather than by a knockout. It seems that in England, Business and Birth knew each other quite well and so got along rather better than they did in other countries. The English bourgeoisie had been able to become landed aristocracy, and the landed aristocracy on its part went in for business without too many worries about "being above all that." Nevertheless the years 1640-1688 in English history mark a period of real fighting—fighting that was stopped only when it was settled that the bourgeoisie were to have their say in government.

You remember the name of Edmund Burke, that great British statesman who spoke so ably on the side of the American colonists in the "taxation without representation" question. When he wrote a series of papers bitterly condemning the French Revolutionists, he was reminded by another English writer of England's own "Glorious Revolution" one hundred years before: "In the name of manhood, in the name of humanity, in the name of common sense . . . what is the irremediable offence, the crime never to be atoned, that the people of France have committed against this country? Is it in having effected a change in their government by the Revolution of 1789? They differ from ourselves in this instance only by being a century behind us. Is it in subjecting their monarch to the axe? The British nation set the example."

In England by 1689, then, and in France after 1789, the fight for the freedom of the market had resulted in a middle-class victory. The year 1789 might well mark the end of the Middle Ages in so far as the French Revolution gave the death blow to feudalism. Within the structure of the feudal society of prayers, fighters, and workers there had arisen a middle-class group. Throughout the years it had gained increasing strength. It had waged a long, hard fight against feudalism, marked particularly by three decisive battles. The first was the Protestant Reformation, the second was the Glorious Revolution in England, and the third was the French Revolution. At the end of the eighteenth century it was at last powerful enough to destroy the old feudal order. In the place of feudalism, a different social system, founded on the free exchange of goods, with the primary object of making profits, was ushered in by the bourgeoisie.

We call that system—Capitalism.

PART II

FROM CAPITALISM TO ?

XIV

Where Did the Money Come From?

Two men wait in line for tickets to the show. Each pays $9.90 for three $3.30 orchestra seats. As one of them leaves the box office window he is joined by two of his friends. They enter the theatre, sit down, and wait for the curtain to rise. The other one leaves the box office window, walks to the sidewalk in front of the theatre, and, holding the tickets in his hand, approaches the passers-by. "Wanna buy three in the centre for tonight?" he asks. Maybe eventually he succeeds in selling them (for $4.40 each), maybe he doesn't. It doesn't matter.

Is there any difference between his $9.90 and the first man's? Yes. Mr. Speculator's money is *capital*, Mr. Theatre-goer's money is not. Wherein lies the difference?

Money becomes capital only when it is used to purchase goods or labour in order to sell again at a profit. Mr. Speculator didn't want to see the show. He paid out $9.90 with the hope of getting it back—plus some more. Therefore his money was acting as capital. Mr. Theatre-goer, on the other hand, paid out his $9.90 with never a thought of getting it back—he simply wanted to see the show. His money was not acting as capital.

Similarly, when the shepherd sold his wool for money, in order to buy bread to eat, he wasn't using that money as capital. But when the merchant paid out the money for the wool, hoping to sell the wool again at a higher price, he was using his money as capital. When money is directed to an undertaking or transaction that yields (or promises to yield) profit, that money becomes capital. It is the difference between selling in order to buy, for use (precapitalist), and buying in order to sell, for gain (capitalist).

But what is it that the typical capitalist buys in order to sell for gain? Is it theatre tickets? wool? autos? hats? houses? No. It is none of these things, and yet it is part of all of them. Talk to an industrial worker. He will tell you that what his boss pays him wages for is his ability to work. It is the worker's labour-power which the capitalist buys to sell for gain, but it is obvious that the capitalist does not sell his worker's labour-power. What he does sell—at a profit—is the goods that the worker's labour has transformed from raw material to finished product. The profit comes from the fact that the worker receives in wages less than the value of what he has produced.

The capitalist owns the means of production—buildings, machinery, raw materials, etc. He buys labour-power. It is from the association of these that capitalist production ensues.

Notice that money is not the only form of capital. A present-day industrialist may have little or no cash, and yet be the possessor of a great deal of capital. He may own the means of production. This, his capital, grows as he buys labour-power.

Once modern industry has started, it makes its own profits, accumulates its own capital very quickly. But where did the capital come from in the beginning—before modern industry had begun? That's an important question because, without the existence of accumulated capital, industrial capitalism, as we know it, would not have been possible. Nor would it have been possible without the existence of a free propertyless, labouring class—people who had to work for others for a living. How were these two conditions created?

You might answer that the capital necessary for starting capitalist production came from those careful souls who worked hard, spent only what they had to, and piled up their savings little by little. People did save, of course, but that's not the way the mass of capital was first accumulated. It's such a pretty story, though, it's a pity it is not entirely true. The true story is not nearly so pretty.

Before the capitalist era, capital was accumulated mainly through commerce—an elastic term meaning not only the exchange of goods, but stretched to include conquest, piracy, plunder, exploitation.

Not for nothing had the Italian city-states enlisted the aid of western Europe in the Crusades. The close of those "religious" wars found Venice, Genoa, and Pisa in control of a rich empire. And the Italian conquerors made the most of their opportunity. A stream of wealth flowed from the East to the waiting hands of their traders and bankers. One of the best authorities on the subject, Mr. John A. Hobson, says of this Italian commerce with the East: "Thus early was laid the foundation of the profitable trade which furnished to western Europe the accumulations of wealth required for the later development of capitalistic methods of production at home."

If Mr. Hobson is correct, then we must look for the first beginnings of capitalist organization in the Italian peninsula. And there, in the thirteenth and fourteenth centuries, and even earlier, is exactly where we find those beginnings.

But great as was this treasure from the East, it was not enough. A new and larger flow of capital was necessary before the era of capitalist production could really get going. It was from the sixteenth century on that capital began to be accumulated in amounts enormous enough to satisfy the need. Karl Marx, another eminent authority on the subject of the evolution of modern capitalism, summarizes it in this way: "The discovery of gold and silver in America, the extirpation, enslavement, and entombment in mines of the aboriginal population, the beginning of the conquest and looting of the East Indies, the turning of Africa into a warren for the commercial hunting of black-skins, signalised the rosy dawn of the era of capitalist production. These idyllic proceedings are the chief momenta of primitive accumulation."

Would you care to listen to a tale of cruelty, murder, and torture that would make activities of our twentieth-century gangsters and racketeers sound like a Sunday-school picnic? Then ask a Mexican or Peruvian Indian to tell you the story of the first contact of his ancestors with the white man in the sixteenth century. The natives were given Christianity—and with it enforced service in the mines, beatings, killings. But what a tremendous store of gold and silver they dug out of the ground to be shipped to the Old World—there to find its way eventually into the hands of the merchants and bankers! (And gold or silver in those hands was not idle; it was used to give credit; it was used either in loans to manufacturers or in trading, to bring in a greater amount of money. In short, it was capital.)

True, Cortez and Pizarro, the conquerors of Mexico and Peru, were Spaniards, and the Spaniards have long been notorious for their harsh treatment of their colonies. But what of the Dutch? Surely their methods were different?

Sir T. S. Raffles, one-time Lieutenant-Governor of the island of Java, says, "No." He described the history of the colonial administration of Holland as "one of the most extraordinary relations of treachery, bribery, massacre, and meanness." He estimated that the profits of the Dutch East Indian Company from 1613 to 1653 were about 640,000 guilders every year.

Here's a sample of the Dutch methods of accumulating that capital. "To secure Malacca, the Dutch corrupted the Portuguese governor. He let them into the town in 1641. They hurried at once to his house and assassinated him, to 'abstain' from the payment of £21,875, the price of his treason. Wherever they set foot, devastation and depopulation followed. Banjuwangi, a province of Java, in 1750 numbered over 80,000 inhabitants, in 1811 only 18,000. Sweet commerce!"

Thus Holland piled up the money it needed to make it the chief capitalistic nation of the seventeenth century.

England next wore the crown as most important capitalist country. Where and how did the English acquire the necessary capital? Through hard work, careful living, and piled-up savings? Don't you believe it.

W. Howitt, in his *Colonisation and Christianity*, published in

London in 1838, quotes a writer in the *Oriental Herald* who has this to say about the British in India: "Our empire is *not* an empire of opinion, it is not even an empire of laws; it has been acquired; it is still governed . . . by the direct influence of force. No portion of the country has been voluntarily ceded . . . we were first permitted to land on the sea coast to sell our wares . . . till by degrees, sometimes by force and sometimes by fraud . . . we have put down the ancient sovereigns of the land, we have stripped the nobles of all their power, and by continual drains on the industry and resources of the people we take from them all their surplus and disposable wealth."

Sounds angry, doesn't he? Well, maybe you'd be angry, too, if you had lived in India in 1769-1770. At that time you'd have seen thousands of natives starving to death. Because there wasn't enough rice? Not at all. There was plenty of rice. Then why the famine? Simply because the English had bought up all the rice and would not sell it again—except at fabulous prices, which the miserable natives could not pay.

Trade with the colonies brought wealth to the mother country. It built up the early fortunes of European merchants. Particularly interesting as a source of capital accumulation was the trade in human beings, the black-skinned natives of Africa. In 1840, Professor H. Merivale delivered a series of lectures at Oxford on "Colonization and Colonies." In the course of one of these lectures he asked two important questions, and then gave an equally important answer: "What raised Liverpool and Manchester from provincial towns to gigantic cities? What maintains now their ever active industry and their rapid accumulation of wealth? . . . Their present opulence is as really owing to the toil and suffering of the Negro as if his hands had excavated their docks and fabricated their steam-engines."

It's fashionable at the present time to poke fun at the pronouncements of the professors. Was Professor Merivale, then, talking through his hat? He was not. He had probably read the petition to the House of Commons sent by the merchants of Liverpool in 1788, in answer to some misguided people who had the bad taste to suggest that the horrible trade in live human beings was unbecoming to a civilized country: "Your Petitioners therefore contemplate with real concern the attempts now making . . . to obtain a total abolition of the African Slave trade, which . . . for a long series of years has constituted and still continues to form a very extensive branch of the commerce of Liverpool. . . . Your Petitioners humbly pray to be heard . . . against the abolition of this source of wealth. . . ."

The Portuguese began the Negro slave trade at the opening of the sixteenth century. The other civilized nations of Christian Europe followed immediately. (The first Negro slaves to be brought to our own country came in a Dutch ship in 1619.) The first Englishman to conceive the idea that there was lots of money to be made by seizing unsuspecting Negroes in Africa, and selling them as "raw material" to be worked to a quick death on plantations in the New World, was John Hawkins. "Good Queen Bess" thought so much of the great work of this murderer and kidnapper that she knighted him after his second slave-trading expedition. It was, then, as *Sir* John Hawkins, who had chosen as his crest a Negro in chains, that he later proudly boasted to Richard Hakluyt of his exploits in this inhuman traffic. Here is Hakluyt's charming recital of Hawkins' account of his first voyage in 1562-1563: "And being amongst other particulars assured, that Negroes were very good merchandise in Hispianola, and that store of Negroes might easily be had upon the coast of Guinea, resolved with himself to make trial thereof, and communicated that devise with his worshipful friends of London. . . . All which persons liked so well of his intention, that they became liberal contributors and adventurers in the action. For which purpose there were three good ships immediately provided. . . . From thence he passed to Sierra Leona, upon the coast of Guinea . . . where he stayed some good time, and got into his possession, partly by the sword, and partly by other means, to the number of 300 Negroes at the least, besides other merchandise which that country yieldeth. With this prey he sailed over the Ocean . . . and [sold] the whole number of his Negroes:

for which he received . . . by way of exchange such quantity of merchandise, that he did not only lade his own 3 ships with hides, ginger, sugars, and some quantities of pearls, but he freighted also two other hulks. . . . And so with prosperous success and much gain to himself and the aforesaid adventurers, he came home."

Queen Elizabeth was impressed with "his prosperous success and much gain." She wanted to be a partner to any profits in the future. So for his second expedition, the Queen loaned a ship to slave-trader Hawkins. The name of the ship was the *Jesus*.

Commerce—conquest, piracy, plunder, exploitation—these were the ways, then, in which the capital necessary to start capitalist production was accumulated. Not without reason did Marx write: "If money . . . 'comes into the world with a congenital bloodstain on one cheek,' capital comes dripping from head to foot, from every pore, with blood and dirt." Commerce—conquest, piracy, plunder, exploitation—these were effective ways. They brought huge profits, fabulous sums—a growing supply of capital.

But more than accumulated capital was necessary before large-scale capitalist production could begin. Capital cannot be used as capital—i.e. to give a profit—until there is labour to yield that profit. So an adequate supply of labour was also necessary.

In the twentieth century, with unemployment everywhere around us, with workers willing and eager to take any job they can find, it is difficult for us to understand that there was a time when getting labourers to work in industry was a real problem. It seems "natural" to us that there should exist a class of people who are eager to enter a factory to work for wages. But it isn't "natural" at all. One man will work for another only when he has to. So long as a man has access to the land where he can produce for himself, he will not work for some one else. The history of the United States proves that. As long as there was cheap or free land in the West, there was a Westward Movement of land-hungry people, which meant that labour was scarce in the East. The same thing happened in Australia: "When the colony at Swan River was founded . . . Mr. Peel . . . took out with him . . . £50,000 and 300 individuals of the labouring classes; but they were all fascinated by the prospect of obtaining land . . . and in a short while he was left without a servant to make his bed, or to fetch him water from the river." Shed a tear for Mr. Peel who had to make his own bed simply because he did not realize that as long as workers have access to their own means of production—in this case, the land—they will not work for some one else.

What is true of workers to whom the land is the means of production is likewise true of those workers whose means of production are their workshop and tools. So long as these workers can use their tools to turn out products which can be sold for enough to give them a living, they will not work for some one else. Why should they?

It is only when workers do not own the land and the tools—it is only when they have become separated from these means of production—that they go to work for another. They do so not because they want to, but because they *have* to, in order to get the wherewithal to buy the food, clothing, and shelter they need in order to live. Stripped of the means of production, the workers have no choice; they must sell the only thing they have left, their capacity to work—their labour power.

The story of how the supply of labour necessary for capitalist production became available must, then, be the story of how the workers were deprived of their means of production: "The process, therefore, that clears the way for the capitalist system can be none other than the process which takes away from the labourer the possession of his means of production; a process that transforms, on the one hand, the social means of subsistence and of production into capital, on the other, the immediate producers into wage-labourers. . . . The immediate producer, the labourer, could only dispose of his own person after he had ceased to be attached to the soil and ceased to be the slave, serf, or bondman of another. To become a free seller of labour-power, who carries his commodity wherever he finds a market, he must further have escaped from the regime of the gilds, their rules for apprentices and journeymen, and the im-

pediments of their labour regulations . . . these new freedmen became sellers of themselves only after they had been robbed of all
their own means of production, and of all the guarantees of existence afforded by the old feudal arrangements. And the history of
this, their expropriation, is written in the annals of mankind in
letters of blood and fire."

It was in England that large-scale capitalism first developed, so
its origins are most clearly traced there. We have seen in the earlier
chapters how the enclosures and rack-renting of the sixteenth century drove many peasants off the land on to the road, where they
became beggars, vagabonds, thieves. Thus early was a free propertyless labouring class created.

Enclosures came again in the eighteenth century and the early part
of the nineteenth. Then they were much more extensive, and so
the army of landless unfortunates who had to sell their labour-power
for wages was increased tremendously. Whereas the enclosures of
the sixteenth century met with a great deal of resistance not only
from the dispossessed, but also from the government, which was
afraid of violence on the part of the masses forced into starvation,
the enclosures of the eighteenth century were put over in legal
form. "Acts of Enclosure" made by a government of the landlords
for the landlords were the order of the day. The labourer with land
became the labourer without land—ready, therefore, to go into
industry as a wage-worker.

Though the enclosure movement is more typical of England, it
did take place to a lesser extent on the Continent. Proof of this is
contained in the following complaint from the peasants of Cheffes,
in France, to their deputies in the Estates-General in 1790: "The
parishioners of Cheffes, in Anjou, make bold to present to you . . .
their wishes, requests and complaints, in regard to the commons
of their parish, of which certain individuals, either rich, or powerful, or greedy, have unjustly taken possession. . . . The community
of this parish . . . has been deprived thereof by a judgment of the
Council rendered in favour of the seigneurs of Cheffes . . . they
have only the said lands for pasturing their cattle, and being at

present deprived thereof, they are without any relief, and reduced to extreme poverty. A new system created by the economists tries to make people believe that the commons were not good for agriculture; powerful lords, men with money, have enriched themselves with the spoils of the country parishes by invading their common lands. . . . Nothing is more precious to certain parishes than the pasture lands; without them the cultivators can keep no cattle, without cattle they have no manure, and how can they hope for good harvests without manure?"

The loss of their common rights, of which these French peasants complain, hit the English peasants very hard also. For successful farming, provision must be made for the maintenance of animals. When the peasants lost their rights to the common, it meant disaster. Naturally they were bitter against the lords who deprived them of their rights to the commons, and against the government which enforced those measures which drove them off the land. Their resentment is shown in this little jingle which was popular at the time:

> The law locks up the man or woman
> Who steals a goose from off the common;
> But leaves the greater villain loose
> Who steals the common from the goose.

Don't get the idea that the landlords were driving the peasants off the land to provide a labour force for industry. That never occurred to them. They were interested only in getting the most profit out of the land. If they could have made more money by not enclosing, they would not have enclosed. But there was more money in it for them by enclosing than by letting the land remain in open fields. Arthur Young in his tour through Shropshire in 1776 points this out: "Rents by the enclosures are generally doubled. . . . Three miles from Daventry came to Bramston an enclosure only a year old. . . . The open field let at 6s. to 10s. an acre; but now it is (on lease) 20s. to 30s."

Perhaps the most infamous example of the sweeping from off the land of the wretched labourers who had always been on it is that of the Duchess of Sutherland in Scotland. The story is told by Marx: "Where there are no more independent peasants to get rid of, the 'clearing' of cottages begins; so that the agricultural labourers do not find on the soil cultivated by them even the spot necessary for their own housing. . . . As an example of the method obtaining in the nineteenth century, the 'clearing' made by the Duchess of Sutherland will suffice here. This person, well instructed in economy, resolved . . . to turn the whole country, whose population had already been, by earlier processes of the like kind, reduced to 15,000, into a sheep-walk. From 1814 to 1820 these 15,000 inhabitants, about 3,000 families, were systematically hunted and rooted out. All their villages were destroyed and burnt, all their fields turned into pasturage. British soldiers enforced this eviction, and came to blows with the inhabitants. One old woman was burnt to death in the flames of the hut which she refused to leave. Thus this fine lady appropriated 794,000 acres of land that had from time immemorial belonged to the clan."

From the sixteenth century to the early part of the nineteenth, in England, the process of depriving the peasant of the land went on. In France, the small peasant owner class grew, but in England, where industrial capitalism developed more rapidly than anywhere else, the small peasant owner class was almost completely wiped out. Dr. R. Price, an eighteenth-century English writer, tells what happened to them: "When this land gets into the hands of a few great farmers, the consequence must be that the little farmers will be converted into a body of men who earn their subsistence by working for others. . . . Towns and manufactures will increase, because more will be driven to them in quest of places and employment. . . . Upon the whole, the circumstances of the lower ranks of men are altered in almost every respect for the worse. From little occupiers of land they are reduced to the state of day-labourers and hirelings."

That's an exact statement of the case. Forced off the land, the "lower ranks of men" had to become day-labourers. The enclosures, then, were one of the chief ways by which the necessary supply of labour was made available.

There were other ways. One of them was not nearly as spectacular or as obvious, but it affected many more people. It was the factory system itself, which finally divorced the labourer from the means of production in industry, as he had already been divorced from it on the land.

In the Journals of the House of Commons for 1806 the report of the committee appointed to "consider the State of the Woollen Manufacture in England" states that "there have long been a few Factories in the neighbourhood. . . . These have for some time been objects of great jealousy to the Domestic Clothiers. The most serious apprehensions have been stated . . . lest the Factory system should gradually root out the Domestic; and lest the independent little Master Manufacturer, who works on his own account, should sink into a Journeyman working for hire."

What were "serious apprehensions" in this 1806 report became reality later. You can easily see why. The factory system with its power-driven machinery, and division of labour, could turn out products much faster and more cheaply than could the hand workers. In the competition between machine work and hand work, the machine was bound to win. It did win—and thousands of "independent little Master Manufacturers" (independent because they had owned the tools, their means of production) sank into the position of "Journeymen working for hire." Many of them went hungry for a long time before they submitted, but in the end they had to submit.

Another House of Commons Report, from the Assistant Hand-Loom Weavers' Commissioners, for 1840, contains this evidence showing why it was useless for the hand-loom weaver to hold on to his own outmoded means of production: "Competition, the great cause of reduction of wages, arising . . . in attempting to gain trade by underselling each other, has produced great changes. The trade of the weaver, who, assisted by his family and others, made a few pieces only, has been absorbed by the great manufacturers. Many of the former masters have been reduced to journeymen; poverty has dispossessed them."

Perhaps the most convincing proof of the fact that the hand worker was licked by the drop in the prices he received due to machine competition, is furnished by this extract from Philip Gaskell's famous book, published in 1836: "From the time of the introduction of steam power, a most extraordinary and painful change has been wrought in the condition of the hand-loom weavers, and their labour may fairly be said to have been crushed beneath the steam engine. . . . The prices paid for weaving a particular kind of cloth, as shown in the following table, will exhibit the extraordinary depreciation which has taken place in the value of this species of labour:

1795	39/9
1810	15/0
1830	5/0

"This is not a solitary instance; it is an example of the entire labour connected with hand-loom manufacture."

That decline in the prices paid for hand-work tells the sad tale. No longer able to earn a living, the weaver sold (if he could) his hand-loom, his means of production. His next step had to be the line in front of the employment office of a factory. There he was joined by other workers of other trades, who had suffered the same experience. Thus machine production, which cannot carry on without a large labour supply, itself ensured that labour supply by ruining the handicraft worker.

And so, there came into existence that propertyless labouring class which, with the accumulation of capital, was essential to industrial capitalism.

When the revolution in the modes of production and exchange, which we have called the change from feudalism to capitalism, occurred, what happened to the old science, the old law, the old education, the old government, the old religion? They changed also. They had to. The practice of law, Model 1800 A.D., was quite different from the practice of law, Model 1200 A.D. So with religious teaching. The world dominated by traders, manufacturers, bankers, required a different set of religious precepts from the world dominated by prayers and fighters. In a society where the object of work was merely to make an adequate living for yourself and family, the Church could denounce profiteers; but in a society in which the primary object of work was to make a profit, then the Church had to sing a different tune. And if the Catholic Church, geared to a feudal-handicraft economy in which the craftsman worked merely to make a living, could not change its teaching fast enough to fit capitalist economy in which the capitalist worked to make a profit, then the Protestant Church could—and did. The Protestant Church split into many different sects, but in all of them, in varying degrees, the capitalist interested in acquisition could find comfort.

Take the Puritans, for example. Where the Catholic lawgivers had warned that the road to riches might be the path to hell, the Puritan, Baxter, told his followers that unless they took advantage of their opportunities for acquiring wealth, they were not serving God. "If God show you a way in which you may lawfully get more than in another way (without wrong to your soul or to any other), if you refuse this, and choose the less gainful way, you cross one of the ends of your calling, and you refuse to be God's steward, and to accept His gifts and use them for Him when he requireth it; you may labour to be rich for God, though not for the flesh and sin."

Or take the Methodists. Wesley, their famous leader, could write: "We ought not to prevent people from being diligent and frugal; we must exhort all Christians to gain all they can, and to save all they can; that is, in effect, to grow rich."

Or take the Calvinists. The Protestant Reformation came in the sixteenth century, the period when opportunities for the accumulation of capital, so necessary for later large-scale capitalist production, were greater than ever before. The teachings of Calvin were particularly in the spirit of capitalist enterprise. Where formerly the Catholic Church had looked with suspicion on the merchant as one whose "lust for gain" was a sin, the Protestant, Calvin, could write: "What reason is there why the income from business should not be larger than that from landowning? Whence do the merchant's profits come, except from his own diligence and industry?" No wonder Calvinism became the creed of the rising bourgeoisie.

Here in America we know best the Puritans, those followers of Calvin who settled New England. Our history books sing the praises of that sturdy band whose aim in life was the glorification of God. We know how they worked toward that end by leading a disciplined life in which thrift and hard work were desirable, and luxury, extravagance, and idleness were undesirable. Think about that for a moment from a different angle. What qualities could be more fitting for an economic system in which the accumulation of wealth on the one hand, and steady habits of work on the other, were the foundation stones, than these same religious ideals converted into daily practice by these followers of Calvin? That man was the best Christian whose every activity was most suited to the acquisition of wealth—to the spirit of capitalism. A perfect tie-up.

Benjamin Franklin is an outstanding example of one in whom that spirit was most alive. In his *Poor Richard's Almanack* he put into simple homely phrases the Puritan key to the best life for the righteous:

"No man e'er was glorious, who was not laborious."

"Hope of gain lessens pain."

"Keep thy shop and thy shop will keep thee."

And in *Advice to Young Tradesmen*:

"In short, the way to wealth, if you desire it, is as plain as the way to market. It depends chiefly on two words, *industry* and *frugality*; that is, waste neither *time* nor *money*. . . . He that gets all he can honestly, and saves all he gets, will certainly become *rich*."

This is the capitalist spirit. For the Calvinist this teaching was not advice in the ordinary sense, it was an ideal of Christian conduct. The best way to work for the glory of God was to put into practice this teaching.

The next time some one tells you that it is "human nature" to desire gain, you can show him how that became human nature. Show him that saving and investing, practically unknown in feudal society, slowly became the thing to do in capitalist society—for the glory of God. So that by the time the nineteenth century came around, "To save and to invest became at once the duty and the delight of a large class. The savings were seldom drawn on, and, accumulating at compound interest, made possible the material triumphs which we now all take for granted. The morals, the politics, the literature, and the religion of the age joined in a grand conspiracy for the promotion of saving. God and Mammon were reconciled. Peace on earth to men of good means. A rich man could, after all, enter into the Kingdom of Heaven—if only he saved."

The accumulation of the capital that came from early commerce, plus the existence of a propertyless labouring class, spelt the beginnings of industrial capitalism. The factory system itself made for the accumulation of a greater supply of wealth. The owners of this new wealth, brought up to believe that theirs was the Kingdom of Heaven if they saved and reinvested their savings, put their capital back into the factories. Thus the modern system, as you and I know it, came into being.

XV

Revolution—In Industry, Agriculture, Transport

THE newspapers of 150 years ago did not run a "Believe It or Not" cartoon with its story of incredible happenings. If they had, the *Birmingham Gazette* for March 11, 1776, would have known immediately where to put this amazing news item: "On Friday last a Steam Engine constructed upon Mr. Watt's new Principles was set to work at Bloomfield Colliery . . . in the Presence of a Number of Scientific Gentlemen whose Curiosity was excited to see the first movements of so singular and so powerful a Machine . . . by this Example the Doubts of the Inexperienced are dispelled and the Importance and Usefulness of the Invention is finally decided. . . . [It was] invented by Mr. Watt . . . after many Years' Study, and a great Variety of expensive and laborious Experiments."

By 1800 the "Importance and Usefulness of the Invention" of Mr. Watt had become so plain to Englishmen that it was in use in 30 collieries, 22 copper mines, 28 foundries, 17 breweries and 84 cotton mills.

The invention of machines to do the work of man was an old, old story. But with the harnessing of machinery to steam power an important change in the method of production came about. The coming of power-driven machinery meant the rise of the factory system on a wide scale. You could have factories without machines, but you could not have power-driven machines without factories.

The factory system with its large-scale efficient organization and division of labour meant a tremendous increase in production. Goods poured out of factories at a great rate. This increase in production was in part due to capital pushing its way towards profits. In part it was the answer to increased demand. The opening up of markets in the newly-discovered lands was one important cause of that increased demand. There was another. Factory-made goods were finding a home market as well as a foreign market. This was due to the growth of population in England itself.

Historians used to argue whether the noticeable increase in the growth of population in England in the eighteenth century was due to an increase in the birth rate or a fall in the death rate. Though both causes were true, it is now thought that the fall in the death rate was the more important. But why should the death rate have fallen? Possibly because the doctors had learned more about their business, which meant, among other things, that people were kept alive who formerly would have died. The records of the Lying-in Hospital in London show an almost unbelievable reduction in the mortality of mothers and children there:

Proportion of deaths	1749–1758	1799–1800
Women	1 in 42	1 in 914
Children	1 in 15	1 in 115

These figures shout the story. Before 1700, the increase in population in England for every one hundred years was about 1,000,000; between 1700 and 1800, however, the increase was 3,000,000!

Perhaps another cause of the growth in population was the fact that people were better fed due to striking improvements in agriculture. (These improvements were themselves, in a measure, the result of the growth of population.) Just as there was an industrial revolution, so there was an agricultural revolution.

Say "1649" to an English schoolboy and he'll respond with "Death of Charles I." He wouldn't think of answering "Introduction of turnips and other root crops from Holland." But why should he? Why were turnips so important?

You have only to look at the table showing the three-field system on p. 5 for the answer. One-third of the land lying fallow meant a tremendous waste. The introduction of turnips and clover meant that the problem of recuperating the ground was solved. A four-course system of

1st year—wheat
2nd year—turnips
3rd year—barley
4th year—clover

was a much-needed improvement. It meant that the land need no longer become "tired out" by the planting of two successive corn crops; it meant also that the waste of letting the land lie fallow was avoided.

The introduction of turnips and clover not only cleansed the soil, but also solved the problem of providing winter food for the cattle. Where formerly cattle would have been killed and salted down for eating throughout the winter, now more cattle could be kept alive.

Experimentation in improving the quality of the breed came at this time, too. That it was successful is proven by this table showing the average weights of animals sold at Smithfield market before and after the beginning of scientific breeding.

	Beginning of 18th century	End of 18th century
Beeves	370 lbs.	800 lbs.
Calves	50 lbs.	148 lbs.
Sheep	28 lbs.	80 lbs.

And just as improvements came in the tools and machinery used in industry, so the eighteenth century saw new and better ploughs, hoes, etc., introduced in agriculture.

It was the enclosure movement, so terrible in its effect on the dispossessed, which made it possible for all these noteworthy improvements in agricultural technique, science, and tools to be adopted on a large scale. It would have been impossible with the old open-field, commons-for-everybody, arrangement.

The growth of population meant that farming could be profitable. Big landowners seeking a profit, at this time made large investments of capital in their farms, and one result was more and better food—which in turn led to a further increase in population.

The revolutions in industry and agriculture were accompanied by a revolution in transportation. Turning out more goods at greater speed, and growing more and better crops, is of no use unless they can be carried to the people who need them. The roads were bad. They were so bad that the Marquis of Downshire in the middle of the eighteenth century had to take along a force of labourers to make the necessary repairs en route, and heave his coach out of the mud so he could complete his journey. What was merely annoying to the Marquis was impossible to the manufacturer anxious to supply the demands of a growing market. Cheap and quick and regular transport was needed. It was needed too for those manufacturers who wanted to take advantage of the benefits arising from concentrating production in a specially suitable area—e.g., cotton in Lancashire.

It was, therefore, in the eighteenth century that improvements in road-making, and the building of canals, were begun. The macadam road (John McAdam, engineer) that you and I know, came at the beginning of the nineteenth century, and was followed by the railroad and the steamship. Meanwhile the beds of rivers had been deepened, and canals dug. The revolution in transport not only made it possible for the home market to widen in every direction; it also made it possible for the world market to become the home market.

The growth of population, the revolutions in transportation, agriculture, and industry,—all these were inter-related. They acted and reacted upon each other. They were the forces making for a new world.

XVI

"The Seed Ye Sow, Another Reaps . . ."

OVERHEARD on a Fifth Avenue bus. "Good Lord! More pickets! I'm getting sick and tired of these strikers parading up and down in front of stores and factories with their Unfair to Organized Labour signs. Why doesn't the government clap them all in jail?"

The indignant lady who made this remark didn't know her history. She thought she had an easy solution to a simple problem. But she was quite wrong. Her solution had been tried again and again and was found to be no solution at all. In England more than one hundred years ago a magistrate wrote to the Home Office his plans for crushing a strike: "The steps I shall propose to take will be to have the men apprehended who have left their employ and to have them sent to the treadmill."

Exactly what the lady suggested—yet written way back in 1830. With what result? Let the lady answer.

What both the magistrate in the nineteenth century and the lady in the twentieth century did not seem to realise was that workers do not go on picket lines because they like to walk up and down carrying signs; nor that workers do not strike because they don't want to work. The causes lie deeper. To discover them we must turn to English history because it was there that the Industrial Revolution first came.

It is a well-known fact that statistics can be made to prove anything. Never did statistics give a more false picture of what was really happening than in the period of the infancy of the Industrial Revolution in England. Every table of figures showed tremendous advances. Production of cotton, iron, coal, any and every commodity, multiplied tenfold. Volume of sales, amount of sales, profits to the owners—they all leaped sky-high. Read these figures and you will be amazed. England, you will feel, must have been that paradise the song-writers have always warbled about. It was—for the few.

For the many it was anything but paradise. In terms of the happiness and well-being of the workers those cheery statistics told horrible lies. One writer pointed this out in a book published in 1836: "Upwards of a million of human beings are literally starving, and the number is constantly on the increase. . . . It is a new era in the history of commerce that an active and increasing trade should be the index, not to the improvement of the condition of the working classes, but to their poverty and degradation: it is an era at which Great Britain has arrived."

That imaginative figure, the Man from Mars, if he had been dropped on the busy isle of England would have thought earth's inhabitants were all madmen. For he would have seen, on the one hand, the great mass of people working hard and long and returning at night to miserable unhealthy hovels, not fit for swine; on the other hand, a few people who never soiled their hands with toil, who nevertheless made the laws which governed the mass, and lived like kings each in his individual palace.

There were, in truth, two Englands. Disraeli pointed that out in his *Sybil*. " 'Two nations; between whom there is no intercourse and no sympathy; who are as ignorant of each other's habits, thoughts, and feelings, as if they were dwellers in different zones, or inhabitants of different planets; who are formed by a different breeding, are fed by a different food, are ordered by different manners, and are not governed by the same laws.'

" 'You speak of . . .' said Egremont, hesitatingly.

" 'THE RICH AND THE POOR.' "

This division was not new. But with the coming of machinery and the factory system the borderline became more marked than ever before. The rich grew richer and the poor, cut off from the means of production, grew poorer. Particularly down and out were those craftsmen who had earned a fairly decent living, and who now, through competition with machine-made goods, were destitute. We get an idea of how desperate their condition was from the evidence of one of them, Thomas Heath, a hand-loom weaver:

"*Question:* Have you any children?

Answer: No; I had two but they are both dead, thanks be to God!

Question: Do you express satisfaction at the death of your children?

Answer: I do; I thank God for it. I am relieved from the burden of maintaining them, and they, poor dear creatures, are relieved from the troubles of this mortal life."

You will agree that to talk in this fashion a man would have to be really down and out, and no mistake.

What of those who, reduced to absolute starvation, could no longer hold out against the machine, and finally entered the factory? What were the conditions in those early factories?

The new machinery which might have lightened labour actually made it worse. It was so very efficient that it was made to perform its magic as long as possible. To the mill-owners the machines represented so much capital which must not be left idle—it must be kept working, ever working. Besides, the smart mill-owner knew that to get all he could out of the machine as quickly as possible was essential, because, with new inventions the machine might soon become obsolete. So hours were long. A sixteen-hour day was not unknown. When two twelve-hour shifts were finally won, the workers looked upon the change as a blessing.

But long hours alone would not have been too bad. The workers were used to that. In their own homes, under the domestic system, they had worked long hours. The real hardship came in learning to get used to the discipline of the factory. To begin at a definite hour, to stop work at a definite hour, to begin again, to keep pace with the movements of the machine—always under the dictation and strict supervision of an ever-present overseer—that was new. And it was hard.

The spinners in a mill near Manchester had to work fourteen hours a day in a temperature of eighty to eighty-four degrees without being allowed to send for water to drink. They were "subject to the following penalties:

	s.	d.
Any spinner found with his window open	1	0
Any spinner found dirty at his work	1	0
Any spinner found washing himself	1	0
Any spinner repairing his drum banding with his gas lighted	2	0
Any spinner spinning with gaslight too long in the morning	2	0
Any spinner heard whistling	1	0"

This seems fantastic, but it was true, and it was not an isolated case. Most of the evils which today we associate only with sweat-shops or backward communities, such as being paid in scrip, or having to buy at a company store, or live in a company house, all these were familiar to the workers in the period of early industrialism.

Capitalists thought they could do as they pleased with what belonged to them. They made no distinction between their "hands" and their machines. That's not quite true. Since machines represented an outlay of money, and men did not, they were more concerned with the welfare of the machines than of the men.

They paid as little in wages as they had to. They were in the market for as much labour-power as they could use at as little cost as was necessary to buy it. Since women and children could tend the machines and would be paid less than men, women and children were given work while the man in the house was often idle. At first factory-owners bought pauper child labour from the Guardians of the Poor; later, because the earnings of the working father and the working mother were not enough to support the family, the children living at home had to enter the mills and the mines. The horrors of industrialism were nowhere better revealed than in the records of child labour in those early days.

Before a committee of Parliament in 1816, Mr. John Moss, at one time a master of apprentices in a cotton mill, gave the following evidence concerning the parish children who were forced into factory work:

"Were they parish apprentices?—All parish apprentices.

"At what age were they taken?—Those that came from London were from about seven to eleven. Those from Liverpool were from about eight or ten to fifteen.

"Up to what period were they apprenticed?—One-and-twenty.

"What were the hours of work?—From five o'clock in the morning till eight at night.

"Were fifteen hours in the day the regular hours of work?—Yes.

"When the works were stopped for the repair of the mill, or for any want of cotton, did the children afterwards make up for the loss of that time?—Yes.

"Did the children sit or stand to work?—Stand.

"The whole of their time?—Yes.

"Were there any seats in the mill?—None. . . . I have found them frequently upon the mill-floors, after the time they should have been in bed.

"Were any children injured by the machinery?—Very frequently."

Again, in 1833, His Majesty's Commissioners issued a report on the Employment of Children in Factories. In that report there is the evidence of eleven-year-old Thomas Clarke, earning 4s. a week (with the aid of his brother) as piecer in a mill. Here is part of his story: "They always strapped us if we fell asleep. . . . Castles used to get a rope about as thick as my thumb, and double it, and put knots in it. . . . I used to go to the factory a little before six, sometimes at five, and work on till nine at night. . . . I worked all night one night. . . . We choosed it ourselves. We wanted to have something to spend. We had been working from six in the morning the day before. We went on working till nine o'clock the next night. . . . I am at the rope walk now. . . . I can earn about 4s. . . . My brother turns for me. He is just seven. I don't give him anything. . . . If it was not my brother, I must give him 1s. a week. . . . I take him with me at six, and keep him till eight."

Understand, child labour was not new. You remember Defoe's description of the domestic system (p. 116). But where formerly children's work was auxiliary to their parents', now it was the foundation of this new system. Where formerly children worked in their own homes, under their parents' eyes, with the hours and conditions set by their parents, now they worked in factories, under the eyes of an overseer whose own job depended on how much work he could drive out of their little bodies, with the hours and conditions set by a profit-seeking mill-owner. Even a West Indian slave-master could take comfort from the long hours worked by children. One of them, talking to three Bradford mill-owners, is reported to have said: "I have always thought myself disgraced by being the owner of slaves, but we never in the West Indies thought it possible for any human being to be so cruel as to require a child of nine years old to work twelve and a half hours a day, and that, you acknowledge, is your regular practice."

This slave-owner might have drawn another comparison. Bad as slave living-quarters were in both the West Indies and our South, it could have been argued that in some respects they were no worse than the homes of the workers in the new factory towns. With the coming of steam power, it was no longer necessary for factory sites to be located near water power, as before. Industry moved near the coal areas, and almost overnight places of no importance became towns, and older towns became cities. In 1770 the rural population of England was forty per cent of the total; by 1841 it had dropped to twenty-six per cent. The figures for the growth of cities show what was happening:

	1801	1841
Manchester	35,000	353,000
Leeds	53,000	152,000
Birmingham	23,000	181,000
Sheffield	46,000	111,000

You recognize the names. Famous places, turning out famous goods. Goods made by workers living in dark, unhealthy, crowded, ugly quarters. Nassau Senior, a noted economist, walked through a part of Manchester in 1837. He described what he saw: "These towns, for in extent and number of inhabitants they are towns, have been erected with the utmost disregard of everything except the immediate advantage of the speculating builder. . . . In one place we found a whole street following the course of a ditch, because in this way deeper cellars could be secured without the cost of digging, cellars not for storing wares or rubbish, but for dwellings for human beings. *Not one house of this street escaped the cholera.* In general, the streets of these suburbs are unpaved, with a dung-heap or ditch in the middle; the houses are built back to back, without ventilation or drainage, and whole families are limited to a corner of a cellar or a garret."

Note particularly the italicized words in the above quotation. The effect of such housing conditions on the health of the poor people who had to live there is evident. Disease and death stalked the poor who were so unfortunate as to have to live in quarters as unsanitary as these. The person who was born on the other side of town was truly lucky, because how long you lived was determined by where you lived—according to the report of Dr. P. H. Holland, who made an investigation of a suburb of Manchester in 1844. "When we find the rate of mortality four times as high in some streets as in others, and twice as high in whole classes of streets as in other classes, and further find that it is all but invariably high in those streets which are in bad condition, and almost invariably low in those whose condition is good, we cannot resist the conclusion that multitudes of our fellow-creatures, *hundreds of our immediate neighbours,* are annually destroyed for want of the most evident precautions."

How did the other nation, the rich, feel about the destruction of their "immediate neighbours"? What was the attitude of the well-to-do toward factory conditions, long hours, child labour? Most of them didn't think about these things at all. When they did they comforted themselves with the thought that what was had to be. Didn't the Bible say, "The poor always ye have with you?" That the Bible had other things to say about the relationship of man to his fellow-man did not bother them—they read only what they wanted to see, and listened to only what they wanted to hear.

So some of the things that you and I today think quite terrible, the rich of that period found fitting and proper. Bad for children to be out of school, working fourteen hours a day? Nonsense! said Mr. G. A. Lee, the owner of a cotton mill in which the hours of labour for children were from 6 A.M. to 8 P.M. "Nothing is more favourable to morals than habits of early subordination, industry, and regularity."

Mr. Lee was concerned with the morals of the poor. So was the president of the Royal Society, Mr. Giddy, who was against the proposal to establish elementary schools for working-class children. This was Mr. Giddy's interesting argument: "Giving education to the labouring classes of the poor . . . would in effect be found to be prejudicial to their morals and happiness; it would teach them to despise their lot in life, instead of making them good servants in agriculture, and other laborious employments to which their rank in society had destined them . . . it would enable them to read seditious pamphlets . . . it would render them insolent to their superiors."

But if we are to believe another witness of the period, far from despising their lot in life the poor had every reason to be thankful for it. Fortunate indeed were those who were part of that great boon to humanity, the factory system. At least that was the belief of Andrew Ure, who wrote in 1835: "In my recent tour . . . I have seen tens of thousands of old, young, and middle-aged of both sexes . . . earning abundant food, raiment, and domestic accommodation, without perspiring at a single pore, screened meanwhile from the summer's sun and the winter's frost, in apartments more airy and salubrious than those of the metropolis in which our . . . fashionable aristocracies assemble . . . magnificent edifices, surpassing far in number, value, usefulness, and ingenuity of construction, the boasted monuments of Asiatic, Egyptian, and Roman despotism. . . . Such is the factory system."

Perhaps it is well to note that Dr. Ure was on a tour of the factories—he didn't work in one.

Long before Dr. Ure began to sing his praise of the factory system, a churchman gave comfort and aid to the miserable poor. No ordinary churchman either—the Archdeacon Paley himself. To those discontented members of the working class who thought they were badly off and the rich were well off, this distinguished churchman brought words of cheer. "Again, some of the necessities which poverty . . . imposes are not hardships, but pleasures. Frugality itself is a pleasure. It is an exercise of attention and contrivance which . . . produces satisfaction. . . . This is lost amidst abundance. There is no pleasure in taking out of a large unmeasured fund. . . . A yet more serious advantage which persons in inferior stations possess is the ease with which they provide for their children. All the provision which a poor man's child requires is contained in two words, 'industry and innocence.' "

And if some of the stupid poor people were too stubborn to believe that poverty was really a pleasure, then the Archdeacon had another one up his sleeve. The poor envied the rich their leisure. What a mistake! It was the rich who were really envious—because leisure is pleasurable only after hard work. Here's the argument: "Another article which the poor are apt to envy in the rich, is their *ease*. Now here they mistake the matter totally. . . . Rest is the cessation of labour. It cannot therefore be enjoyed, or even tasted, except by those who have known fatigue. The rich see, and not without envy, the refreshment and pleasure which rest affords to the poor."

Archdeacon Paley wrote these comforting words in 1793. This, you remember, was the time when the poor in France were trying to unseat the privileged in their country. The French Revolution was a bloody affair. The rich in England didn't like it. They hated the thought that the horrible French idea of "Off with their heads!" might cross the Channel and infect their own down-and-outs. So this friend of the poor, the Archdeacon, cautioned any poor Englishmen who were inclined to be too hot-headed: "The change, and the only change, to be desired, is that gradual and progressive im‐ provement . . . which is the natural fruit of successful industry. . . . This may be looked forward to . . . in a state of public order and quiet; it is absolutely impossible in any other. . . . To covet the stations or fortunes of the rich, or so however to covet them, as to wish to seize them by force, or through the medium of public up‐ roar and confusion, is not only wickedness, but folly."

The English poor took the churchman's advice. They did not "seize the fortunes of the rich." But as time went on, they did look for "that gradual and progressive improvement" which he promised was "the natural fruit of successful industry." It didn't come. So they fought for it.

For example, they fought for shorter hours of labour. And they were joined in that fight by some of the rich who were humane enough to agree with them that a fourteen- or sixteen-hour day was too long. Some of these rich people carried the fight into Parlia‐ ment. They made speeches in favour of limiting the hours of work to ten a day. They persuaded some of their fellow-members to vote with them for a bill to that effect. This displeased a great many people, among them Dr. Ure. He was outraged—for an interesting reason: "It will certainly appear surprising to every dispassionate mind, that ninety-three members of the British House of Commons could be found capable of voting that any class of grown-up arti‐ sans should not be suffered to labour more than ten hours a day— an interference with the freedom of the subject which no other legislature in Christendom would have countenanced for a moment. The Gloucestershire manufacturers justly characterized the proposal as 'worthy of the darkest ages.'"

Dr. Ure, like Archdeacon Paley, was a friend of the working‐ man. So he and the Gloucestershire manufacturers were indignant at this proposal to interfere with the labourer's freedom to work as long as his employer pleased. What would become of the English‐ man's historic liberties if Parliament took from him his inalienable right to be worked to death?

This argument—that to limit the hours of labour was to interfere with a man's natural liberty, was very important. It was used again and again in America as well as in England. The manufacturers who advanced it (curiously enough, the workmen themselves didn't mind having their natural rights in this respect disregarded) got it from that great economist, Adam Smith, the apostle of *laissez-faire*. It was true, as we have seen, that Smith, the arch-opponent of the restrictive policies of mercantilism, came out strongly against such interference. The manufacturers could quote from the *Wealth of Nations*: "The property which every man has in his own labour, as it is the original foundation of all other property, so it is the most sacred and inviolable. The patrimony of a poor man lies in the strength and dexterity of his hands; and to hinder him from employing this strength and dexterity in what manner he thinks proper without injury to his neighbour, is a plain violation of this most sacred property. . . . To judge whether he is fit to be employed may surely be trusted to the discretion of the employers whose interest it so much concerns."

Adam Smith, of course, had written this in opposition to mercantilist regulation and restraint. It might have been argued that the manufacturers were putting something over when they used this quotation, written in 1776, to fight against another kind of regulation. But let us suppose that it was fair for them to quote Smith. What was not fair was for them to forget what Smith said when it was not in their interest. This habit of selecting from Smith whatever justified their actions, and overlooking in Smith whatever was contrary to their actions, was useful to the ruling class—and disastrous to the working class. It was done for over a hundred years.

What could the workers do to improve their lot? What would you have done? Suppose you had made a decent living as a knitter of hosiery by hand. Suppose you witnessed the erection of a mill, into which went machines which soon turned out so much hosiery at such cheap prices that the living you could make became less and less decent until you were on the verge of starvation. You would look back to the days before the machine had come, and

what had been barely a decent living would appear in your daydream as a luxurious living. Then you would look about you and
shudder at the poverty you were in. You would ask yourself the
cause as you had already done a thousand times, and you would
come to the same conclusion—the machine. It was the machine
which threw men out of work and lowered the price of goods. The
machine—there was the enemy.

When desperate men came to this conclusion, the next step was
inevitable.

Machine-wrecking.

Lace-frames, hosiery-frames, weaving-machines, spinning-ma-
chines—any and all machines which seemed to certain workers in
certain places to have brought misery and starvation—were destroyed, either smashed or burnt. The machine-wreckers, called
Luddites, in fighting against machinery felt they were fighting for
a standard of life. All their pent-up hatred of the machine was
released, as they set about their riotous task singing such ditties
as this:

> "Around and around we all will stand
> And sternly swear we will.
> We'll break the shears and windows, too,
> And set fire to the tazzling mill."

You can easily imagine the result of this violence. Property had
been destroyed; machines had been broken to pieces by mobs. The
men who owned the machines acted quickly. They appealed to the
law. And the law was not slow in answering their appeal. In 1812
Parliament passed a bill to make machine-wrecking punishable by
death. But before the bill was passed, during the debate on the subject, one member of the House of Lords made his maiden speech
in opposition to the measure. He reminded the law-makers that the
cause of the destruction of machinery had been the destruction of
men: "But whilst these outrages must be admitted to exist to an
alarming extent, it cannot be denied that they have arisen from
circumstances of the most unparalleled distress. The perseverance

of these miserable men in their proceedings tends to prove that nothing but absolute want could have driven a large and once honest and industrious body of the people into the commission of excesses so hazardous to themselves, their families, and the community. . . . In the foolishness of their hearts they imagined that the maintenance and well-doing of the industrious poor were objects of greater consequence than the enrichment of a few individuals by any improvement in the implements of trade, which threw the workmen out of employment and rendered the labourer unworthy of his hire. . . .

"You call these men a mob, desperate, dangerous, and ignorant. . . . Are we aware of our obligations to the mob? It is the mob that labour in our fields, serve in our houses—that man your navy and recruit your army—that have enabled you to defy all the world, and can also defy you when neglect and calamity have driven them to despair."

The name of the man who made this speech on February 27, 1812, is familiar to you. It was Lord Byron.

Machine-wrecking was not a wise plan. Even if it had succeeded, it could not have solved the workers' problems. They were barking up the wrong tree. It was not the machine which was the cause of their woe—it was the machine-owner, who not as openly, but just as effectively as the landowner who enclosed the land, was cutting them off from their means of production.

The workers soon learned that the destruction of machinery was no way out for them. Some workers tried other methods. Here, for example, is the pitiful petition of a group signing themselves "The Poor Weavers." It was written to their employers in Oldham, England, in 1818: "We the Weavers of this Town and Neighbourhood respectfully request your attention to the wretched situation to which we have a long time been exposed, owing to the extreme depression of our Wages, and request you to call a Meeting among yourselves, and try if there cannot be some alleviation made to our sufferings, by an advance thereof, as you well know they are not adequate to purchase the common Necessaries of Life. We are of opinion that if you would exert yourselves as a body, the thing might be accomplished without affecting your profits, which we are far from wishing to injure."

There were other petitions. Hundreds of them. Petitions sent not to employers—that was soon given up as useless—but to Parliament. Many went unheeded, but others received some attention. There were already some laws on the statute-books that should have helped to relieve the misery of the working class. Now more laws were passed as a result of these petitions, and as a result, too, of investigations by committees of the law-makers which proved beyond a doubt that conditions were as horrible as the workers said they were.

But laws on the statute-books are one thing. And laws put into effect are another. The workers found that out. They found out, too, that the same law could be applied in one way to them and in quite another way to the employing class.

Sometimes this was true because when the workers brought their complaints to court they found that the magistrate who heard their case was the very employer against whom they were complaining! Small chance of a fair trial under those circumstances.

But the tie-up didn't have to be that close. It was enough that in most cases the magistrates were of the same class as the employers. Or where they were not of the same class, then they thought in the same way about the same things. The workers were looked down on, the employers were looked up to. Magistrates began with the idea that the workers ought to be thankful for the few crumbs thrown them; and that the employers were to be thanked for throwing their workers some crumbs. Under such conditions the dice were heavily loaded against the working class. In *The Town Labourer*, two eminent historians summarize what was happening: "Parliament did not concede much to the working classes, but the concessions, such as they were, lost all their value from the refusal of the magistrates to carry out legislation that was obnoxious to the masters. . . . The magistrates, for the most part, seem to have taken it for granted, that if the masters would not obey the law, nothing could be done to enforce obedience. . . . As they could not persuade the masters to obey the law, they sent the men to prison for trying to make them do so."

That keen observer, Adam Smith, believed that this was not a happen-so of this particular moment, but was a generalization true for all capitalist countries, at all times. The employers in looking to their hero for sanction for their deeds were careful not to dwell too long on this passage from the *Wealth of Nations*: "Civil government, so far as it is instituted for the security of property, is, in reality, instituted for the defence of the rich against the poor, or of those who have property against those who have none at all."

This truth the workers learned from bitter experience. What could they do about it? A seemingly obvious remedy suggested itself. If they won for themselves the right to vote, then they could bring pressure to bear on the law-makers to make government a government of and for the many instead of of and for the few. They felt that they had to win for themselves a say in the selection of the law-makers. Where the law was made by the workers it would be made for them. The law put obstacles in their path—it was made by the bosses—if the workers could help to make the laws, then they'd stand a chance. If the government could protect landowners by corn laws, and manufacturers by duties, then it could protect the workingmen's wages and hours. So they fought for the right to vote.

Today in the United States and in England we are so used to political democracy that we are inclined to believe that it always existed. Of course this is not true. The right to vote, for all citizens, both in this country and in European countries, was not granted willingly—it came as the result of struggle. In England the working class lined up behind the Chartist movement, which called for:

1. Universal suffrage (male).
2. Payment of members elected to the House of Commons. (This would make it possible for poor people to run for office.)
3. Annual parliaments.

4. No property qualification for candidates.
5. Voting by ballot, to prevent intimidation.
6. Equal electoral districts.

The Chartist movement itself slowly petered out. Nevertheless, one after another these demands were finally won (except that calling for annual parliaments). The Chartists had fought for political democracy because they felt it was a weapon in the struggle for better conditions. Stephens, a Methodist parson, addressing a working-class meeting in Manchester, told his hearers: "Chartism, my friends, is no political movement, where the main point is your getting the ballot. Chartism is a knife-and-fork question; the Charter means a good house, good food and drink, prosperity, and short working-hours."

Parson Stephens was an optimist. The working class won its fight for political democracy, but the good things that he predicted would result from it did not come. At least they came only in part, and then not alone through the vote. Perhaps the most important factor in winning for the workers better conditions, higher wages, and shorter hours was their own organization fighting for their own interests—the trade union.

The trade union was not new. It was one of the earliest forms of workmen's organizations, growing naturally out of the old journeymen's association. When, however, the importance of capital in industry became so great, the workmen's associations changed in character from the gild type to the trade union of today, a body of workmen in one trade organized to get better conditions, to defend their own interests, relying on themselves.

Trade unions did not spring up overnight. It took a long time for the feeling of unity of class interest to grow up, and until that happened real organization on a national scale was impossible. With the Industrial Revolution, trade-unionism took tremendous strides. This had to happen because the Industrial Revolution brought with it the concentration of workers into cities, the improvements in transportation and communication so essential to a nation-wide organization, and the conditions which made a workers' movement so necessary. Thus working-class organization grew with capitalist development, which produced both the class, the class sentiment, and the physical means of co-operation and communication. Trade-unionism is strongest in those countries which are most industrialized, where the factory system has led to the growth of large cities. This was pointed out by Friedrich Engels in 1844: "If the centralization of population stimulates and develops the property-holding class, it forces the development of the workers yet more rapidly. The workers begin to feel as a class, as a whole; they begin to perceive that, though feeble as individuals, they form a power united; their separation from the bourgeoisie, the development of views peculiar to the workers and corresponding to their position in life, is fostered, the consciousness of oppression awakens, and the workers attain social and political importance. The great cities are the birth-places of labour movements; in them the workers first began to reflect upon their own condition and to struggle against it; in them the opposition between proletariat and bourgeoisie first made itself manifest; from them proceeded the Trades-Unions, Chartism, and Socialism."

The Industrial Revolution which came first to England spread to other countries. It is still on its way into some. And though it doesn't always follow the English model in every country, varying in conditions, or in the attitude of the rich, or in reform legislation passed by the governing body, nevertheless on one point every country has repeated the history of England. Everywhere there has been a war on the trade unions.

It's an old war. Combinations of workmen to better their conditions were declared illegal as early as the fourteenth century, and every century thereafter the law put down such combinations. In 1776, Adam Smith wrote on the subject: "What are the common wages of labour depends everywhere upon the contract usually made between those two parties, whose interests are by no means the same. The workmen desire to get as much, the masters to give as little, as possible. The former are disposed to combine in order to raise, the latter in order to lower, the wages of labour.

"It is not, however, difficult to foresee which of the two parties must, upon all ordinary occasions, have the advantage in the dispute. . . . The masters, being fewer in number, can combine much more easily; and the law, besides, authorizes, or at least does not prohibit, their combinations, while it prohibits those of the workmen. We have no acts of parliament against combining to lower the price of work; but many against combining to raise it."

What Smith wrote in 1776 was (and is) true in every capitalist country of the world. Even where the law did prohibit manufacturers' associations as well as workers' associations, enforcement was most often directed against the employees, not the employers. In England, in France, in Germany, in the United States, the law came down hard on trade unions.

For a quarter of a century in England, the Combination Laws made it illegal for workers to join together in associations to protect their interests. When they did—then the law could be swift in its judgment. "Nine Stockport hatters were sentenced to two years' imprisonment in 1816 for conspiracy. The judge (Sir William Garrow), in summing up, remarked, 'In this happy country where the law puts the meanest subject on a level with the highest personages of the realm, all are alike protected, and there can be no need to associate. . . . A person who like Mr. Jackson has employed from 100 to 130 hands, common gratitude would teach us to look upon as a benefactor to the community.' "

For the hatters who dared to join a union—two years' imprisonment; for Mr. Jackson who was kind enough to employ them— praise. Re-read the judge's first sentence. Could he really have meant what he said?

In France, as in England, combinations to raise wages were declared illegal. The judges were sorry for the workers who persisted in running afoul of the law. According to Levasseur, they advised the workers against joining together, but the workingmen had found that divided they were weak, united they were strong, so they persisted in their union activities: "Judges inflicted punishment, without always applying the full vigour of the law. 'The court,' they said, 'has been indulgent; but let this be a lesson to you, and remember that if work brings comfort and consideration, coalitions will only bring you prison and poverty.' The workingmen . . . did not learn the lesson. The only memory which remained with them was that the strike of 1822 had raised their wages to 35 centimes an hour, that the strike of 1833 had raised wages to 40 centimes, and they struck work in 1845 to get a wage of 50 centimes."

In Germany, too, workers were on to the fact that trade unions gave them the power they sorely needed to improve their lot. In 1864 the printers in Berlin petitioned the Prussian Chamber of Deputies: "Filled with the conviction that the improvement in the social condition of the working classes requires firstly the abolition of the restrictions imposed on the workers in the present legal code, the undersigned printers' journeymen petition: Considering . . . that the economic law of supply and demand does not even assure to the worker . . . the minimum necessary for bare subsistence; that the individual worker is actually not in a position . . . to raise his wages, and that therefore the right of coalition . . . is a demand both of justice and of reason. . . . The regulations on the industrial code of 1845, which prohibit the free association of workmen . . . shall be abolished."

Everywhere the same story. Workers pleading and fighting for the right to join together in an effort to make the odds against them more equal. In the United States two items from a report on the year 1935 by the Methodist Federation for Social Service will be enough to show how fierce the struggle for unionization has been: "Weirton, W. Va. . . . A vicious campaign of terror has been launched against the active union members. . . . Every day some member of the union is beaten up by a gang of men wearing masks. The first man to get this treatment was taken for a ride and then left fifteen miles out of town, where his assailants left him for dead. . . . To date there have been five men seriously beaten, the last one a president of one of the Amalgamated Association lodges. . . .

"The whole record shows clearly that the struggle between the privileged and the underprivileged in this country is rapidly and

generally developing into violent action. . . . At least seventy-three
workers, sharecroppers, Negroes, were killed in economic struggles
and lynchings during the year; no employer."

But in spite of every effort, both legal and illegal, to crush them,
trade unions have persisted. It has not been easy. Union members
have been railroaded into jail; union treasuries have been seized;
unions have had to go underground—to become "benefit societies"
or "social clubs"; union weapons, such as striking and picketing,
have been blunted—yet the trade unions still live. They are the
workers' most powerful means of obtaining what they desire—a
better standard of living.

Over a century ago, in England, a great poet addressed himself
"To the Men of England." His poem may well serve as a summary
to this chapter on the conditions following the Industrial Revolution
and the workers' response to those conditions.

> Men of England, wherefore plough,
> For the lords who lay ye low?
> Wherefore weave with toil and care
> The rich robes your tyrants wear?
>
> Wherefore feed, and clothe, and save,
> From the cradle to the grave,
> Those ungrateful drones who would
> Drain your sweat—nay, drink your blood?
>
> Wherefore, Bees of England, forge
> Many a weapon, chain, and scourge
> That these stingless drones may spoil
> The forced produce of your toil?
>
> Have ye leisure, comfort, calm,
> Shelter, food, love's gentle balm?
> Or what is it ye buy so dear
> With your pain and with your fear?

The seed ye sow, another reaps;
The wealth ye find, another keeps;
The robes ye weave, another wears;
The arms ye forge, another bears.

Sow seed—but let no tyrant reap;
Find wealth—let no impostor heap;
Weave robes—let not the idle wear;
Forge arms—in your defence to bear. . . .
—PERCY BYSSHE SHELLEY

XVII

Whose "Natural Laws"?

THINGS fall down, not up. You know what would happen to you if you jumped out of the window. The physicists have obliged us with an explanation of this. Newton formulated a law of gravitation, one of a series of natural laws which, we are told, describe the physical universe. Knowledge of these natural laws enables you to plan your actions and reach a desired goal. Act in ignorance or disregard of them and you suffer the consequences.

In like manner, the economists at the time of the Industrial Revolution developed a series of laws which, they said, were as true for the social and economic world as were the laws of the scientists for the physical world. They formulated a set of doctrines which were the "natural laws" of economics. They were quite superior about their findings. They wouldn't argue about whether the laws were good or bad. No point in such a discussion. Their laws were fixed, eternal. If men were wise and acted in accordance with the principles they expounded, well and good, but if men were stupid, and did not act in accordance with their natural laws, they would suffer the consequences.

Now it may or may not be true that these economists in their search for truth were sublimely indifferent to the practical results of their enquiries. But they were flesh-and-blood men who lived in a certain place at a certain time. Which means that the problems with which they dealt were those which arose in that place and at that time. And their doctrines affected powerful groups in society who consequently adopted or rejected these doctrines in accordance with their own interest and saw the "truth" in that light.

Just as the rise of the merchant class after the Commercial Revolution brought with it the theory of mercantilism, just as the doctrines of the Physiocrats with their stress on land as the source of wealth, were developed in the agricultural country of France, so the rise of the industrialists during the Industrial Revolution in England brought with it economic theories based on the conditions of the time. We call the theorizing of the Industrial Revolution "classical economics."

You are already familiar with some of the doctrines of Adam Smith, who may be termed the founder of the classical school. Other prominent classical economists were Ricardo, Malthus, James Mill, McCulloch, Senior, and John Stuart Mill. They did not all agree with Smith or with one another. But on some fundamental general principles they were all in agreement.

And heartily in accord with these principles were the business men of the period. For an excellent reason. Classical theory was admirably suited to their particular requirements. From it they were able to select with great ease natural laws which were complete justification for their actions.

The business man kept his eye open for the main chance. He was eager for profits. Along came the classical economists who said that was exactly what he should be interested in. Nor was that all. There was still greater comfort for the enterprising business man. He was advised that every minute of the time that he was looking toward his own profit he was helping the state as well. Adam Smith said so. Here, for example, was a perfect prescription made to order for a grasping moneymaker who might be kept awake nights by a troublesome conscience. "Every individual is continually exerting himself to find out the most advantageous employment for whatever capital he can command. It is his own advantage, indeed, and not that of the society, which he has in view. But the study of his own advantage naturally, or rather necessarily, leads him to prefer that employment which is most advantageous to the society."

Get the idea?

The welfare of society is bound up with that of the individual. Give every person an absolutely free hand, tell him to make as much profit as he can, appeal to his self-interest, and, lo and behold, all of society is better off! Work for yourself and you are serving the general good. What a send-off for business men straining at the leash, anxious to run the race toward more and more profits! Clear the track for the *laissez-faire* special!

Should the government regulate hours and wages of labour? To do so, said the classical economists, would be an interference with natural law and would therefore be futile.

What then, was the function of government? To preserve the peace; to protect property; to keep hands off.

Competition must be the order of the day. It kept prices low and ensured the success of the strong and efficient, while getting rid of the weak and inefficient. It followed that monopoly—whether of capitalists to boost prices or of trade unions to boost wages—was a violation of natural law.

These broad concepts, you remember, had been outlined by Adam Smith in answer to mercantilist regulation, restriction, and restraint. He wrote his great book in 1776, just at the beginning of the Industrial Revolution. The classical economists who took up these doctrines and expanded them and popularized them further, wrote at the time that the Industrial Revolution, from the point of view of increased production of goods and rise to power of the capitalist class, was making great headway. They added other "natural laws" of their own, which fitted the conditions of the times.

An Essay on the Principle of Population, by Thomas R. Malthus, was one of the most famous books of the period. It was first published in 1798, partly as an answer to a book by William Godwin, the father-in-law of Shelley. Godwin, in his *Enquiry Concerning Political Justice*, published in 1793, held that all governments were evil, but that progress could be made, and mankind could achieve happiness, through the use of reason. Malthus wanted to fight the dangerous beliefs of Godwin; he wanted to prove that great improvement in the lot of mankind was impossible—which would be a good reason for being content with what was and not trying to stage a revolution as the French had done.

He attacks Godwin in these words: "The great error under which Mr. Godwin labours throughout his whole work, is, the attributing almost all the vices and misery that are seen in civil society to human institutions. Political regulations, and the established administration of property, are with him the fruitful sources of all evil, the hotbeds of all the crimes that degrade mankind. Were this really a true state of the case, it would not seem a hopeless task to remove evil completely from the world; and reason seems to be the proper and adequate instrument for effecting so great a purpose. But the truth is that, though human institutions appear to be the obvious and obtrusive causes of much mischief to mankind; yet, in reality, they are light and superficial, they are mere feathers that float on the surface, in comparison with those deeper-seated causes of impurity that corrupt the springs and render turbid the whole stream of human life."

What were those "deeper-seated causes" that make for the misery of mankind? Malthus' answer was that population increases faster than the food to keep the population alive. The result was that there came a time every so often when there were more mouths to feed than there was food to feed them. "Population, when unchecked, increases in geometrical ratio. Subsistence increases only in an arithmetical ratio. . . . This implies a strong and constantly operating check on population from the difficulty of subsistence. This difficulty must fall somewhere; and must necessarily be severely felt by a large portion of mankind. . . .

"The population of the Island [England] is computed to be about seven millions; and we will suppose the present produce equal to the support of such a number. In the first twenty-five years the population would be fourteen millions; and the food being also doubled, the means of subsistence would be equal to this increase.

In the next twenty-five years the population would be twenty-eight millions; and the means of subsistence only equal to the support of twenty-one millions. In the next period the population would be fifty-six millions, and the means of subsistence just sufficient for half that number. And at the conclusion of the first century the population would be one hundred and twelve millions, and the means of subsistence only equal to the support of thirty-five millions; which would leave a population of seventy-seven millions totally unprovided for."

This, said Malthus, doesn't really happen in fact. Because death (in the form of "epidemics, pestilence and plague . . . and famine") steps in and takes its toll of the increasing population, so that it comes level with the food-supply. "The superior power of population is repressed, and the actual population kept equal to the means of subsistence by misery and vice."

So the reason the labouring classes were poor, said Malthus, was not because profits were too high (man-made reason), but because population increases faster than subsistence (natural law). Could nothing, then, be done to improve the condition of the poor? "Nothing," said Malthus—in the first edition of his book. "It is, undoubtedly, a most disheartening reflection, that the great obstacle in the way to any extraordinary improvement in society, is of a nature that we can never hope to overcome."

But in the second edition of his book, published in 1803, Malthus did find a way. Besides misery and vice, a third check to population growth was possible—"moral restraint." No strike, no revolution, no charity, no government regulation, could help the poor in their misery—they were themselves to blame because they bred so fast. Let them not marry so early. Let them practise "moral restraint"— not have such large families—and thus they could hope to help themselves. Who served society best, the woman who married and had many children, or the old maid? Malthus votes for the old maid: "The matron who has reared a family of ten or twelve children and whose sons, perhaps, may be fighting the battles of their country, is apt to think that society owes her much. . . . But if the subject be fairly considered and the respected matron weighed in the scales of justice against the neglected old maid, it is possible that the matron might kick the beam."

It was cheering news to the rich that the poor had only themselves to blame for their poverty.

After Adam Smith, the most important of the classical economists was David Ricardo. He was a London Jew who made a large fortune as a stockholder. His book *The Principles of Political Economy and Taxation*, published in 1817, is held by many to be the first which treats of economics as a science. You will find Adam Smith's *Wealth of Nations* easy reading as compared with Ricardo's work. One reason is that Smith is a much better writer. Another and perhaps more important reason is that where Smith is concrete and makes use of everyday familiar examples to illustrate his ideas, Ricardo, on the other hand, is abstract and makes use of imaginary examples which may or may not have some semblance of reality. Scientific books in general are difficult and dull. Ricardo's is no exception. Nevertheless, what he had to say was tremendously important and he ranks as one of the greatest economists who ever lived.

In our limited space we can consider only a few of his doctrines, very briefly. The first is known as "the iron law of wages." What workers receive for their labour had claimed the attention of writers before Ricardo. In 1766, Turgot, in a small book entitled *Reflections on the Formation and Distribution of Wealth*, said: "The mere workman, who depends only on his hands and his industry, has nothing but such part of his labour as he is able to dispose of to others. He sells it at a cheaper or a dearer price; but this high or low price does not depend on himself alone; it results from the agreement he has made with the person who employs him. The latter pays him as little as he can help, and as he has the choice from among a great number of workmen, he prefers the person who works cheapest. The workmen are therefore obliged to lower their price in opposition to each other. In every species of labour it must, and, in effect, it does, happen, that the wages of the workman is confined merely to what is necessary to procure him a subsistence."

Turgot left it at that. Ricardo developed the idea, so the iron law of wages is associated with him. That workers get only enough wages to keep themselves and their families alive is stated in these terms by Ricardo: "The natural price of labour . . . depends on the price of the food, necessaries, and conveniences required for the support of the labourer and his family. With a rise in the price of food and necessaries, the natural price of labour will rise; with the fall in their price, the natural price of labour will fall."

But you and I know that there are times when workers receive more than enough to live on, and other times when they receive less than enough. Ricardo takes that into account. He distinguishes between the "market price" of labour and its natural price: "The market price of labour is the price which is really paid for it, from the natural operation of the proportion of the supply to the demand; labour is dear when it is scarce and cheap when it is plentiful. However much the market price of labour may deviate from its natural price, it has, like commodities, a tendency to conform to it."

To prove the truth of the last sentence, that market price tends to conform to natural price, Ricardo borrows a leaf from Malthus' book. He says that when the market price is high, when workers are receiving in wages more than enough for their families to live on, then they will tend to increase the size of their families. And more workers will bring wages down. When the market price is low, when workers are receiving in wages less than they need to keep their families alive, then their numbers will be reduced. And fewer workers will bring wages up.

This then was Ricardo's law of wages—in the long run, workers can never receive more than what "is necessary to enable the labourers . . . to subsist and to perpetuate their race, without either increase or diminution."

For a better understanding of the law of rent, the most famous of Ricardo's doctrines, we must look into the controversy over the Corn Laws which was raging in England at the time when Ricardo's

Principles appeared. The antagonists in the dispute were the landowners and the manufacturers.

The Corn Laws were a kind of protective tariff on wheat (in England, wheat is known as corn). Wheat could not be imported until the price of home wheat had reached a certain height (this varied from time to time).

The idea had been to encourage the cultivation of wheat at home so that England would have enough supplies in case of an emergency. Cultivation was encouraged by assuring the English farmer a good price for his grain. He need not fear the competition of outside wheat, because none was admitted into the country until his own wheat had reached a certain price. This meant a good profit, unless the home crop was too heavy for the demand—which did not happen in England from 1790 on.

Because of the Napoleonic wars, wheat shot up in price and more and more land was turned to cultivation. Landowners wanted the price of wheat to be high, because that meant higher rents, which meant money in their pockets. Manufacturers did not want the price of wheat to be high, because that meant an increase in the cost of workers' subsistence, and therefore discontent, strikes, and eventually higher wages, which meant money out of their pockets. So the fight raged, landlords shouting for protection and manufacturers shouting for free trade.

Ricardo was in the middle of this fight. His sympathies were with the manufacturers, since he himself belonged to the class of the rising bourgeoisie. It is not surprising, then, to learn that, among other things, the natural laws he discovers which explain the nature of rent, show that "all classes, therefore, except the landlords, will be injured by the increase in the price of corn."

How does he arrive at this conclusion? By proving that the higher the price of corn the higher rents will be. Rent arises, argues Ricardo, because the soil is limited and differs in fertility. "If all land had the same properties, if it were unlimited in quantity and uniform in quality, no charge could be made for its use. . . . It is only, then, because land is not unlimited in quantity and uniform in quality, and because, in the progress of population, land of an inferior quality . . . is called into cultivation, that rent is ever paid for the use of it. When, in the progress of society, land of the second degree of fertility is taken into cultivation, rent immediately commences on that of the first quality, and the amount of that rent will depend on the difference in the quality of these two portions of land.

"When land of the third quality is taken into cultivation, rent immediately commences on the second, and it is regulated as before by the difference in their productive powers. . . . With every step in the progress of population, which shall oblige a country to have recourse to land of a worse quality, to enable it to raise its supply of food, rent on all the more fertile land will rise."

According to Ricardo the Corn Laws, by raising the price of wheat, made the farmers turn to poorer lands for wheat-raising. When this happened rents were paid on the more fertile lands. As time went on, the poorer soil came increasingly into cultivation and rent went up and up. And this rent came to the landowners not at all because they worked for it. They did nothing—and yet their rents rose. "The interest of the landlord is always opposed to that of the consumer and manufacturer. Corn can be permanently at an advanced price only because additional labour is necessary to produce it; because its cost of production is increased. The same cost invariably raises rent, it is therefore for the interest of the landlord that the cost attending the production of corn should be increased. This, however, is not the interest of the consumer; to him it is desirable that corn should be low relatively to money and commodities, for it is always with commodities or money that corn is purchased. Neither is it the interest of the manufacturer that corn should be at a high price, for the high price of corn will occasion high wages, but will not raise the price of his commodity."

That last was the rub, of course. In so far as workers were bound to get a subsistence wage, according to Ricardo's own law of wages, it didn't matter to them whether corn was high or low—their wages went up when corn was high, just as they went down when corn was low. But it did matter to the manufacturers who could not sell their products for more just because corn was dearer and therefore wages higher. Ricardo goes on to compare the respective services of landlords and manufacturers and the landlord is again found lacking: "The dealings between the landlord and the public are not like dealings in trade, whereby both seller and buyer may equally be said to gain, but the loss is wholly on one side and the gain wholly on the other."

The industrialists added the natural laws of Ricardo to their armoury of weapons against protection. They wanted the Corn Laws abolished and the era of free trade inaugurated. Parliament, however, was controlled by the landlords, and so the Corn Laws remained for a long time (until 1846). Meanwhile some of the landlords, who found it so difficult to see any advantage to the country in cheap wheat, did become concerned over factory conditions and hours of labour. Humanitarians shouting for correction of the evils of industrialism now found themselves aided by powerful landlords who wanted to get even with the manufacturers for their hostility to the Corn Laws. Parliamentary committees were appointed which looked into conditions and made their reports. Efforts were made to pass laws reducing the hours of labour. There was, of course, tremendous opposition on the part of manufacturers, who predicted that they would be ruined if their workers were not kept at the machines as long as they had been in the past. But the combined efforts of workers, humanitarians, and landlords were successful, and Factory Acts restricting hours and regulating conditions did come into being. And the agitation for further restriction and regulation continued.

One of the classical economists, Nassau Senior, worked out a doctrine which "proved" that hours could not be reduced further, because what profit the employer made came out of the last hour of work—take that away and you cut out the profit, and thus wreck the industry altogether. "Under the present law, no mill in which persons under eighteen years of age are employed . . . can be worked more than . . . twelve hours for five days in the week, and nine on Saturday. Now, the following analysis will show that in a mill so worked the whole net profit is derived *from the last hour*."

Senior's analysis was based on a purely imaginary example in which the arithmetic was correct but the conclusions were wrong. That was proven every time a factory reduced hours—and continued in business.

Much more damaging to the workers than Senior's last-hour analysis was the wage-fund doctrine. This was more damaging because it was believed and taught by most of the economists. The last-hour principle was used to fight the agitation for shorter hours; the wage-fund doctrine was used to fight the agitation for higher pay.

Workers joined trade unions and went on strike because they wanted an increase in wages. "Pure madness," said the economists. Why? Because there was a certain fund set aside for the payment of wages. And there was a certain number of wage-earners. The amount the workers got in wages was determined by these two factors. And that was that. Trade unions couldn't do anything about it.

John Stuart Mill put it this way: "Wages not only depend upon the relative amount of capital and population, but cannot under the rule of competition be affected by anything else. Wages . . . cannot rise, but by an increase of the aggregate funds employed in hiring labourers, or a diminution in the number of the competitors for hire; nor fall, except either by a diminution of the funds devoted to paying labour, or by an increase in the number of labourers to be paid."

Very simple. No hope for the workers unless the wage-fund was increased or the number of labourers decreased. If any of the workers were pig-headed and insisted that higher wages were needed to keep them alive, they might be given a lesson in elementary mathematics: "There is no use in arguing against any one of the four fundamental rules of arithmetic. The question of wages is a question of division. It is complained that the quotient is too small. Well, then, how many ways are there to make a quotient larger? Two ways. Enlarge your dividend, the divisor remaining the same, and the quotient will be larger; lessen your divisor, the dividend remaining the same, and the quotient will be larger."

The illustrations for a page of such an arithmetic lesson might look like this:

How get more wages? How increase the quotient?
1st way—enlarge the dividend.

2nd way—lessen the divisor.

All very plain. Two ways of getting higher wages. The second way, "lessen the divisor"—i.e. decrease the number of workers, was an old bit of advice to the workers. Malthus had called it "moral restraint."

The first way, "enlarge the dividend," i.e. increase the size of the wage-fund, could be brought about, according to Senior, "By allowing every man to exert himself in the way which, from experience, he finds most beneficial; by freeing industry from the mass of restrictions, prohibitions, and protecting duties, with which the Legislature sometimes in well-meaning ignorance, sometimes in pity, and sometimes in national jealousy, has laboured to crush or misdirect her efforts." Let business alone and the result would be more money in the fund set aside for wages. The business men agreed.

The wage-fund theory was the manufacturers' and economists' stock answer to the claims of workmen and unions. The workers had no use for it because they knew it to be untrue. They knew that trade-union action did win them higher wages. They simply did not believe that there was a fixed fund set aside in advance out of which their wages were paid. What they had learned in practice was confirmed in theory by Francis Walker, an American economist writing in 1876. Walker exploded the wage-fund theory with this argument: "A popular theory of wages . . . is based upon the assumption that wages are paid out of capital, the saved results of the industry of the past. Hence, it is argued, capital must furnish the measure of wages. On the contrary, I hold that wages are . . . paid out of the product of present industry, and hence that production furnishes the true measure of wages. . . . An employer pays wages to purchase labour, not to expend a fund of which he may be in possession. . . . The employer purchases labour with a view to the product of the labour; and the kind and amount of that product determine what wages he can afford to pay. . . . It is, then, for the sake of future production that the labourers are employed, not at all because the employer has possession of a fund which he must disburse; and it is the value of the product . . . which determines the amount of the wages that can be paid, not at all the amount of wealth which the employer has in possession or can command. Thus it is production, not capital, which furnishes the motive for employment and the measure of wages."

Excellent proof of the truth of Walker's argument that wages are not an "advance" to the worker paid out of capital is furnished by the practice common today in the textile mills of Japan and India, where wages are "held back." In Japan "the wages earned by the girls in the silk filatures and smaller cotton factories are usually paid directly to the parents. . . . These wages may be paid half-yearly or, as in the case of the silk filatures, at the end of the year's labour . . .

[and in India] wages are paid a month or six weeks in arrears. . . .
The mills even charge nine-per-cent interest if they give short advances up to the next pay day on wages already earned."

But it was not necessary to wait for twentieth-century proof of the
falsity of the wage-fund theory. The working class had denounced
it from the start as being contrary to their own experience. Walker
in 1876 gave numerous examples from American life to prove that
there was no truth in it. And seven years before Walker finally
drove the last nail in the coffin of the wage-fund theory, even the
economists were admitting that this natural law was not a law at
all. John Stuart Mill was the man whose *Principles of Political
Economy*, first published in 1848, had done so much to popularize
the doctrine; in reviewing a book for the *Fortnightly Review*, in
May, 1869, he published this retraction: "The doctrine hitherto
taught by all or most economists (including myself) which denied it
to be possible that trade combinations can raise wages, or which
limited their operations in that respect to the somewhat earlier at-
tainment of a rise which the competition of the market would have
produced without them—this doctrine is deprived of its scientific
foundation, and must be thrown aside."

This was a brave thing for J. S. Mill to do. He had made a mistake
and he admitted it honestly and fully. But for the workers it was
too late—this denunciation of a doctrine which had plagued them
for more than half a century. They had little use for a science which
provided the enemy with a whole arsenal of cannon-shot every time
workers tried to make an advance; they had little use for a science
which offered them practically no hope of ever improving their lot
in life; they had little use for a science which at every turn served
the interests of the employing class.

That the workers had real grounds for such distrust of the science
of economics was admitted by one of the leading followers of the
classical school, Professor J. E. Cairnes. In his *Essays in Political
Economy*, published in 1873, Cairnes pointed out that economics
had become a bourgeois-class weapon: "Political Economy too often
makes its appearance, especially in its approaches to the working

classes, in the guise of a dogmatic code of cut-and-dried rules, a system promulgating decrees, 'sanctioning' one social arrangement, 'condemning' another, requiring from men not consideration, but obedience. Now when we take into account the sort of decrees which are ordinarily given to the world in the name of Political Economy —decrees which I think I may say in the main amount to a handsome ratification of the existing form of society as approximately perfect—I think we shall be able to understand the repugnance, and even violent opposition, manifested toward it by people who have their own reasons for not cherishing that unbounded admiration for our present industrial arrangements which is felt by some popular expounders of so-called economic laws. When a workingman is told that Political Economy 'condemns' strikes . . . looks askance at proposals for limiting the hours of labour, but 'approves' the accumulation of capital, and 'sanctions' the market rate of wages, it seems not an unnatural response that 'since Political Economy is against the workingman, it behoves the workingman to be against Political Economy.' It seems not unnatural that this new code should come to be regarded with suspicion, as a system possibly contrived in the interest of employers, which it is the workmen's wisdom simply to repudiate and disown."

It was true that "Political Economy was against the workingman." It was also true that it was for the business man—particularly the business man of England. The teachings of the classical economists spread to France and to Germany, and in the first quarter of the nineteenth century the famous books on economics published in those countries were, in the main, either translations or expositions of the works of the English classical economists. But it gradually became plain, to thinkers in both these countries, that classical doctrine was not merely business man's doctrine, but in some respects it was peculiarly *English* business man's doctrine. Not that the classical economists had consciously set out to help the English business man. That hadn't been necessary. In so far as they lived in England at a definite time, their doctrines had to be coloured by their environment. They were—and the economists and business men of other countries found it out.

Take free trade, for example. Adam Smith had preached it, and Ricardo and the others that followed him had preached it, too. They stood for world-wide free trade; not only internal barriers must be removed, but the barriers between countries must be taken down as well. Ricardo states the case for free international exchange quite plainly: "Under a system of perfectly free commerce, each country naturally devotes its capital and labour to such employments as are most beneficial to each. This pursuit of individual advantage is admirably connected with the universal good of the whole. By stimulating industry, by rewarding ingenuity, and by using most efficaciously the peculiar powers bestowed by nature, it distributes labour most effectively and most economically: while, by increasing the general mass of productions, it diffuses general benefit and binds together, by one common tie of interest and intercourse, the universal society of nations throughout the civilized world. It is this principle which determines that wine shall be made in France and Portugal, that corn shall be grown in America and Poland, and that hardware and other goods shall be manufactured in England."

Now Ricardo, in this quotation, may be right or wrong about the value of international free exchange of goods. But there was no question but that he was absolutely right *for England at the time he wrote*. The Industrial Revolution had come to England first; English manufacturers had a head start on manufacturers anywhere in the world, in method, in kinds of machinery, in transportation facilities; the English were able and ready to cover the earth with the products of their factories. So international free trade was right up their street.

For that very reason, it was not suited to the business men of other countries. Alexander Hamilton in America instituted a protective-tariff system in Washington's administration. Other countries had had tariff barriers, too, but under the influence of English classical economics they were beginning to flirt with free-trade ideas.

In 1841, at the moment when the English song on the superlative virtues of international free trade was becoming quite popular in other countries, Friedrich List published his *National System of Political Economy*, attacking it. List was a German, and in the Germany of that day industry was still young and undeveloped. He had spent some years in the United States, where he found the same thing true of American industry. List saw that if international free trade were established it would take the industries of countries, not on a par with England, a long time to catch up—if they ever could at all. He said he was for free trade—but only after the less advanced nations had caught up to the more advanced. "Any nation which, owing to misfortunes, is behind others in industry, commerce, and navigation, while she nevertheless possesses the mental and material means for developing those acquisitions, must first of all strengthen her own individual powers, in order to fit herself to enter into free competition with more advanced nations."

He said cheapness wasn't everything, that cheap things could be bought too dear. What made a country great was not its stock of values at any particular time, but its capacity to produce values. *"The causes of wealth* are something totally different from *wealth itself*. A person may possess wealth . . . if, however, he does not possess the power of producing objects of more value than he consumes, he will become poorer. . . . *The power of producing wealth* is, therefore, infinitely more important than *wealth itself*. . . . This is still more the case with entire nations . . . than with private individuals."

List suggests that England, having become great before free trade was its motto, was now trying to make it impossible for other nations to follow suit: "It is a very common clever device that when anyone has attained the summit of greatness, he kicks away the ladder by which he has climbed up, in order to deprive others of the means of climbing up after him."

List, therefore, comes out for protection, for tariff walls, behind which infant industries, assured of the home market, can grow until they can stand on their own legs. Only when they had gathered strength were they to be sent into the free trade world to fight. List was a powerful exponent of the national as opposed to the international system of economy. His ideas had great influence particularly in Germany and the United States.

List, with his strong advocacy of Protection *vs.* the Free Trade doctrine of Adam Smith and his followers, was one of a growing number of disbelievers in the infallibility of the classical school. Classical economics, so popular and so powerful in the first half of the nineteenth century, started to lose some of its strength in the second half. At that time there began to appear the works of a man who, while accepting some of the principles expounded by the classicists, carried them along a different path to a far different conclusion. He, too, was a German. His name was Karl Marx.

XVIII

"Workingmen of All Countries, Unite!"

"IF I only had a million dollars!" How often you and I have toyed with this delightful idea. It comes to most of us every time the newspapers run the pictures of the lucky winners of the Irish Sweepstakes. In similar fashion, there have always been people who spent a good deal of their time in speculating on better societies than the one in which they lived. Often these speculations never got beyond the daydream stage; but occasionally the dreamers really let themselves go, worked hard on their ideas, and completed their utopias— visions of the ideal society of the future.

As a matter of fact, the task wasn't difficult. Almost anyone with imagination could have done it. All you had to do was to look around and you'd know what to avoid. You saw poor people everywhere; in your utopia you eliminated poverty. You saw waste in the production and distribution of goods; in your utopia you formulated a method of production and distribution which was one hundred per cent efficient. You saw injustice of every kind; in your utopia you provided for honest courts presided over by honest judges (or you might even fix it so courts and judges were totally unnecessary). You saw sickness, misery, unhappiness; in your utopia you brought health, wealth, and happiness to everyone.

Perhaps the most important first principle of the utopian schemers was the abolition of capitalism. In the capitalist system they saw only evil. It was wasteful, unjust, without a plan. They wanted a planned

222

society which would be efficient and just. Under capitalism the few who did not work lived in comfort and luxury through their ownership of the means of production. The utopians saw in the common ownership of the means of production the production of the means to the good life. So in their visionary societies they planned that the many who did the work would live in comfort and luxury through their ownership of the means of production. This was Socialism—and this was the dream of the utopians.

And then came Karl Marx.

He, too, was a Socialist. He, too, wanted to improve the condition of the working class. He, too, wanted a planned society. He, too, wanted the means of production to be owned by all of the people. But—and this is very important—he planned no utopia. He wrote practically nothing on how the Society of the Future would operate. He was tremendously interested in the Society of the Past, how it arose, developed, and decayed, until it became the Society of the Present; he was tremendously interested in the Society of the Present because he wanted to discover the forces in it which would make for further change to the Society of the Future. But he spent no time on and had no concern for the economic institutions of Tomorrow. He spent almost all of his time on a study of the economic institutions of Today. He wanted to know what made the wheels go round in the capitalist society in which he was then living. The name of his greatest work was *Capital—A Critical Analysis of Capitalist Production*.

It was through his analysis of capitalist society that he came to the conclusion that Socialism would come—he didn't dream it into existence as the utopians had done. Marx thought that Socialism would come about as the result of definite forces at work in society, with an organized revolutionary working class necessary to usher it in. Just as classical economics may be called business man's economics because in it the business man could find aid and comfort, so the economics of Marx may be called workingman's economics because in it the workingman could find his important place in the scheme of things and could derive hope for the future.

The fundamental point of Marx's economic doctrine is that the capitalist system is based upon the exploitation of labour.

It was easy to see that in the days of slavery the labourer—i.e., the slave—was getting a raw deal. Everyone would agree to that. The more tender-skinned might even exclaim in a rage: "How shocking! That one man should work for another is absolutely wrong! It's a good thing slavery has been abolished."

Similarly, it was easy to see that in the feudal period, the labourer —i.e., the serf—was getting a raw deal. There was no question about that. No question, because it was quite plain that he, like the slave, had to work for another man—his lord. He worked, say, four days a week on his own land, and the other two days on his lord's. In both cases, the exploitation of the worker was evident.

But it was *not* easy to see that in capitalist society the worker was still getting a raw deal. Presumably the worker is a free agent. Unlike the slave or serf he does not *have* to work for this master or that lord. Presumably, he can work or not, as he pleases. And having chosen the boss for whom he will work, the labourer receives his pay for his work at the end of the week. Surely this was different— this was not exploitation of labour?

Marx disagreed. He said that the labourer in capitalist society was being exploited just as he had been in slave and feudal society. Marx said that the exploitation in capitalist society was hidden, masked. He tore the mask off by his exposition of the theory of surplus value.

In this theory he takes over Ricardo's labour theory of value held, in varying degrees, by most of the classicists from Adam Smith to John Stuart Mill. According to this doctrine, the value of goods depends on the amount of labour needed to produce them. Marx quotes a famous economist, our own Benjamin Franklin, as a believer in this labour theory of value. Marx writes: "The celebrated Franklin, one of the first economists after William Petty, who saw through the nature of values, says, 'Trade in general being nothing else but the exchange of labour for labour, the value of all things is justly measured by labour.'"

Marx makes a distinction between goods in general and commodities. Commodity production is the kind typical of capitalist society. "The wealth of those societies in which the capitalist mode of production prevails, presents itself as 'an immense accumulation of commodities,' its unit being a single commodity. Our investigation must, therefore, begin with the analysis of a commodity."

A good becomes a commodity when it is produced, not for consumption directly, but for exchange. A coat made by a man for himself is not a commodity. A coat made to be sold to someone else—to be exchanged for money or for another article—is a commodity. "Whoever directly satisfies his wants with the produce of his own labour, creates, indeed, use-values, but not commodities. In order to produce the latter he must not only produce use-values, but use-values for others, social use-values." The man who makes a coat, not to wear himself, but for exchange, for sale, has produced a commodity.

Now the important question is, at what rate will it exchange? What determines the value of this commodity? Compare this coat with another commodity—a pair of shoes. As goods, as means of satisfying human wants, there doesn't seem much in common between them. Nor between them and other commodities—bread, pencils, sausages, etc. But they can only exchange because of something which they have in common, and what they have in common, says Marx, is that they are products of labour. All commodities are the products of labour. Value, therefore, or the rate at which commodities exchange, is determined by the amount of labour embodied in them. And that amount of labour is measured by the extent of its duration—i.e. labour-time. "We see, then, that which determines the magnitude of the value of any article is the amount of labour socially necessary, or the labour-time socially necessary for its production. . . . The value of one commodity is to the value of any other, as the labour-time necessary for the production of the one is to that necessary for the production of the other."

If then, the coat took sixteen hours to produce, while the pair of shoes took eight hours, the coat will have twice as much value, and one coat will exchange for two pairs of shoes. Marx realized

that the kinds of labour in the two cases weren't quite the same—
the coat embodied the labour of the spinner, weaver, tailor, etc.;
while other kinds of labour went into the shoes. But, says Marx,
all labour is the same, and therefore comparable, in the sense that
it is the expenditure of human labour-power. Simple, unskilled,
average labour and skilled labour are comparable, the latter being
just a multiple of the former, so that one hour's skilled labour =
e.g., two hours' unskilled.

So the value of a commodity is determined, says Marx, by the
social labour-time necessary to produce it. "But," you will object,
"that would mean that the commodity produced by a slow, inefficient worker would be worth more than a commodity produced
by an able, fast worker, since it would take the slow worker more
time to complete it." Marx anticipated that objection and answered
it this way: "It might seem that if the value of a commodity is
determined by the *quantity of labour bestowed upon its production*,
the lazier a man, or the clumsier a man, the more valuable his
commodity, because the greater the time of labour required for
finishing the commodity. This, however, would be a sad mistake.
You will recollect that I used the word '*social* labour,' and many
points are involved in this qualification of '*social*.' In saying that
the value of a commodity is determined by the *quantity of labour*
worked up or crystallized in it, we mean the *quantity of labour
necessary* for its production in a given state of society, under certain
social average conditions of production, with a given social average
intensity, and average skill of the labour employed."

In a factory employing, say, two hundred workmen, some will
work better than others. But there is an average quality of labour.
Those who work better than this average are cancelled out against
those who work below it. Suppose the average, or socially necessary, labour-time required to make a coat equals sixteen hours.
Some workers need less time, some need more, but these are minor
deviations from the general standard. It is the same with the means
of production, the machinery which labour uses in producing goods.
In the textile industry as a whole, some plants may be working

with out-of-date looms. Some may be working with the very latest models which have not yet been generally adopted. But again there is an average level of equipment—the aboves and belows cancel each other out, and therefore socially necessary labour-time means average labour working with average instruments. This, of course, changes with different times and places, but at any one time, in any one country, there is this general average standard to which labour and the means of production conform.

So what? Suppose we grant that the value of a commodity is determined by the labour-time socially necessary for its production. What has that to do with proving that in capitalist society labour is exploited, that the propertied class lives on the labour of the class without property? What has that to do with proving that the worker, like the serf, works only part of the time for himself and part of the time for his boss?

Everything.

The wage worker in capitalist society is a free man. He does not belong to a master, as in slavery, nor is he tied to the soil, as in serfdom. We have already seen (Chapter XIV) how he was "freed" not only from his master, but also from the means of production. We have seen how the means of production (land, tools, machinery, etc.) came to be owned by a small group, and were no longer distributed generally among all workers. Those who do not own the means of production can make their living only by hiring themselves out—for wages—to those who do. Of course the worker doesn't sell himself to the capitalist (that would make him a slave), but he sells the only commodity he possesses—his capacity to work, his labour-power.

"For the conversion of his money into capital, therefore, the owner of money must meet in the market with the free labourer, free in the double sense that as a free man he can dispose of his labour-power as his own commodity, and that on the other hand he has no other commodity for sale, is short of everything necessary for the realization of his labour-power."

At what rate must this free labourer sell his commodity—i.e., what is the value of his labour-power? The value of labour-power, like the value of any other commodity, is determined by the amount of labour necessary to produce it. In other words, the value of the worker's labour-power is equal to all the things necessary for him to live, and, since the supply of labour must go on, to raise a family. What this sum of things includes is different at different times and places. (For example, it differs today in the U.S. and in China.) The worker is paid wages in return for his labour-power. Those wages will always tend to equal a sum of money which will purchase for the worker the commodities he requires to reproduce his labour-power both in himself and in his children.

Marx puts it this way: "The value of labour-power is the value of the means of subsistence necessary for the maintenance of the labourer. . . . His means of subsistence . . . must be sufficient to maintain him in his normal state as a labouring individual. His natural wants, such as food, clothing, fuel, and housing, vary according to the climatic and other physical conditions of his country. On the other hand, the number and extent of his so-called necessary wants . . . are themselves the product of historical development, and depend, therefore, to a great extent on the degree of civilization of a country . . . on the habits and degrees of comfort in which the class of free labourers has been formed. . . .

"The owner of labour-power is mortal. . . . The labour-power withdrawn from the market by wear and tear and death must be continually replaced by, at the very least, an equal amount of fresh labour-power. Hence the sum of the means of subsistence necessary for the production of labour-power must include the means necessary for the labourer's substitute—i.e., his children—in order that this race of peculiar commodity-owners may perpetuate its appearance in the market."

This simply means that the labourer will get, in return for his labour-power, wages, which will be just enough to keep himself and his family alive, with enough more (in some countries) to buy a radio, or a car, or a ticket to the movies occasionally.

Notice in the above quotation that Marx refers to "this race of peculiar commodity-owners." What is "peculiar" about the worker's commodity, labour-power? It is peculiar in that, unlike any other commodity, *it can create more value than it is itself worth*. When the workman hires himself out, he sells his labour-power not merely for the time it takes to produce the value of his own wages, but for the length of the full working day. If the working day is ten hours, and the time necessary to produce the value of the labourer's wages equals six hours, then there will be four hours left during which time the labourer is working *not for himself, but for his employer*. The six hours Marx calls *necessary labour-time*, the four hours *surplus labour-time*. Of the value of the total product of the ten hours' labour, six-tenths will equal wages, and four-tenths will equal *surplus value* which is appropriated by the employer and forms his profits.

"The value of a commodity is determined by the *total quantity of labour* contained in it. But part of that quantity of labour is realized in a value, for which an equivalent has been paid in the form of wages; part of it is realized in a value for which *no* equivalent has been paid. Part of the labour contained in the commodity is *paid* labour; part is *unpaid* labour. By selling, therefore, the commodity *at its value*, that is, as the crystallization of the *total quantity of labour* bestowed upon it, the capitalist must necessarily sell it at a profit. He sells not only what has cost him an equivalent, but he sells also what has cost him nothing, although it has cost the labour of his workman. The cost of the commodity to the capitalist and its real cost are different things. I repeat, therefore, that normal and average profits are made by selling commodities not *above*, but *at their real values*."

Marx's theory of surplus value thus solves the mystery of how labour is exploited in capitalist society. Let us summarize the whole process in brief sentence form:

The capitalist system is concerned with the production of goods for sale, commodities.

The value of a commodity is determined by the socially necessary labour-time which has gone into its production.

The worker does not own the means of production (land, tools, factories, etc.)

In order to live, he must sell the only commodity he does own, his labour-power.

The value of his labour-power, like that of the commodities, is the amount needed to reproduce it—in this case, the amount needed to keep him alive.

The wages paid to him, therefore, will be equal to only what is necessary for his maintenance.

But this amount the worker can produce in a part of his working day (less than the whole).

This means that only part of the time will the worker be working for himself.

The rest of the time he will be working for the boss.

The difference between what the worker receives in wages, and the value of the commodity he produces, is surplus value.

Surplus value goes to the employers—the owners of the means of production.

It is the source of profits, interest, rent—the returns to the owning classes.

Surplus value is the measure of the exploitation of labour in the capitalistic system.

Karl Marx was a keen student of American history and so was probably familiar with the writings and speeches of Abraham Lincoln. We don't know whether or not Abraham Lincoln ever had the opportunity to read any of the works of Karl Marx. But we do know that on some subjects their thinking was similar. Witness this from Abraham Lincoln: "No good thing has been or can be enjoyed by us without having first cost labour. And inasmuch as most good things are produced by labour, it follows that all such things of right belong to those whose labour has produced them. But it has so happened, in all ages of the world, that some have laboured, and others have without labour enjoyed a large proportion of the fruits. This is wrong and should not continue. To secure to each labourer the whole product of his labour, or as nearly as possible, is a worthy object of any good government."

That's by Abraham Lincoln. He too was on to the fact that labour does the work, and that in having to share with capital, it is, in a sense, being robbed. He goes further. Read his last sentence again and you will see that he wants something to be done about it. So did the Utopians. So did Marx. But they differed very much about the method of doing it.

The Utopian Socialists "in working out their utopias . . . worried but little as to whether the great industrial forces at work in society would permit of the contemplated change." They believed that all that was necessary was to formulate a plan for an ideal society, interest the powerful or the rich (or both) in the scheme, experiment with it on a small scale, and then rely on the sweet reasonableness of people to bring it into being.

Thus, Robert Owen, famous English Socialist, wrote a book the thesis of which can be gathered from its title, *Book of the New Moral World*. Does he call for a revolt of the working class to bring about the change to his new society? He does not. At the end of his book he writes a letter to His Majesty, William IV, King of Great Britain. It runs: "The book . . . unfolds the fundamental principles of a *New Moral World*, and it thus lays a new foundation on which to reconstruct society and recreate the character of the human race. . . . Society has emanated from fundamental errors of the imagination, and all the institutions and social arrangements of man over the world have been based on these errors . . . under your reign, Sire, the change from this system, with all its evil consequences, to another founded on self-evident truths, ensuring happiness to all, will, in all probability, be achieved."

And Charles Fourier, famous French Socialist, also looked beyond the working class to the men with money to help inaugurate his experiments with a new order: "Once he announced publicly that he would be at home every day at a certain hour to await any philanthropist who felt disposed to give him a million francs for the development of a colony based on Fourieristic principles. For twelve years thereafter he was at home every day, punctually at noon, awaiting the generous stranger, but, alas, no millionaire appeared."

The followers of Saint-Simon, another French Socialist, were contemptuous of Fourier's proposals. But they too thought collaboration with the bourgeoisie was necessary to bring about social change. In their organ, the *Globe*, on November 28, 1831, they published this revealing item: "The working classes cannot rise unless the upper classes reach out their hand. It is from these latter that the initiative should come."

Marx ridiculed these proposals of the Utopians. He thought they were fantastic. In the *Communist Manifesto*, written jointly in 1848 with Friedrich Engels, his life-long friend and collaborator (Engels published Volumes II and III of *Capital*, unfinished at Marx's death), Marx and Engels show their disapproval of the Utopian Socialists. "They want to improve the condition of every member of society, even that of the most favoured. Hence, they habitually appeal to society at large, without distinction of class; nay, by preference, to the ruling class. For how can people, when once they understand their system, fail to see in it the best possible plan of the best possible state of society?

"Hence they reject all political, and especially all revolutionary, action; they wish to attain their ends by peaceful means, and endeavor, by small experiments, necessarily doomed to failure, and by the force of example, to pave the way for the new social Gospel. . . .

"They still dream of experimental realization of their Social Utopias, of founding isolated 'phalansteres' [Fourier] of establishing 'Home Colonies,' of setting up a 'Little Icaria' [Etienne Cabet, another French Socialist]—duodecimo editions of the New Jerusalem, and to realize all these castles in the air, they are compelled to appeal to the feelings and purses of the bourgeois."

It was this "appeal to the feelings and purses of the bourgeois" which particularly irritated Marx and Engels. For them the change to the new society was to be brought about, not through the efforts of the ruling class, but rather through the revolutionary action of the working class. Writing to Bebel, Liebknecht, and other German radicals, in September, 1879, they express themselves quite clearly on this point: "For almost forty years we have stressed the class struggle as the immediate driving force of history, and in particular the class struggle between the bourgeoisie and the proletariat as the great lever of the modern social revolution; it is therefore impossible for us to coöperate with people who wish to expunge this class struggle from the movement. When the International was formed we expressly formulated the battle-cry: the emancipation of the working class must be achieved by the working class itself. We cannot, therefore, coöperate with people who say that the workers are too uneducated to emancipate themselves and must first be freed from above by philanthropic bourgeois and petty bourgeois."

What did Marx and Engels mean when they called the class struggle the "immediate driving force of history," and the class struggle between bourgeoisie and proletariat the "great lever of the modern social revolution"? The answers to these questions can be found only by examination of the way they looked at history.

What is your philosophy of history? Do you believe that historical events are largely a matter of chance, that they are merely accidents with no connecting theme running throughout? Or do you believe that historical changes are due to the power of ideas? Or do you believe that historical movements can be traced to the influence of great men? If you adhere to any of these philosophies, then you are not a Marxist. The school of historians, of which Marx was the founder and the most brilliant exponent, explains the movement of history, the changes which take place in society, as the result—the working out—of the economic forces of society.

To this school things are not independent of each other, but interdependent; history merely appears to be a jumble of disordered facts and happenings; but in reality it is not a jumble; it conforms to a definite pattern of laws which can be discovered.

Engels explains the roots of Marx's philosophy in these terms: "In this system—and herein is its great merit—for the first time the whole world, natural, historical, intellectual, is represented as a process—i.e., as in constant motion, change, transformation, development; and the attempt is made to trace out the internal connection that makes a continuous whole of all this movement and development. From this point of view the history of mankind no longer appeared as a wild whirl of senseless ideas . . . but as the process of evolution of man himself."

The economics, politics, law, religion, education, of every civilization are tied together; each depends on the other and is what it is because of the others. Of all these forces the economic is the most important—the basic factor. The keystone of the arch is the relations which exist between men as producers. The way in which men live is determined by the way they make their living—by the mode of production prevailing within any given society at any given time.

Marx states it in this way: "I was led by my studies to the conclusion that legal relations as well as forms of state could neither be understood by themselves, nor explained by the so-called general progress of the human mind, but that they are rooted in the material conditions of life . . . In the social production which men carry on they enter into definite relations. . . . These relations of production correspond to a definite stage of development of their material powers of production. The sum total of these relations of production constitutes the economic structure of society—the real foundation, on which rise legal and political superstructures and to which correspond definite forms of social consciousness. The mode of production in material life determines the general character of the social, political, and spiritual processes of life. It is not the consciousness of men that determines their existence, but, on the contrary, their social existence determines their consciousness."

This philosophy gives us a tool for the analysis and interpretation of history. The way men earn their living—the mode of production and exchange—is the basis of every society. "The manner in which wealth is distributed, and society divided into classes . . . is dependent upon what is produced, how it is produced, and how the products are exchanged." Likewise, conceptions of right, of justice, of education, etc.—the set of ideas which each society has—are suited to the particular stage of economic development which that particular society has reached. Now what is it that brings about social and political revolution? Is it simply a change in men's ideas? No. For these ideas depend on a change that occurs first in economics—in the mode of production and exchange.

Man progresses in his conquest of Nature; new and better methods of producing and exchanging goods are discovered or invented. When these changes are fundamental and far-reaching, social conflicts arise. The relationships that grew up with the old mode of production have become solidified; the old ways of living together have become fixed in law, in politics, in religion, in education. The class that was in power wants to retain its power—and comes into conflict with the class that is in harmony with the new mode of production. Revolution is the result.

This approach to history, according to the Marxists, makes it possible to understand an otherwise incomprehensible world. By looking at historical events from the point of view of class relationships resulting from the way men earn their living, what has been unintelligible becomes intelligible for the first time. With this concept of history as an instrument we can understand the transition from feudalism to capitalism and from capitalism to communism.

Because they studied the past from this viewpoint Marx and Engels were able to give to the bourgeoisie its proper place in history. They didn't say that capitalism and the capitalists were wicked —they explained how the capitalist mode of production grew out of earlier conditions; they emphasized the revolutionary character of the bourgeoisie in its period of growth and struggle with feudalism. "We see then: the means of production and exchange on whose foundation the bourgeoisie built itself up, were generated in feudal society. At a certain stage in the development of these means of production and exchange . . . the feudal relations of property became no longer compatible with the already developed productive forces; they became so many fetters. They had to burst asunder; they were burst asunder.

"Into their places stepped free competition, accompanied by a social and political constitution adapted to it, and by the economical and political sway of the bourgeois class."

So the transition from feudalism to capitalism came about because both new productive forces and a revolutionary class (the bourgeoisie) were present. This must always be true. The old order will not be replaced by the new society because men wish it. No. The new productive forces must be present, and with them a revolutionary class whose function it is to understand and direct.

So it was with the change from feudalism to capitalism, and so it will be, said Marx and Engels, with the change from capitalism to communism.

But it was one thing to look at the society of the past and describe what had happened; it was another thing to look at the society of the present and describe what *would* happen. What proof did Marx and Engels have to offer that capitalism must, like feudalism, pass from the stage of history? What proof did they have to offer that capitalism would break down internally, that the forces of production were hemmed in and were prevented from developing and expanding in freedom, by the relations of production?

Marx and Engels, way back in 1848, analyzed capitalist society and pointed to certain characteristics within the system of production itself which, they argued, spelled its doom. They pointed to:

The growing concentration of wealth in the hands of the few.

The crushing of the many small producers by the few big ones.

The increasing use of machinery, displacing more and more workers, and creating an "industrial reserve army."

The increasing misery of the masses.

The recurrence of periodic breakdowns in the system—crises—each one more devastating than the last.

And most important—the fundamental contradiction in capitalist society—the fact that while *production* itself is becoming more and more *socialized*—the result of collective effort and labour, *appropriation* is *private*—individual. Labour creates, capital appropriates. Under capitalism, creation by labour has become a joint undertaking, a coöperative process with thousands of labourers working *together* (often to produce only one thing—e.g., the auto). But the products, produced socially, are appropriated, not by the producers, but by the owners of the means of production—the capitalists. And there's the rub—the source of the trouble. Socialized production vs. capitalistic appropriation.

All this is summarized in a striking passage in Marx's *Capital*: "One capitalist always kills many. Hand in hand with this central-ization, or this expropriation of many capitalists by few, develops, on an ever-extending scale, the coöperative form of the labour process . . . the transformation of the instruments of labour into instruments of labour only usable in common. . . . Along with the constantly diminishing number of the magnates of capital . . . grows the mass of misery, oppression, slavery, degradation, exploita-tion; but with this, too, grows the revolt of the working class . . . disciplined, united, organized by the very mechanism of the process of capitalist production itself. The monopoly of capital becomes a fetter upon the mode of production. . . . Centralization of the means of production and socialization of labour at last reach a point where they become incompatible with their capitalist integument. This integument is burst asunder. The knell of capitalist private property sounds. The expropriators are expropriated."

Marx and Engels looked forward to the time when the social forces of production could no longer be hemmed in by the limita-tions imposed by private property and individual appropriation; they anticipated that the resulting conflict would lead to the estab-lishment of a new harmonious society. A society in which the own-ership and control of the means of production would be transferred from the hands of the few capitalist appropriators to the many proletarian producers.

But how would this change be effected? By the actions of men. And who were the men who would effect the change? The pro-letariat. Why? Because it suffers most from the contradictions of capitalism, because it is not interested in preserving a system based on private property in which it does not get its just share. The development from capitalism to communism is inherent within capitalism itself, and the instrument of the transition is the proletariat.

Marx was not an armchair revolutionist who was content with telling the other fellow what to do and why he should do it. No, he lived his philosophy. And in so far as his philosophy was not merely an explanation of the world, but also an instrument to change the world, he himself, as a sincere revolutionist, had to be not above the struggle, but a fighting part of it. He was.

When he realized that the instrument to abolish capitalism was the proletariat, he naturally devoted his attention to the training and organization of the working class for its economic and political struggles. He was the most active and influential member of the International Working Men's Association (the First International) established in London on September 28, 1864. Two months after it was founded, on November 29, 1864, Marx wrote to Dr. Kugelmann, a German friend: "The Association, or rather its Committee, is important because the leaders of the London Trades Unions are in it. . . . The leaders of the Parisian workers are also connected with it."

Marx and Engels attached very great importance to trade unions; "The organization of the working class as a class by means of the trade unions . . . is the real class organization of the proletariat in which it carries on its daily struggles with capital, in which it trains itself. . . ."

Trains itself for what? For the struggle for higher wages, shorter hours, better conditions? Yes, of course. But for a much more important struggle as well—the struggle for the complete emancipation of the working class, through the abolition of private property. Since it is from the private ownership of the means of production that all the evils of capitalism flow, the cardinal point in the program of Marx and Engels was the abolition of private property which is the basis of exploitation. "The immediate aim of the Communists is the . . . formation of the proletariat into a class, overthrow of the bourgeois supremacy, conquest of the political power by the proletariat. . . . The distinguishing feature of Communism is not the abolition of property generally, but the abolition of bourgeois property. But modern bourgeois private property is the final and most complete expression of the system of producing and appropriating products, that is based on class antagonism, on the exploitation of the many by the few.

"In this sense, the theory of the Communists may be summed up in the single sentence: Abolition of private property. . . .

"You [the bourgeoisie] are horrified at our intending to do away with private property. But in your existing society, private property is already done away with for nine-tenths of the population; its existence for the few is solely due to its non-existence in the hands of those nine-tenths. You reproach us, therefore, with intending to do away with a form of property, the necessary condition for whose existence is, the non-existence of any property for the immense majority of society.

"In one word you reproach us with intending to do away with your property. Precisely so; that is just what we intend. . . .

"It has been objected, that upon the abolition of private property all work will cease, and universal laziness will overtake us.

"According to this, bourgeois society ought long ago to have gone to the dogs through sheer idleness; for those of its members who work acquire nothing, and those who acquire anything do not work."

So private property in the form in which it exists in capitalist society—giving to the owning class the right to exploit others—was to be abolished. But how? By asking the property-holders to give up their property? By voting their property rights out of existence? Indeed no, said Marx and Engels.

How then? What was the method they advocated?

Revolution.

"The Communists disdain to conceal their views and aims. They openly declare that their ends can be attained only by the forcible overthrow of all existing social conditions. Let the ruling classes tremble at a Communistic revolution. The proletarians have nothing to lose but their chains. They have a world to win.

"Workingmen of all countries, unite!"

This ringing challenge to the ruling class, this appeal to revolution, was first published in February, 1848. It is an interesting fact that one month *before* its publication, complete sanction for revolution was given by that great American, Abraham Lincoln, in a speech in the House of Representatives, January 12, 1848: "Any people anywhere, being inclined and having the power, have the right to rise up and shake off the existing government and form a new one that suits them better. This is a most valuable, a most sacred right—a right which we hope and believe is to liberate the world."

Why did Lincoln talk about the right "to rise up and shake off the existing government"? Why not bring about the desired changes within the framework of the old government?

Possibly because he thought that couldn't be done. Possibly because he believed with Marx and Engels that "the executive of the modern State is but a committee for managing the common affairs of the whole bourgeoisie."

This means simply that in the fight between those who have property and those who have not, the haves find in the government an important weapon against the havenots. The state power is used in the interests of the ruling class—in our society, this means in the interests of the capitalist class.

As a matter of fact, according to the Marxists, that is the reason the State comes into being in the first place. Modern society is divided into the oppressors and the oppressed, the bourgeoisie and the proletariat. There is a conflict between the two. The class that rules economically—that owns the means of production—also rules politically. And "political power . . . is merely the organized power of one class for oppressing another."

We are led to believe that the State is above class—that governments represent all of the people, the high and the low, the rich and the poor. But actually, since economic society today is based on private property, it follows that any attack on the citadel of capitalism—i.e., on private property—will be met with the resistance of the State, carried to the length of violence if necessary.

In effect, so long as classes exist, then the State cannot be above class—it must be on the side of the rulers. Adam Smith expressed it in this way: "Whenever the legislature attempts to regulate the difference between masters and their workmen, its counsellors are always the masters."

And a great authority nearer our own times gave, in unmistakable terms, his opinion that our government was controlled by the controllers of our economic life. In 1913 President Woodrow Wilson wrote: "The facts of the situation amount to this: that a comparatively small number of men control the raw material of this country; that a comparatively small number of men control the waterpowers . . . that the same number of men largely control the railroads; that by agreements handed around among themselves they control prices, and that that same group of men control the larger credits of the country. . . . The masters of the government of the United States are the combined capitalists and manufacturers of the United States."

But even granting that the machinery of the State is in control of the ruling class, does it therefore follow that the only way for the proletariat to capture control is through forcible overthrow of the government? Why not use the ballot-box? Why not attain power through democratic procedure? Why doesn't the proletariat vote itself in?

These are important questions—the cause of bitter strife among the workers themselves. One answer commonly made by revolutionists is that force *must* be used, blood *must* flow, not because they want to use violence, but because the ruling class will not give up without it. There is a strong case for this argument. Marx, had he been alive in 1932, might have used the following news dispatch to the *New York Herald Tribune* in support of it:

> BULGARIA, MONARCHY,
> HAS COMMUNIST CAPITAL
>
> BUT REDS' SWEEP OF SOFIA
> COUNCIL TO BE SHORT-LIVED
>
> SOFIA, Bulgaria, Sept. 26—The sweeping victory of the Communists in yesterday's municipal elections caused great surprise and much embarrassment here.
>
> Out of thirty-five seats in Sofia's city council, the Communists won twenty-two, against ten for the allied governmental bloc and the Democrats and three for the Zankoff party. Since the parliamentary elections, in 1931, the Communists have more than doubled their votes, while the governmental bloc has lost 50 per cent of its followers.
>
> Sofia is the first European capital, outside of Russia, to go Communist, and the anomaly becomes even more striking when it is remembered that Bulgaria is a monarchy and that *the residence of King Boris is only a few minutes' walk from the city hall.*
>
> *For this, and other reasons,* a Communist city administration *will not be tolerated.* As soon as the election results were known, Premier Nicolas Mushanoff announced his intention to dissolve the city council before it assembles. It also is probable that the Communist party will be declared illegal and forbidden throughout Bulgaria.
>
> The Communist victory was due to the desperate economic situation, which led many persons in no way connected with Bolshevism to vote Communist out of protest.

In this case, the Communists, according to this conservative Republican newspaper, won the victory. Nevertheless they were to be denied the right to take office, and even the right to exist in the future. What did this newspaper reporter have in mind when he wrote "For this *and other reasons*"? What indeed, but that the victory for the Communists meant that the private property of the ruling class was threatened?

Marx and Engels tried to prepare the working class for events to come. To be ready the workers must be conscious as a class, organized as a class, must understand their rôle in historical development. They must be prepared to expropriate the expropriators; to abolish private property and with it classes and class rule.

Marx and Engels felt that the breakdown of capitalism was coming. That breakdown, if the workers were not ready, would mean chaos; if the workers were ready, it would mean socialism. "Then for the first time, man, in a certain sense, is finally marked off from the rest of the animal kingdom, and emerges from mere animal conditions of existence into really human ones. . . . Only from that time will man himself, more and more consciously, make his own history—only from that time will the social causes set in movement by him have, in the main and in a constantly growing measure, the results intended by him. It is the ascent of man from the kingdom of necessity to the kingdom of freedom."

XIX

"I Would Annex the Planets If I Could . . ."

OF COURSE all this was dangerous stuff.

The labour theory of value, as expounded by the classical economists at the beginning of the Industrial Revolution, had served a useful purpose. The bourgeoisie, then the progressive class, had fashioned it into a weapon against the unprogressive but politically powerful landowning class, which was shown up as enjoying, without working, the fruits of other people's labour. In the hands of Ricardo, who used it together with his theory of rent to assail the landlords, the labour theory of value was O.K.

But in the hands of Marx it was decidedly not O.K. Marx had accepted the labour theory of value and had carried it along further, to what he thought was its logical conclusion. The result, in the eyes of the bourgeoisie, was disastrous. For now the tables were turned completely. What had been their weapon in *their* fight against *their* enemy had been forged into a weapon for use by the proletariat against *them*!

Deliverance was, however, near at hand. For a few years after *Capital* appeared, the economists came forward with an entirely new theory of value. Three men in three different countries—Stanley Jevons in England (1871), Karl Menger in Austria (1871), and Léon Walras in Switzerland (1874)—each working independently, hit upon this new conception at practically the same time. Like the classical economists, and like Marx and Engels, they soon had their followers, who both explained and expanded their doctrines. Corrections, revisions, and additions were made, but the central idea in their theory remains today the pivot of orthodox economics.

The explanation of value given by these economists is called the marginal utility theory. On the second page of his *Theory of Political Economy* Jevons announces his break with the past: "Repeated reflection and enquiry has led me to the somewhat novel opinion that value depends entirely upon utility." Now utility is really just another word for usefulness, and expresses the feeling of the man who is going to buy the commodity toward that commodity. If he wants it very badly, it has great utility for him; the more he wants it, the greater the utility, the less he wants it, the smaller the utility. Its utility to him measures the value he will place upon it, and therefore measures the price he will be willing to pay.

It will be seen what a sharp break this was with the past—with the classical school no less than with the Marxist. For them the value of a commodity depended on the labour required to make it, but Jevons said, "Labour once spent has no influence on the future value of any article." This shifts the emphasis in economic theory from production to consumption, from the costing department to the marketplace. It is a much more difficult theory to understand, because while it is fairly easy to think of an article taking so much labour to produce, it is not so easy to think of it having so much utility. Labour cost is something you can measure—that is to say, it is an *objective* standard. But utility differs for each man; it varies with the amount of satisfaction which he expects to get from the commodity once he has bought it; that is to say, it is a *subjective* standard.

Now it is quite easy to see that different people get different amounts of satisfaction from the same commodity. Or, in other words, the same commodity has different amounts of utility for different people. But the same commodity sells at the same price—i.e. it has the same value. (For most modern economists price is just value expressed in money, although for Marx this was not true.) Then if utility measures value, how can different amounts of utility be sold for the same price? This is where the idea of the "margin" comes in, and it is important to understand it because if you read any modern textbook of economic theory you will find hundreds of references to "marginal utility" and "marginal productivity" and "marginal cost," etc.

Let us suppose that for some reason or other there are only a hundred thousand motor-cars on the market. There will be some prospective buyers who are so rich, and want a motor-car so much, that they are willing to pay almost any price for it. Then there will be others who also want a motor-car, but perhaps they aren't so rich, or else they think that if the car is going to be too expensive, they'd rather spend their money on something else. After them come people who are willing to pay a fair amount for an auto, but have to be rather careful because they haven't got too much money to spend, and there are lots of other things they can do with their limited amount of money which will give them nearly as much satisfaction as the car. If the car is going to cost more than something else which will give them just as much satisfaction, of course they won't buy it. "We buy just as many pounds of tea or anything else as we think are worth the price which we have to pay, and then we stop. If the price were higher we should buy fewer, and if it were lower we should buy more, just because of this variation of utility which Jevons has been pointing out. So the utility of our final purchase goes along with the price. . . ." And so it goes on until the two sides balance. Somewhere or other there will be the hundred-thousandth buyer who is willing to give a price at which the automobile manufacturer is willing to sell; some purchasers would be willing to pay more, and there might be thousands who would buy a car if it cost just a little less. But there are only 100,000, and if the manufacturer wants to sell them all, he's got to sell them at a price which suits the purse and tastes of the hundred-thousandth buyer. He could get a higher price if he were willing to sell fewer cars. He could sell more if he were willing to sell at a lower price. But if he has only 100,000 to sell, and wants to sell them all, he has to suit the pocket of the man who can only just afford to buy. If he finds that there aren't 100,000 purchasers willing to pay the amount he asks, he's either got to withdraw some cars from the market and sell fewer; or if he wants to sell them all he has to lower the price in order to get at the people with smaller purses or different tastes. He can't sell the same car in a free market at one price to one man, and at another price to another man.

Of course this hundred-thousandth, or marginal, buyer, isn't any particular man—he is any one of the whole 100,000, just as the car he buys may be any one of the 100,000 cars. In the theoretical explanation of the way the market works, and the way market price is settled, he is the man who represents marginal demand. If the price were higher, he could get other things for his money which would afford him greater satisfaction. If the price were lower, a larger number of buyers would be in the field and the supply would be too small; the manufacturer would put up his price until he'd excluded from the market those who were only willing to pay the lower price but no more.

Now look at it the other way round, and start the explanation from the demand side. Let us say that there are 1,000 people willing to pay $1,000 for a refrigerator, and another thousand who would be willing to pay $750, but no more. That makes 2,000 people willing to pay at least $750. And so we go down the scale (reaching people who have less and less money) until we get to 5,000,000 people willing to pay at least $50. The question is, how many of them will be able to buy a refrigerator, and what will it cost? (We will pretend, just to make things simple, that there is only one sort of refrigerator.) This will depend on whether the manufacturer of refrigerators thinks it worth while to turn out 5,000,000 at that price. If, even with mass production, a refrigerator costs him more than $50, of course he won't do it, or if it leaves him such a tiny margin that it isn't worth his trouble, he will look around for something else to put his capital into that is going to bring him in higher profits. Then there won't be any 5,000,000 refrigerators produced. The manufacturer has a marginal use for his capital just as the consumer has a marginal use for his money. He won't put it into making refrigerators if he is going to get bigger profits from investing it in something else. He will put just so much of his capital into making refrigerators as is worth while—if he put in less, he'd be missing a good opportunity (and the existence of that opportunity would soon attract more capital looking round for profits), and if he put in more the industry would be "over-capitalized" and couldn't pay dividends. He finds that there are 3,000,000 people willing to pay $150 for a refrigerator, and that this just about gives him the right amount of profits; he couldn't get more by investing in anything else, and if he turned out more the price would go down and his profits would fall, and so capital would turn away from that industry.

Of course this all sounds very complicated—and it is! But the general idea underlying "marginal utility" is really quite simple, and you can see it illustrated around you every day. The amount of satisfaction you get from an article depends on how much of it you already have. The larger the supply you already have, the less satisfaction you get from some more of it. Suppose a boy's baseball team is all set to start the game, but they have no bat. Then the opportunity comes to get one. Do they hesitate to pay the price for it? They do not. Now suppose they have four bats to begin with. The opportunity comes to get a fifth. Do they rush with the same speed to pay the price for it? Indeed they don't. The marginal utility of bats has for them fallen so low that they probably don't even pause to buy that fifth bat.

The more you have of a thing the less you want any more of the same thing. If you have ten suits of clothes it is obvious that an extra suit would mean much less to you than a second suit would mean to a man with only one. Jevons put the same idea, using water as an illustration: "Water, for instance, may be roughly described as the most useful of all substances. A quart of water per day has the high utility of saving a person from dying in a most distressing manner. Several gallons a day may possess much utility for such purpose as cooking and washing; but after an adequate supply is secured for these uses, any additional quantity is a matter of indifference. All that we can say, then, is, that water, up to a certain quantity, is indispensable; that further quantities will have various degrees of utility; but that beyond a certain point the utility appears to cease . . . the very same articles vary in utility according as we already possess more or less of the same article."

This idea of marginal utility is used to explain the difference in the value of, say, bread and diamonds. On first sight you would think that bread should cost more than diamonds, because it has so much more utility. But the supply of bread is so large that an extra loaf or two makes very little difference, whereas the supply of diamonds is so small in relation to the number of wealthy people who are willing to pay a lot for them that they command a very high price.

The argument that utility *doesn't* correspond to value, otherwise iron would cost more than gold "hopelessly confounds the importance of the *whole* of a commodity with the ordinary subject of valuation, the *unit* of the commodity taken separately and sold separately. The purposes to which the useful commodity ministers are conceived as all the purposes, taking them all together. . . . The world, says Cairnes, would get on better without gold than without iron—that is, better without *any* gold than without *any* iron. But if we take the utility thus, so to speak, in a lump, surely we must take the value of the things in the same way. If we do that, the supposed opposition between utility and value promptly vanishes, since if the world, as a whole, had to buy all the iron in one lot or have none at all, and to buy all the gold or have none at all, it would doubtless bid more for the iron than for the gold, and then the value of (all) the iron would be greater than that of (all) the gold.

"The confusion . . . between the commodity as a whole and the unit of the commodity bought and sold is most manifest in his comparison of *a* diamond with *coal*. Like should be compared with like: coal as a whole is not only more useful, but more valuable than diamonds as a whole."

But whatever the economists said—and their controversies are endless on this as on other questions—and whatever theory wins out for the time being, the capitalists themselves realized that, be the reason what it may, if they could control the supply of an article they could also control its price. The value of a commodity might fall because it took less time to produce, or because the quantity had increased and therefore the marginal utility was less, but there was no doubt at all that manipulation of the supply carried with it the power to fix prices. And the power to fix prices affects profits.

If 5,000 commodities can be turned out at a cost of $10 per unit, and sold at $11 a unit, this gives a total profit of $5,000, or 10 per cent, on capital invested. If only 4,000 are turned out, the cost of production goes up to $10.50, but the price is pushed up to $12.50, leaving a total profit of $8,000, or 19 per cent. The company which can control the supply will therefore regulate it to give the greatest profit. It won't be concerned with turning out more goods to satisfy a wider demand at a lower price unless in doing so it can increase profits. The economies of mass production might make it possible to turn out 100,000 at $7 each, and the market might be able to absorb them at $8 each. But this only gives 14 per cent profit!

You remember how the Dutch merchants in the sixteenth century cut down the production of spices in order to keep up the price. Those early monopolies had been broken, but we shall see how new and vastly more powerful monopolies came in the modern world, when the output of goods became so great that there was a danger of prices falling too low for profits.

The manufacturers of England had made a good thing out of the head start they had in the Industrial Revolution. In the first half of the nineteenth century the problem in England was not so much where to sell its manufactured goods, but how to turn them out fast enough to fill the orders which came from all over the known world. But along about the last quarter of the nineteenth century there came an important change. The free-trade policy advocated by England had never "taken" in the United States, where, you remember, a protective tariff was in effect almost from the country's beginning. Tariff walls in the United States were made higher after the Civil War. In Russia, a general protective tariff went into effect in 1877; in Germany in 1879; in France in 1881. Now English manufacturers no longer had a clear field—their goods had difficulty in jumping the tariff barriers. Now England's best customers no longer needed to take her goods—they could make their own, they could serve themselves. Behind tariff walls "infant" industries were fast becoming "giant" industries.

Not figuratively, but literally. From 1870 onward is the period of "trusts" in the United States, of "cartels" in Germany. Competition was replaced by monopoly. Little men were driven out of business by big men. Little business was either crushed by Big Business, or merged with it to make still larger Big Business. Everywhere there was growth, amalgamation, concentration—giant industries in the making, giant industries heading for monopoly.

The gradual replacement of competition by monopoly was not an encroachment from the outside, but a development of competition itself. Monopoly arose from within competition—an illustration of the truth that each system, or event, or whatever, carries *within itself* the seeds of its own transformation. Monopoly wasn't an outside invader that charged in and conquered competition. It was the natural outgrowth of competition itself.

You know the story of the revolution in the means of communication and transportation following our Civil War period. More and better railways were built, bigger and better steamships sailed up and down rivers and across the oceans; the telegraph was improved and its use became widespread. With rapid, regular, and cheap means of communication and transport, it was both possible and economical to bring production necessities together and concentrate them in one locality; with the tremendous advance in technology, with more and more patents for efficient machinery being taken out all the time, it was possible to go in for mass production and a greater division of labour. The time was ripe for large-scale production which would result in decreasing costs per unit at the same time that production was increasing. It was at last possible for Combination to enter the field of battle—and win the victory.

What was possible was done.

Business is a fight. Ask anyone who's in it. Now there's a saying in the fight game that "a good big man will lick a good little man." In the business game this was proven true. Two companies are competing in a certain business. One company takes a crack at the other by lowering the price of its goods. The other company hits back by lowering the price still further. This goes on. Punches—in the form of still lower prices—fly back and forth. Soon prices are below the cost of production. Who will win the contest? It is obvious that the firm that can produce at the lowest cost will have the advantage. It is obvious, too, that the larger the scale of production, the lower the cost of production. This means that the big fellow has an initial advantage. But it is staying-power that counts. And staying-power in this fight is measured by the reserves of capital, which determine how long you can stick it out. The firm with the greater amount of capital is the big fellow. Lowered prices leave him scarred, but they leave the little fellow punch-drunk—and before long, completely out. Marx, who probably never saw a prize fight, had a permanent ringside seat at the continual fight of business vs. business. He reported it in this fashion: "The battle of competition is fought by cheapening of commodities. The cheapness of commodities depends . . . on the productiveness of labour, and this again on the scale of production. Therefore the larger capitals beat the smaller. . . . Competition . . . always ends in the ruin of many small capitalists, whose capitals partly pass into the hands of their conquerors, partly vanish."

That last sentence indicates that there is a difference between ordinary prize fights and that of business vs. business. In the former, the loser is knocked out and the victor leaves the ring seeking new and more profitable conquests. In the latter the victor does the same—but very often, before leaving the ring, he acts the part of a cannibal. He gobbles up the loser and then steps forth Bigger than Ever, Ready to Meet all Comers.

The bigger he gets the harder it is to defeat him. Other fighters try—and lose. The Big Fellow becomes Champ. No one can stand up against him—at least for a time.

Out of free competition trusts were formed. Sometimes the fight was fair. Often the fight was foul (even from the point of view of the business world, which has learned to take blows below the belt in its stride). But fair or foul, the fight was bitter. The men who ran the businesses which lost out, were often ruined; they could not fight again; sometimes they went mad, occasionally they committed suicide.

But an authority on the subject, John D. Rockefeller, Jr., the son of the greatest trust-maker, thought the result was worth the cost. In a talk to students of Brown University on the subject of trusts he said: "The American Beauty Rose can be produced in its splendour and fragrance only by sacrificing the early buds which grow up around it."

The first "American Beauty" in the trust field was in oil. By 1904 the Standard Oil Company controlled over 86 per cent of the refined illuminating oil of the country. What happened in oil happened also in steel, sugar, whisky, coal, and other products. Trusts were everywhere formed which attempted to bring monopolistic order out of competitive chaos.

They were gigantic. They were efficient. They were powerful. Because they were these things they were able to reduce costs by economies in production, marketing, and management. They did what they could to eliminate wasteful competition. They tried to obtain control over the production of commodities so they would be able to fix output and price. They did either or both—whichever brought the greater profit. It was larger profits they were interested in according to students of the trust movement: "A trust is any form of industrial organization, in the production or distribution of any commodity, which possesses sufficient control over the supply of that commodity to be able to modify the price to its own advantage."

The trust was able "to modify the price to its own advantage." So were other large-scale organizations. The trust was American. Pools, combines, associations, cartels, were other forms of monopoly that became common, too, both here and abroad. The cartel was most common in Germany. "The term cartel designates an association based upon a contractual agreement between enterprisers in the same field of business which, while retaining their legal independence, associate themselves with a view to exerting a monopolistic influence on the market."

This simply means that the various big producers, instead of carrying on a war to the finish through cutting prices, then combining into one company, remain separate organizations but do not compete with each other—they agree as to the division of the market and as to prices.

The specific case of the Ruhr Coal Cartel shows how it was done: "A central selling syndicate or company was formed . . . the shares of which were held by the separate companies. This syndicate was the sole agent for the sale of coal. It secured statistics from the separate coal companies. It appointed an Executive Committee which made certain arrangements for a uniform price and payment. The mine-owners sold all their coal and coke to the syndicate. . . . It fixed penalties for breach of agreements and enforced a common policy. The syndicate would appoint a Commission to determine the proportion of output allowed to each mine. . . . It would fix a minimum selling-price and when selling in competitive districts it would sell at this, and in non-competitive areas it would sell above or below this, according to the demand and output available."

In England, too, there was this tendency for competing groups to form associations to eliminate competition among themselves. Let the various witnesses before the Committee on Trusts tell their own story: "Our association was formed for the purpose of regulating the trade and avoiding unnecessary competition. . . .

"Our association was formed for the purpose of agreeing on prices and has been the means of preventing cutting, which went on considerably before the association was formed, the result being that most of the firms were making no profits or very small profits. . . .

"Competition was so severe . . . that no one could make anything out of the trade. Manufacturers were producing more than was really required, and were concerned only with cutting one another's throats."

After hearing the witnesses the committee came to this important conclusion: "We find that there is at the present time [1919] in every important branch of industry in the United Kingdom an increasing tendency to the formation of Trade Associations and Combinations, having for their purpose the restriction of competition and the control of prices."

That last line tells the story—"restriction of competition and control of prices." This practice was a far cry from the traditional theory of the classical economists—the theory that competition among the producers and sellers of commodities would keep prices down to cost of production (including a reasonable rate of profit); the theory that with each individual looking to advance his own self-interest, the supply of an article would adjust itself to the demand at the right price.

With the growth of monopoly, supply and demand did not adjust themselves—they were adjusted; with the growth of monopoly, prices were not made through competition in the free market— the market was no longer free and prices were fixed.

Besides the monopoly that came to industry there was another, equally important if not more so—the monopoly in banking. Marx had foreseen this when he said that with large-scale "capitalist production an altogether new force comes into play—the credit system. Not only is this itself a new and mighty weapon in the battle of competition. By unseen threads it, moreover, draws the disposable money, scattered in larger or smaller masses over the surface of society, into the hands of individual or associated capitalists. It is the specific machine for the centralization of capitals."

Industry was run largely on credit, and so the financiers who had control of the credit system were in the seats of power. When industrialists, large or small, monopolists or otherwise, wanted money with which to expand their business, they had to go cap in hand to the bankers. When a group of men wanted to start a business and decided to sell stock to raise money, they had to go cap in hand to the bankers whose function it became to float issues of stock. Money was everywhere needed and the money of the nation was to be found in the vaults of the bankers—or in some place to which they alone had access.

The more money bankers could control the greater their power. A Money Trust grew up in every great industrial country. The era of monopoly in industry was the era of monopoly in banking as well. That this was true, certainly by 1911, is proven by these words of Woodrow Wilson, at that time Governor of New Jersey: "The great monopoly in this country is the money monopoly. So long as that exists, our old variety and freedom and individual energy of development are out of the question. A great industrial nation is controlled by its system of credit. Our system of credit is concentrated. The growth of the nation, therefore, and all our activities are in the hands of a few men."

Very often it happened that these "few men," the financiers, were the same men who were the heads of the industrial monopolies. There were "interlocking directorates," which meant that the important men in the banking world were on the boards of directors of the great trusts or giant corporations in which they were "interested"—that is, in which their banks had invested large sums.

But they didn't have to be so closely connected. It was enough that the bankers held the purse-strings—that gave them the power to dictate policy to the industrial firms. This was demonstrated in clear fashion by the letter sent in 1901 by one of the "Big Four" Berlin banks to the board of directors of a German cement syndicate: "We learn . . . that the next general meeting of your company . . . may be called upon to take measures which are likely to effect alterations in your undertakings to which we cannot subscribe. We deeply regret that, for this reason, we are obliged to withdraw herewith the credit which has been allowed you. If the general meeting referred to does not decide upon anything inacceptable to us, and if we receive suitable guarantees on this matter for the future, we shall have no objection to negotiating with you the opening of new credits."

If the financiers could call the tune in this abrupt fashion to a big syndicate, just imagine how great a measure of control they could—and did—exercise over the small fry in the industrial world.

The situation was well described by Supreme Court Justice Louis D. Brandeis in a book he wrote back in 1912, aptly entitled, *Other People's Money*. He said: "The dominant element in our financial oligarchy is the investment banker. Associated banks, trust companies, and life insurance companies are his tools. Controlled railroads, public service, and industrial corporations are his subjects. Though properly but middlemen, these bankers bestride as masters America's business world, so that practically no large enterprise can be undertaken successfully without their participation or approval. These bankers are, of course, able men possessed of large fortunes; but the most potent factor in their control of business is not the possession of extraordinary ability or huge wealth. The key to their power is Combination—concentration intensive and comprehensive."

After 1870, then, capitalism old-style became capitalism new-style; the capitalism of free competition became the capitalism of monopolies. That was a change of tremendous importance.

Large-scale monopoly industry brought with it greater development of the productive forces than ever before. The power of industrialists to produce goods grew at a more rapid rate than the power of their countrymen to consume them. (This means, of course, consumption *at a profit*—people could always use more goods, but they couldn't always pay for them.)

The monopolists were in a position at home to regulate the supply to fit the demand, and they did so. This was sensible business practice and brought high profits. But it left a good part of their productive plant idle, and that condition of affairs always tends to give captains of industry a headache. They didn't want to make only enough goods to sell at home. They wanted to use their plants all the time to turn out as much goods as possible. That meant they had to sell goods outside the home country. They *had* to find foreign markets which would absorb their surplus manufactures.

Where to find them? They could try dumping their goods on other rich nations, as England had done for years. But there they increasingly ran into high tariff walls behind which their competitors had been able to seize the market of that country. Witness this complaint by Jules Ferry, a French Prime Minister in 1885: "What our great industries lack . . . what they lack more and more, is markets. Why? Because . . . Germany is covering herself with barriers; because, beyond the ocean, the United States of America have become protectionist, and protectionist to an extreme degree."

Nations like Germany and the United States were no longer a free market for other nations' goods—they were themselves competing for the markets of the world. Here was a serious situation; within the great industrial nations the capacity to produce had outstripped the capacity to consume; all of them had a surplus of manufactured goods for which they had to find outside markets.

Where to find them?

There was one answer—colonies.

We are so accustomed to seeing the whole of the map of Africa colored in various hues to show ownership by different European nations that we are apt to forget that this was not always so. Less than seventy years ago practically all of Africa belonged to the people who inhabited it. It was in the era of monopoly capitalism that surplus manufactures presented itself as a problem to captains of industry everywhere. They thought they found the answer to the problem in—colonies. And it was then that the map of Africa was changed.

David Livingstone, famous missionary-explorer, was lost in the heart of Africa. James Gordon Bennett, the owner of the *New York Herald*, sent Henry Morton Stanley to Africa to find him. What an assignment! And miracle of miracles, Stanley succeeded. He not only found Livingstone, but he made further explorations. Then he delivered a series of lectures on his exploits. We may be certain that he interested his audiences. We may be certain, too, that never did he talk to more interested audiences than the cotton merchants of Manchester and the iron manufacturers of Birmingham who heard him say: "There are forty millions of people beyond the gateway of the Congo, and the cotton-spinners of Manchester are waiting to clothe them. Birmingham foundries are glowing with the red metal that will presently be made into ironwork for them and the trinkets that shall adorn those dusky bosoms, and the ministers of Christ are zealous to bring them, the poor benighted heathen, into the Christian fold."

Stanley was suggesting to troubled captains of industry a way out of their dilemma of what to do with their surplus manufactures. Colonies—that was the answer.

Captains of industry in other industrial countries found the same answer to the same problem at the same time. After 1870, England, France, Belgium, Italy, and Germany joined in the scramble for colonies as a market for surplus goods. America's turn was to come in 1898. In that year Republican Senator Albert J. Beveridge told an interested group of Boston business leaders: "American factories are making more than the American people can use; American soil is producing more than they can consume. Fate has written our policy for us; the trade of the world must and shall be ours. And we will get it as our mother (England) had told us how. We will establish trading-posts throughout the world as distributing points for American products. We will cover the ocean with our merchant marine. We will build a navy to the measure of our greatness. Great colonies governing themselves, flying our flag and trading with us, will grow about our posts of trade."

Besides being a market for surplus goods, colonies could serve another useful purpose. Large-scale mass production needs vast supplies of raw materials. Rubber, oil, nitrates, sugar, cotton, tropical foodstuffs, minerals—these and a host of others, were raw materials which were necessary to monopoly capitalists everywhere. Captains of industry did not want to be dependent upon other countries for raw materials essential to themselves. They wanted to own or control the sources of those necessary raw materials. One of the most recent imperialistic ventures, that of Italy in Ethiopia, had this as one cause, according to the *New York Times* of August 8, 1935.

ITALY WOULD RAISE
                    COTTON IN ETHIOPIA

Believes Crops of That Product and Coffee
        Would Make Up for Her
        Expenses.

LARGE IMPORTS ARE CITED

ROME, Aug. 7.—Italy's primary hopes of profit in Ethiopia are based on development of products that would affect its trade with North and South America—cotton and coffee.

Whatever may be the outcome of its expectations in gaining gold, iron ore, platinum, copper and other minerals, Italy has reason to believe that cotton and coffee will compensate it for the billions of lire expended in East Africa.

Italy's imports of cotton average 740,000,000 lire yearly, mostly paid to the United States, and of coffee about 185,000,000—a total of nearly 1,000,000,000 lire representing 13.5 per cent of Italy's total imports.

So desire for control of the sources of raw materials was a second factor making for imperialism. The first, you remember, was the necessity of finding a market for surplus goods. There was another surplus, also looking for a suitable market, which was the third and perhaps most important cause of imperialism. This was the surplus of capital.

Monopoly industry brought huge profits to its owners. Super-profits. More money than the owners knew what to do with. It sounds unbelievable, but in some cases the profits were so great that the trust-makers could not possibly spend all their money, even if they had tried.

They didn't try. They saved their money. So did others—millions of small savers who put their money into banks, insurance companies, investment houses, etc. The result was an over-accumulation of capital.

Now that sounds funny. How could there be too much money? Were there no ways to be found for the useful employment of capital? Surely there were roads to be built, hospitals to be erected, tenement houses to be torn down, and decent living quarters put up in their stead? Surely there were a hundred and one businesses at home where money could be invested?

There were. Rural areas needed better roads, workers needed decent houses, and small businesses were crying for expansion—yet economists spoke of "surplus" capital. And there was no doubt of it—millions of dollars (and francs, and pounds, and marks) were being exported to other lands.

Why?

Because capital does not ask, "What is needed?" Not at all. What it does ask is, "How much can I get for my money?" The answer to that second question determines where the saved surplus capital will be invested. Lenin, a disciple of Marx, and the leader of the Russian Revolution, explained this in his book *Imperialism*, written in 1916: "It goes without saying that if capitalism could develop agriculture, which today lags far behind industry everywhere, if it could raise the standard of living of the masses . . . there could be no talk of a surplus of capital. . . . But then capitalism would not be capitalism. . . . As long as capitalism remains capitalism, surplus capital will never be used for the purpose of raising the standard of living of the masses, for this would mean a decrease in profits for the capitalists: instead it will be used to increase profits by exporting the capital abroad, to backward countries. In these backward countries profits are usually high, for capital is scarce, the price of land is relatively low, wages are low, raw materials are cheap."

That is what happened. The surplus capital which had to find an outlet found one in the backward countries—in colonies. Places in need of railways, electricity and gas systems, roads, etc., places rich in natural resources, where "concessions" on mines and plantations were obtained—it was in these colonial areas that surplus capital found opportunities for profitable investment.

Nor was that all. Apart from the profits which were drawn directly from investment, loans were usually so arranged that a large part of the loan was spent in the home country. Thus when England made loans to Argentina for the construction of railways, most of the rails, rolling stock, etc., were purchased in England—at a profit to English manufacturers. The export of surplus capital here led to the export of surplus goods as well. Thus both the investor and the manufacturer found it in their joint interests to collaborate in the policy of controlling or seizing colonial areas. This was one aspect of that alliance between finance and industry which characterizes modern economic society to such an extent that it has been called the age of finance capital. This means that finance—the control of vast sums of capital, plus industry, which utilizes that capital for profit-making purposes, is the dominating force in the world today.

The alliance of industry and finance seeking profits in markets for goods and capital was the mainspring of imperialism. So J. A. Hobson thought back in 1902, when he published his pioneer study of the subject: "Imperialism is the endeavour of the great controllers of industry to broaden the channel for the flow of their surplus wealth by seeking foreign markets and foreign investments to take off the goods and capital they cannot sell or use at home."

That's the *why* of imperialism. *How* the controllers of industry "broaden the channel for the flow of their surplus wealth" is another story with which you are probably familiar. There have been many ways—the latest examples are those of Italy's "mission of civilization" in Abyssinia, and Japan's "penetration" of China. In the old days, back in the last quarter of the nineteenth century, particularly in Africa, the procedure was simpler. "In almost every case the first steps towards partition and the incorporation of African territory in European States were taken by traders or capitalist companies working in coöperation with explorers or through their own agents. The usual procedure was for the explorer or agent to penetrate some distance inland from the coast and induce the chiefs or kings, by gifts of cloth or alcohol, to sign so-called treaties with the joint-stock companies. According to the treaties, these African rulers, whose signature consists of a mark, ceded the whole of their territory to joint-stock companies in exchange for a few yards of cloth or a few bottles of gin. Nearly all the Central African possessions of European States rest upon such titles. . . . In less than twenty years the whole of Central Africa was partitioned and incorporated in the Empires of Britain, France, Germany, Belgium, Portugal, and Italy."

Sometimes these shrewd explorers—traders—capitalists honestly thought that in stealing the country from its inhabitants they were performing a God-given mission for the good of the natives. Cecil Rhodes, one of the greatest of the empire-builders, thought so. At any rate, that's what he said: "I contend that we are the first race in the world, and that the more of the world we inhabit the better it is for the human race. . . . If there be a God, I think what He would like me to do is to paint as much of the map of Africa British red as possible."

The natives in the conquered territories were often quite peculiar. They didn't seem to understand that what the white man was doing was for their good. They were very apt to become confused by what one set of white men—the missionaries—preached to them, and what the other set of white men—the capitalists—did to them. Sometimes, in their ignorance, they rebelled, and then, unfortunately, it became necessary to teach them a lesson. Soon big shiny ships from the mother country steamed into their harbors. They were filled with troops who carried rifles and bombs and machine-guns—the weapons of civilization—and the lesson was taught.

It had been taught with the aid of the military power of the home government. The governments ever ready to "protect the lives and property" of their subjects, helped in other ways, too. For example, to help defray the costs of administration, of bringing hospitals, schools, good roads, etc., to the colony, the government instituted a tax which the natives had to pay in money. Now the natives had no money. But there was a way out—they could earn the money to pay the tax by working on the plantations or in the mines of the white owners. It was true that the pay was miserably low; it was true, too, that the natives could feed themselves without working in mines or plantations. But the tax had to be paid—which meant they had to work. What happened if they didn't? An observer of conditions in the French West African colonies in 1935 tells us of one remedy for non-payment: "A village in the southern Soudan was unable to pay the taxes; the native guards were sent, took all the women and children of the village, put them into a compound in the centre, burned the huts, and told the men they could have their families back when the taxes were paid."

It is impossible to talk quite generally of the treatment of colonial peoples because it varied from time to time and from place to place. But the atrocities were general—no imperialist nation had clean hands. Mr. Leonard Woolf, a recognized student of the subject, wrote: "Just as in national society in Europe there have appeared in the last century clearly defined classes, capitalists and workers, exploiters and exploited, so too in international society there have appeared clearly defined classes, the imperialist Powers of the West and the subject races of Africa and the East, the one ruling and exploiting, the other ruled and exploited."

Understand, a country did not have to become a colony to be "ruled and exploited." Where the backward countries were not directly imperialized they were carved out into "spheres of influence"—e.g., China, in which all the major powers have certain acknowledged interests. Or South America, which is pretty well "shared" by England and the United States. These two countries, without exactly taking possession of any South American republics, were ever ready to furnish them with capital which was used as a whip to get certain money-making rights by treaty, or by formal concession. And in such cases everywhere it was made quite clear that there were always cruisers, airplanes, and battalions ready to enforce the claim, the concession, or the exclusive trading monopoly.

It was not an accident that governments had come to the aid of their manufacturers and bankers in their search for markets for goods and capital. One observer of British affairs in 1921 found it inevitable: "British trade at present in the autumn of 1921 is under the paramount control of large combines, governed and directed by the large money and banking trusts whose power . . . is so great as to give them in all cases control of the levers that set trade in motion. More than this, their power of advising the Government of the day is such that . . . the Government (composed as it is today of the moneyed classes) cannot act except in accordance with the money trade trusts' advice."

That was in England. For President Taft in the United States the path of justice was indeed straight, but it was not narrow—there was room on it for intervention in behalf of "our capitalists": "While our foreign policy should not be turned a hair's breadth from the straight path of justice, it may well be made to include active intervention to secure for our merchandise and our capitalists opportunity for profitable investment."

Once embarked on a course of intervention in behalf of "our capitalists," governments found themselves on a long journey. Capital, like the Man on the Flying Trapeze, "floats through the air with the greatest of ease" and it's quite a job to keep up with it to see that it is safe. Major-General Smedley D. Butler was entrusted with part of the job. His description of it is picturesque—he disagrees with President Taft about being able to stick on the path of justice while intervening for Big Business: "I spent thirty-three years and four months in active service as a member of our country's most agile military force—the Marine Corps. I served in all commissioned ranks from a second lieutenant to major-general. And during that period I spent most of my time being a high-class muscle man for Big Business, for Wall Street, and for the bankers. In short, I was a racketeer for capitalism. . . .

"Thus I helped make Mexico and especially Tampico safe for American oil interests in 1914. I helped make Haiti and Cuba a decent place for the National City Bank boys to collect revenues in. . . . I helped purify Nicaragua for the international banking house of Brown Brothers in 1909-1912. I brought light to the Dominican Republic for American sugar interests in 1916. I helped make Honduras 'right' for American fruit companies in 1903. In China in 1927 I helped see to it that Standard Oil went its way unmolested.

"During those years I had, as the boys in the back room would say, a swell racket. I was rewarded with honors, medals, promotion. Looking back on it, I feel I might have given Al Capone a few hints. The best *he* could do was to operate his racket in three city districts. We Marines operated on three *continents*."

We can gather from Major-General Butler's experiences that imperialism, begun at the end of the nineteenth century, is still with us. It is—in intensified form. It's easy to see why this has to be. Monopoly in industry is not decreasing. It is growing. And with it, as we have seen, goes imperialism.

In an illuminating study of the *Modern Corporation and Private Property* by two experts on the subject, we find some startling facts and figures about the size, wealth, and control of the modern giant corporations in America today. There are in the United States about 300,000 non-banking corporations. But of this number, about 200 control one-half of the corporate wealth! Fifteen of these 200 had assets of over a billion dollars each. And one of them, the American Telephone and Telegraph Company, "controls more wealth than is contained within the borders of twenty-one of the states in the country."

But perhaps the best way of understanding to what extent monopoly rules the roost, is to follow the authors of the study mentioned above in their exposition of how you and I in our daily lives are affected all the time by some of these 200 largest corporations. "These great companies form the very framework of American industry. The individual must come in contact with them almost constantly . . . he is continually accepting their service. If he travels any distance he is almost certain to ride on one of the great railroad systems. The engine which draws him has probably been constructed by the American Locomotive Company or the Baldwin Locomotive Works; the car in which he rides is likely to have been made by the American Car and Foundry Company or one of its subsidiaries. . . . The rails have almost certainly been supplied by one of the eleven steel companies on the list; and coal may well have come from one of the four coal companies, if not from a mine owned by the railroad itself. Perhaps the individual travels by automobile—in a car manufactured by the Ford, General Motors, Studebaker, or

Chrysler companies, on tires supplied by Firestone, Goodrich, Good-year, or the United States Rubber Company. . . .

"Perhaps, on the other hand, the individual stays in his own home in comparative isolation and privacy. What do the largest two hundred companies mean to him there? His electricity and gas are almost sure to be furnished by one of these public-utility companies: the aluminum of his kitchen utensils by the Aluminum Company of America. His electric refrigerator may be the product of General Motors Company, or one of the two great electric equipment companies, General Electric and Westinghouse Electric. The chances are that the Crane Company has supplied his plumbing fixtures, the American Radiator and Standard Sanitary Corporation his heating equipment. He probably buys at least some of his groceries from the Great Atlantic and Pacific Tea Company . . . and he secures some of his drugs, directly or indirectly, from the United Drug Company. The cans which contain his groceries may well have been made by the American Can Company; his sugar has been refined by one of the major companies, his meat has probably been prepared by Swift, Armour, or Wilson, his crackers put up by the National Biscuit Company. . . .

"If he seeks amusement through a radio he will almost of necessity use a set made under the licence of the Radio Corporation of America. When he steps out to the movies he will probably see a Paramount, Fox, or Warner Brothers' picture (taken on Eastman Kodak film) at a theatre controlled by one of these producing groups. No matter which of the alluring cigarette advertisements he succumbs to, he is almost sure to find himself smoking one of the many brands put out by the 'big four' tobacco companies, and he probably stops to buy them at the United Cigar store on the corner."

There you have it, anywhere and everywhere—monopoly. The same story is true of the other great industrial nations of the world. Now what happens when these various giants, in control of their national markets, meet on the international markets? Fireworks! Competition—long, hard, bitter. And then—agreements, associations, cartels, on an international basis. The monopoly "capitalists partition the world, not out of personal malice, but because the degree of concentration which has been reached forces them to adopt this method in order to get profits. And they partition it 'in proportion to capital,' 'in proportion to strength.' . . . But strength varies with the degree of economic and political development."

After international combines have divided up the world market, it would seem that competition must cease and a period of lasting peace begin. But this does not happen because the strength relations are continually changing. Some companies grow larger and more powerful, while others decline. Thus what was fair at one moment becomes unfair later. There is discontent on the part of the stronger group, and a struggle for a larger quota follows. This often leads to war.

The same is true of political control of colonies. Seventy years ago there were still a lot of "free" areas as yet unattached. Today that is no longer true. If there is to be a redivision the have-nots must seize what they want—from the haves. Germany, Italy, and Japan want colonies today. Italy and Japan are grabbing what they can. Germany is arming—in preparation for the grab to come. Imperialism leads to war.

But war doesn't settle anything permanently. The hostilities which can no longer be resolved by bargaining round a table do not disappear because the bargaining is done with the arguments of high explosives, poison gas, maimed men, and mutilated corpses. No. Monopoly capitalism must have its outlet for surplus goods and capital, and the hostilities will continue so long as it continues. The hunt for markets must go on.

Cecil Rhodes, outstanding imperialist, felt this keenly. The acquisition of new markets became part of him; the annexation of new territories was part of his life-blood. The imperialist urge is perhaps best illustrated in a statement he once made to a friend: "The world is nearly all parcelled out, and what there is left of it is being divided up, conquered, and colonized. To think of these stars that you see overhead at night, these vast worlds which we can never reach. I would annex the planets if I could; I often think of that. It makes me sad to see them so clear and yet so far."

Rhodes died too soon. What a pity! For in a laboratory on the desert of New Mexico, Professor R. H. Goddard has been experimenting with a rocket ship that is to make a flight to the moon. In a mountain fastness in Wales the British Interplanetary Society carries on its work of perfecting a rocket capable of reaching the planets. If only Rhodes had lived!

However, there may be comfort for his soul in the thought that his spirit still survives, stronger than ever before. When the Man in the Moon greets the first passenger on the first rocket ship, that passenger will undoubtedly reply with a question whispered into his host's ear, "How would you like to borrow some money to fix up your old canals and build some new ones? Now just sign here, and my bank will take care of all the details. . . . There you are. . . . Thank you."

XX

The Weakest Link

"IN THESE crises a great part not only of the existing products, but also of the previously created productive forces, are periodically destroyed. In these crises there breaks out an epidemic that, in all earlier epochs, would have seemed an absurdity—the epidemic of over-production. Society suddenly finds itself put back into a state of momentary barbarism; it appears as if a famine, a universal war of devastation, had cut off the supply of every means of subsistence; industry and commerce seem to be destroyed; and why? Because there is too much civilization, too much means of subsistence, too much industry, too much commerce."

No, this was not written yesterday.

It can be found in the *Communist Manifesto* written by Marx and Engels almost a hundred years ago, way back in 1848. It was not a daring prophecy—it was a description of what happened to capitalist society every few years, at that time. That it has continued to happen is known to all of us who were above the age of ten in 1929. That quotation has a familiar ring because you and I are living through the greatest economic crisis the world has ever known.

There have always been crises in all periods of history. But there is a marked difference between those that occurred before capitalism grew up and those that have occurred since. Before the eighteenth century the most common type of crisis was that due to crop failure, war, or some abnormal event; such a crisis was marked by a shortage of food and other necessities which caused prices to rise. But the crises that we know, the crises that came into being with the coming of the capitalist system, are not due to abnormal events —they seem to be part and parcel of our economic system; these crises are marked not by a shortage, but rather by an overabundance; in these crises, prices do not rise, they fall.

You know the other characteristics of crises and depression—unemployment, both of labour and of capital, falling profits, and a general slowing down of industrial activity, both in production and in trade. The paradox of poverty in plenty is everywhere visible.

Is there a lack of raw materials? Not at all. The cotton-growers are anxious to sell their cotton. Is there a lack of capital equipment? Not at all. The factory-owners are eager to see the spindles and looms in their silent mills running again. Is there a lack of labour? Not at all. The unemployed textile-workers are more than willing to get back into the mill to make the very cotton cloth they lack.

No. The raw materials, the capital equipment, and the labour necessary for production are all available, yet production does not take place. Why?

The economists are not agreed on the answer.

But on one fact they are in agreement. And unless you understand that fact at the outset, the causes of crises will be a closed book to you.

The all-important fact is simply this: in the capitalist system, commodities are produced not for use, but for exchange—at a profit. In our society, minerals are dug out of the earth, crops are harvested, men are given jobs, the wheels of industry are set in motion, and goods are bought and sold, only when the owners of the means of production—the capitalist class—can see a chance to make a profit. This was well put by Walter Lippmann in his column in the *Herald Tribune* on July 13, 1934: "There is no use talking about recovery under present conditions unless capitalists, large and small, begin to invest in enterprise for the purpose of earning a profit. They will not do it to earn a Blue Eagle. They will not do it for patriotism's sake or as an act of public service. They will do it because they see a chance to make money. This is the capitalist system. That is the way it works."

According to Professor F. A. von Hayek, Mr. Lippmann is right: "In the modern exchange economy, the entrepreneur does not produce with a view to satisfying a certain demand—even if that phrase is sometimes used—but on the basis of a calculation of profitability."

Professor Hayek is one of the leading economists alive today. He does not have much in common with the economists who look at society from the point of view of the working class. But on the important fact that it is profit alone that makes the wheels go round, we find him in agreement with Friedrich Engels. Here is part of a letter which Engels wrote in 1865: "Too little is produced. . . . But *why* is too little produced? Not because the limits of production . . . are exhausted. No, but because the limits of production are determined not by the number of hungry bellies, but by the number of *purses* able to buy and to pay. The moneyless bellies, the labour which cannot be utilized *for profit* and therefore cannot buy, is left to the death-rate."

In the writings of Thorstein Veblen, one of the most original of American economists, we find the same truth expressed in his famous acid style: "The business man's place in the economy of nature is to 'make money,' not to produce goods. . . . The highest achievement in business is the nearest approach to getting something for nothing . . . it should . . . be noted that there is next to no business enterprise, if any, whose chief end is not profitable sales, or profitable bargains which mean the same thing as profitable sales . . . the profits of business come out of the product of industry; and industry is controlled, accelerated, and slowed down with a view to business profits."

One further bit of evidence that under capitalism goods are produced not for use, but for profit. This quotation is from *Business Cycles*, by Wesley C. Mitchell, an outstanding study by an outstanding American economist: "Where business economy prevails natural resources are not developed, mechanical equipment is not utilized, workman-like skill is not exercised, scientific discoveries are not applied, unless conditions are such as to promise a money profit to those who direct production."

Here then is a parade of expert witnesses of different economic complexions, who all give the same testimony—that in the capitalist system production does not take place unless it promises to yield a profit. If, however, these same witnesses were asked to testify why, periodically, that promise is not performed, there would be no such unanimity of opinion. Economists agree on what makes the system work, but they emphatically do not agree on what makes it not work. The system breaks down—that is, profits fall—in a period of crisis. What are the causes of these breakdowns? What are the causes of crises? Let us examine some of the answers of the economists.

There are some economists who even today, after more than a century of crises coming again and again almost in a regular pattern, still cling to the belief that the causes must be found not within the system itself, but outside of it. Of this school, Professor Mitchell writes: "Some economists despaired of finding any theory which would account for all crises in the same way. To these men a crisis is an 'abnormal' event produced by some 'disturbing cause,' such as the introduction of revolutionary inventions . . . tariff revisions, monetary changes, crop failures, changes in fashion, and the like. This view . . . points to the conclusion that each crisis has its own special cause which must be sought among the events of the preceding year or two."

For another group, the special cause of crises is physical. W. Stanley Jevons announced in 1875 that spots on the sun, famine in India, and crises in England came at about the same time. What had one to do with the other? Watch closely. The sun's radiation affects the weather; the weather affects the harvest; the harvest, good or bad, affects the income of the farmers; the income of the farmers affects the extent of the demand for manufactured goods. Blame it on the sun!

Or rather, blame it on the planet Venus. So says Mr. Henry L. Moore, father of the theory of eight-year "generating cycles." But why Venus? Because every eight years Venus comes between the sun and the earth, and you can guess that with Venus in his path much of Apollo's radiation will never reach earth!

So much for the physical causes of crises. Professor A. C. Pigou, the Cambridge economist, is the leader of a school which attributes booms and depressions to psychological causes—errors of optimism and pessimism on the part of captains of industry. In the "variations in the expectations of business men" Professor Pigou finds the root cause of the ups and downs of industry. When things are going well, business men become optimistic about their chances of increasing their profits. They want to expand production. They borrow more money from the banks and invest it freely in industrial equipment—either enlarging their plants or buying newer machinery, etc. "When these [expectations] are good, they lead business men to increase their borrowings, in part from the banks, thus directly pushing up the rate of interest and indirectly, by bringing more purchasing power into circulation, pushing up prices." Then, however, the goods produced on this wave of optimism have to stand the test of the market. Will they sell for the new high prices? They will not. In one case after another it is seen that the optimism was unjustified, so a deep psychological distrust and pessimism take hold of the business world, and production is slowed down. "The activity which is developed in industry under the influence of an error of optimism finally materializes in the form of commodities seeking a market. So long as these are in process of being created . . . exceptional activity continues. [Then it is found that the optimism was too great—i.e. the optimism does not survive the test of the market.] When this test has been applied to a number of things and found wanting for a fair number, confidence is shaken. The fact that errors of optimism have been made and prospective profits exaggerated is discovered and recognized widely. . . . As a consequence the flow of business activity is checked."

At this point over-optimism gives way to over-pessimism. Production is slowed down considerably, investment in industry practically ceases, and whatever goods are sold come out of stock carried over from before. Then after a while demand increases again, profits rise again, business men cheer up again, and over-optimism is generated again.

The great importance Pigou and the psychological school place on the expectations of business men as responsible for booms and depressions is shown in the following quotation, "While not, indeed, for the present inquiring *how* these varying expectations themselves come about, we conclude definitely that they, and not anything else, constitute the immediate and direct causes or antecedents of industrial fluctuations."

For another school of economists there is real truth in the old proverb that "money is the root of all evil." They feel that our system of exchange—our monetary system—is defective. They want that defective system regulated. Professor J. M. Keynes, one of the leading exponents of the "regulation of money" school, writes: "Unemployment, the precarious life of the worker, the disappointment of expectation, the sudden loss of savings, the excessive windfalls to individuals, the speculator, the profiteer—all proceed, in large measure, from the instability of the standard of value."

The key words in this quotation are the last, "the instability of the standard of value." Not much proof is needed to convince us that our money is unstable—we know it from experience. Shoppers know that a dollar will buy so many pounds of butter one month and more (or less) another month. And how often have we heard comments like this, "Yes, but the dollar is worth more (or less) now than it used to be." Or, "The first time I was in Paris I got twenty-five francs for my dollar, but this year I got only seventeen."

Our primers of economics tell us that "money is just a medium of exchange." The regulation of money experts argue that it is a bad medium because it isn't stable. Unlike other measures, it's not fixed. A dozen means twelve—it doesn't mean fifteen one day and eight the next. But the value of our monetary unit varies. That's bad and should be remedied—say these economists. What they're arguing for is currency and credit control which will establish a stable relationship between the amount of goods produced and the amount of money in the pockets of the consumers.

For example. With the growth of industry and the expansion of production, the output of goods increases. Unless the money in circulation is increased to keep pace with the increased flow of goods, prices will fall. You can see why. Suppose there are 500 shirts on the market and the consumers have $500 to pay for them. Each shirt will sell for $1. Now suppose that the shirtmakers improve their machinery and turn out 1,000 shirts. Then, other things being equal, unless an additional $500 is put into the hands of the consumers, the price of the shirts will drop to 50 cents apiece.

The monetary economists argue that crises are the effects of the rise and fall in the general price level, due to increase or decrease of the volume of money in circulation. When business is good, money goes round faster and the banks issue larger and larger amounts of credit. It's true they charge high interest rates, but that isn't enough to stop manufacturers who see business expanding and want to make all the profit they can while the going is good. This is how prosperity leads to a boom.

When that happens, the credit-controllers—the banks—get rather scared and begin to feel that the credit structure is becoming top-heavy. "Values are inflated," they say. So they draw in their horns, stop granting new loans, and demand that loans already made be paid back. But this the manufacturers—or many of them—can't do, because they've invested their loans in their businesses, and haven't made enough yet to pay back. When they can't pay back, they are bankrupt. Their plants are closed down, their employees are dismissed, and the distress spreads in ever-widening circles, because the orders to the producers of raw materials cease, and the workmen who are thrown out of work no longer exercise an effective demand for goods. The slowing down of production, the cessation of demand, the accompanying crash in prices, spread depression over the whole field of national economy like a contagious disease. People are afraid to invest, and banks are afraid to lend; and so the money piles up in the banks instead of being used to finance industry and trade.

The monetary economists argue that such topheavy borrowing wouldn't take place if business men didn't feel that prices were going to go up and up. Manufacturers borrow at high rates only because they believe that the expected rise in prices will be enough to pay the interest, and provide still higher profits. If prices remained stable they wouldn't engage in violent and unjustified expansion of production. To cure the evil, these economists propose that the money unit be standardized so that it will keep in line with the rise and fall of productive output. Professor Irving Fisher of Yale University has worked out a plan for a "compensated dollar" which he says will do the trick. It will buy the same market-basket full of goods yesterday, today, and tomorrow.

Fisher and Keynes argue that it is silly and dangerous for man to continue to use an imperfect monetary system when a perfect one can be invented. Says Professor Keynes: "The best way to cure this mortal disease of individualism [price movements resulting in booms and depressions] is to provide [by currency and credit control] that there shall never exist any confident expectation either that prices generally are going to fall or that they are going to rise. . . .

"We can no longer afford to leave it [the standard of value] in the category of which the distinguishing characteristics are possessed in different degrees by the weather, the birth-rate, and the Constitution—matters which are settled by natural causes or are the resultant of the separate action of many individuals acting independently, or require a Revolution to change them."

Other economists, however, are not convinced that manipulating the currency to correspond with productive output is a good thing. Here is the dissenting opinion of Professor Hayek: "The reasons commonly advanced as a proof that the quantity of the circulating medium should vary as production increases or decreases are entirely unfounded. It would appear rather that the fall of prices . . . which necessarily follows when, the amount of money remaining the same, production increases, is not only entirely harmless, but is in fact the only means of avoiding misdirections of production."

Much more popular than any of these theories of the causes of crises is that advanced by Mr. John A. Hobson. You are probably familiar with Mr. Hobson's analysis. It is his argument that during periods of prosperity, incomes to capital grow much more than wages to labour. The rich get richer—at an unbelievable rate. Their incomes swell. No matter how much they spend on themselves, they still have money left over. What they can't spend, they save. Their huge sums of money are invested in industry, and the result is a tremendous increase in the equipment for turning out goods—in productive capacity. The new and better equipment does its job. The goods pour out of the factories on to the market. But the workers are not getting enough in wages to enable them to buy this ever-increasing output. The goods are unsold, they pile up in ware-house and store, and prices drop disastrously. Production becomes unprofitable. When that happens, production is curtailed. The re-sult is unemployment, depression, and a reduction in the size of the incomes of the rich. Over-saving stops.

Then slowly the consumers catch up on the pile of accumulated goods, industries which are running find they can no longer do without new or improved equipment, and so gradually production works up again, and the whole cycle of prosperity, boom, crisis, depression, is on us once more.

Those people who are disturbed by the very existence of extremes of rich and poor find Mr. Hobson's analysis especially suited to their taste. For whether you think of it as the theory of "over-saving" or from another angle, as the theory of "under-consumption," it boils down to the unequal distribution of wealth as the essential cause of crises.

Here it is in the words of Mr. Hobson: "These 'surpluses,' so far as they are not taken by taxation, form the irrational or wasteful factor in our economic system. As income they have no justification, moral or economic. Their low utility for purposes of consumption or enjoyment leads to their accumulation as savings for investment

in excess of the requirements and possible uses of the economic system as a whole . . . this unearned surplus . . . is the direct cause
of the stoppage of industry, the collapse of prices, and the unemployment classed under the term trade depression. The application
of this surplus . . . to enlarge the spending power and consumption
of the workers and the community, will remedy these chronic mal-
adjustments by raising the aggregate power of consumption to keep
pace with every increase of productive power. . . . To increase the
proportion of the general income that comes to the wage-earners
whether through high wages . . . or through increasing social
services, is the essential condition for the maintenance of full employment in those industries that are most prone to periods of
depression and unemployment."

Mr. Hobson states his case convincingly. And because many of us
are disturbed by evidences of distress everywhere around us we want
to believe that his argument for higher wages and increased social
services is the correct one. But we must not let our desires lead us
into swallowing it whole. Recall, at this time, that the purpose of
production in the capitalist system is to make a profit. Mr. Hobson
says that crises come because capitalists invest too much; that workers do not get enough in wages to buy back the goods produced by
over-capitalized industry; that therefore profits fall.

But Professor Hayek says this is not true. Professor Hayek says
profits fall because capitalists do not invest enough. He argues not
for the expansion of social services, but for their reduction; not for
an increase in wages, but for a decrease: "Certain kinds of state
action, by causing a shift in demand from producers' goods to consumers' goods, may cause a continued shrinking of the capitalist
structure of production and therefore prolonged stagnation . . . the
granting of credit to consumers, which has recently been so strongly
advocated as a cure for depression, would in fact have quite the
contrary effect; a relative increase of the demand for consumers'
goods could only make matters worse."

It is impossible in a few pages to do justice to Professor Hayek's
complicated theory. But for our purpose it is sufficient to point out

that Hobson and Hayek find exactly opposite causes for the fall in profits which is a crisis; that to effect a cure for the disease of falling profits they offer contrasting remedies.

And the interesting thing is that they are both right—and wrong. Hobson is right in arguing that higher wages and expanded social services would provide a necessary market for the increasing supply of commodities; he is wrong in that raising wages means lowering the immediate profits of production. Hayek is right in arguing that lower wages and restricted social services would increase the immediate profits of production; he is wrong in that lowering wages means destroying the market for the increasing supply of commodities. Hobson is concerned with restoring the market (and so profitability) by increasing the purchasing power of the masses; Hayek is concerned with restoring profitability by decreasing the purchasing power of the masses (wage-cuts).

And here, according to the followers of Karl Marx is the dilemma of capitalism—*it cannot do both*. Therefore, they argue, crises are inevitable under capitalism. Whereas all the other economists see this or that or the other thing as the cause of crises, but suggest that if you adopt their particular remedy all will be well, Marx said that there was no way out within the capitalist system. To get rid of crises, he wrote, you must get rid of capitalism.

Marx's analysis of crises is inherent in his entire theory. His theory of capitalist production and his theory which explains the breakdown of capitalist production are one—and they have the same roots.

The essential purpose of the capitalist system of production is to make a profit. Now Marx was able to prove that there was a *tendency for the rate of profit to fall*. Nor was this a happen-so. It had to be. The structure of the capitalist productive system made it inevitable. Let us see why. (It would be a good idea, at this point, for you to read again, carefully, pages 224 to 230 on Marx's labor theory of value.)

Marx divides capital into two parts—constant and variable. Constant capital is that part which is spent on plant, machinery, tools, raw materials, etc. Variable capital is that part which is spent on buying labour power—on wages. Constant capital gets its name from the fact that in the process of production its value remains constant —into the final product, just its original value is transferred, no more and no less. Variable capital gets its name from the fact that in the process of production its value varies—into the final product more than its original value is transferred. Whereas constant capital is barren in that it creates no new value in the productive process, variable capital is creative in that it (and it alone) does create new value in the productive process. It is the variable capital which creates more value than it is itself worth—surplus value. It is the variable capital (living labour-power) from which profits are derived.

So in manufacture, the capitalist's capital is divided thus:

C (total capital) $=$ c (constant capital) $+$ v (variable capital).

Now how much of C will be devoted to c and how much to v? There is no doubt, says Marx, and here everyone will agree with him, that with the development of capitalism, an ever-increasing share of the total capital, C, is being put into constant capital, c. As you know, more and better machinery is being introduced into modern industry all the time. This machinery is truly miraculous— but it costs money—lots of it. And it displaces labour. Which simply means that increasingly, the proportion of variable capital, v, to total capital, C, is growing smaller; and conversely, the proportion of constant capital, c, to total capital, C, is growing larger. Here it

is in shorthand, $\dfrac{v}{C}$ diminishes

              while $\dfrac{c}{C}$ increases.

This fact that, relatively, constant capital grows while variable capital diminishes, is of tremendous importance. For, you remember, it is v and v alone which is the source of surplus value, or profit. This means that, as v diminishes, so there is a tendency for the rate of profit to fall. As the proportion of constant to total capital gets higher, according to Marx "the same rate of surplus value, with the same degree of labor exploitation, would express itself in a falling rate of profit. . . . If it is furthermore assumed that this gradual change in the composition of capital is not confined to some individual spheres of production, but occurs more or less in all . . . then the gradual and relative growth of the constant over the variable capital must necessarily lead to *a gradual fall of the average rate of profit,* so long as the rate of surplus value . . . remains the same."

Now a fall in the rate of profit is a serious business. It is a threat to the very aim of the capitalists, which is to obtain the largest amount of profit they can. But there is a way out, temporarily, for the capitalists. They find that it is possible to increase their amount of profit even though the rate of profit is falling. Here is an example (surplus value is represented by *s*, and we assume that the rate of surplus value is the same in each case, 100 per cent):

C	c	v	s
$1,500	1,000	500	500
$4,000	3,000	1,000	1,000

Since surplus value, s, is created only by variable capital, v, the rate of surplus value is always the relation of s to v, or $\frac{s}{v}$. But although the profits come only from the amount spent on wages (v), the capitalist reckons his profit as a profit on total capital invested (C). Therefore he estimates his rate of profit as the relation of s to C, or $\frac{s}{C}$.

So in the example given above, in the first case, the rate of profit is $\frac{\$500}{\$1,500}$, or 33 1/3 per cent; in the second case, it is $\frac{\$1,000}{\$4,000}$, or only 25 per cent. But though the *rate* of profit has fallen, the *amount* of profit has risen, from $500 to $1,000.

Notice, however, what was necessary in order to make this possible. Variable capital from which alone the profit can come, had to be *doubled*; and because the modern technique of production requires a continually increasing amount of constant capital as compared to variable, while v was doubled, c *had to be tripled*. And there's the rub. In order to increase the amount of profit, capitalists are compelled to accumulate more and more capital. There is no choice in the matter. If accumulation of capital stops, then the amount of profit (as well as the rate) falls.

Every individual capitalist knows this. Competition in the market has taught him that he must save his money and put ever-increasing amounts back into the business—or go down in the fight. He must accumulate, ever accumulate, so that his total capital can be increased sufficiently to beat off the falling rate of profit.

The well-meaning people who advocate the payment of high wages to workers have overlooked this point. The capitalist, however, knows that the more he pays his workers the less he has in profits—which means that the accumulation which is essential for him to continue to make a profit is slowed down—not speeded up. This from his point of view, must not happen—because when accumulation ceases, profits cease.

He solves that part of the dilemma, then, by paying as low wages as possible. This leaves him free to continue the necessary policy of ever-increasing accumulation. But ever-increasing accumulation means that an ever-increasing amount of commodities is thrown on the market. And here he runs into the other half of the shears of the economic contradiction, the lack of purchasing power of the workers to absorb the output. For low wages mean that the commodities he makes cannot be bought and paid for.

Marx's analysis comes to this: the capitalists must maintain profits by keeping down wages; but in doing so they destroy the purchasing power on which the realization of profit depends. Low wages make high profits possible, but at the same time they make profits impossible because they reduce the demand for goods.

Insoluble contradiction.

.   .   .   .

About ninety years ago, Thomas Carlyle put his finger on the crisis confronting the capitalist system: "What is the use of your spun shirts? They hang there by the million unsaleable; and here, by the million, are diligent bare backs that can get no hold of them. Shirts are useful for covering human backs; useless otherwise, an unbearable mockery otherwise. You have fallen terribly behind with that side of the problem!"

If it was true at the time that Carlyle wrote that "you have fallen terribly behind with that side of the problem!" how much more true is it today when we are in the midst of the greatest crisis in world history?

People everywhere are grappling with the problem. In the Soviet Union, they are attempting to solve it by the Marxist method of replacing capitalism; in other parts of the world they are attempting to solve it by patching up and controlling capitalism.

XXI

Russia Has a Plan

SEVENTEEN years before the end of the nineteenth century Karl Marx died.

Seventeen years after the beginning of the twentieth century Karl Marx lived again.

What had been theory with Marx was put into practice by his disciples—Lenin and the other Russian Bolsheviks—in their seizure of power in 1917. Before that time the teachings of Marx had been familiar to a small group of devoted followers; after that time the teachings of Marx had the spotlight of the world focussed on them. Before that time Communists could only promise that their theory, if put into practice would create a new and better world; after that time Communists could point to one-sixth of the earth's surface and say: "Here it is. Look at it. It works."

How was it possible for the Bolsheviks to seize power in the first place? What conditions were present which made the revolution successful? For of one fact concerning revolution we may be certain, and that is that carrying through a successful revolution is no easy task to be accomplished by anybody, anywhere, at any time. No. Revolution is an art, and Lenin, the leader of the Bolsheviks, emphasized that important truth.

"To be successful, the uprising must be based not on a conspiracy, not on a party, but on the advanced class. This is the first point.

285

The uprising must be based on the *crucial point* in the history of the maturing revolution, when the activity of the vanguard of the people is at its height, when the *vacillations* in the ranks of the enemies, and *in the ranks of the weak, half-hearted, undecided friends of the revolution are at their highest point*. This is the third point. . . . But once these conditions exist, then to refuse to treat the uprising *as an art* means to betray Marxism and the revolution."

This was written one month before the Bolsheviks seized power. There were many among his own followers who agreed with Lenin that the conditions he enumerated must exist before a revolution could be successful. But many of these same people did not agree with him on what was the *exact moment* when those necessary conditions did exist. And therein lay the genius of Lenin. He sensed the very moment when the conditions were truly ripe, when to act was to succeed, and to delay was to fail.

On the very eve of the seizure of power he had to bend all his energies to the task of convincing his followers that the time had come to strike. On October 7-14 he completed an article entitled *Will the Bolsheviks Retain State Power?* in which he analysed, one by one, all the various arguments that were being presented against revolutionary action then and there. Here is his answer to one of those objections. "The fifth argument is that the Bolsheviks will not retain power because 'the circumstances are exceptionally complicated.'

"Oh, wiseacres! They are prepared perhaps to tolerate revolution, but without 'exceptionally complicated circumstances.'

"Such revolutions never occur, and in the yearnings after such revolutions there is nothing but the reactionary lamentation of the bourgeois intellectual. Even if a revolution starts in circumstances which seem not so very complicated, the revolution itself, in its development, always gives rise to exceptionally complicated circumstances. For a revolution, a real, deep, 'people's revolution,' to use Marx's expression, is the incredibly complicated and painful process of the dying of the old and the birth of the new social order, the adjustment of the lives of tens of millions of people. A revolution is the sharpest, most furious, desperate class struggle and civil war. Not a single great revolution in history has escaped civil war, and no one who does not live in a shell could imagine that civil war is conceivable without 'exceptionally complicated circumstances.'

"If there were no exceptionally complicated circumstances, there would be no revolution. If you fear wolves, do not go into the forest."

Here was the writing of a revolutionist who knew what lay ahead, who had counted the cost, but was not frightened; a revolutionist who thought the goal of a socialist state, controlled by and for the working class, was worth the terrific price that had to be paid. Because Lenin knew the art of revolution, he triumphed.

We are fortunate that so magnificent a reporter as John Reed was an eyewitness to most of the events that ushered in what the Communists call a new civilization. In his *Ten Days That Shook the World* he gives us an unforgettable picture of those stirring times. Here is part of his description of a meeting of the Soviet Congress in Petrograd, November, 1917: "Now Lenin, gripping the edge of the reading-stand, letting his little winking eyes travel over the crowd as he stood there waiting, apparently oblivious to the long-rolling ovation, which lasted several minutes. When it finished, he said, simply, 'We shall now proceed to construct the Socialist order!' "

That was 1917. Fifteen years after Lenin so dramatically announced the beginning of the construction of "the Socialist order," Walter Duranty, correspondent for the *New York Times*, wrote that the framework was finished: "1932 may be said to mark the completion of the framework of that Socialist order at which the revolution was aimed.

"The building itself is far from complete, but the steel framework which will hold the finished edifice of socialism can now be seen in stark outline against the Eastern sky. Finance, industry, and transportation, public health and recreation, art and science, commerce, agriculture—every branch of national life is fitted to the arbitrary pattern of collective effort for collective benefit, instead of individual effort for individual profit."

Mr. Duranty, in his last sentence, has put his finger on the essential part of the Soviet programme. The key words are "collective" instead of "individual." You would have expected that one of the first steps that followers of Karl Marx would take in their construction of the socialist order would be the abolition of private ownership of the means of production. That's exactly what happened. In the U.S.S.R. the land, factories, mines, mills, machinery, banks, railways, etc., are no longer the property of private individuals. Practically all these means of production and distribution are in the hands of the government, or of bodies appointed or approved by the government and under its control.

That's fundamental.

To understand its true significance we must contrast it with capitalist society. It means, according to the Russians, that one man can no longer exploit another—*A* cannot profit from *B's* labour; it means that it is no longer possible for anyone to climb the ladder of money accumulation on the backs of "his" workers; it means that it is no longer possible for an auto manufacturer to announce to the newspapers on one day that anyone who really wants a job can get one, and on the next day shut down his plants and throw 75,000 workers out of their jobs. He cannot do that, because they are no longer *his* plants—they belong to all the people, collectively. It means, say the Russians, that class divisions are wiped out—the extremes of owner and worker, capitalist and proletariat, rich and poor, are gone. The "expropriators are expropriated."

In a special cable to the *New York Times* on April 22, 1936, Harold Denny, Moscow correspondent, reported this proud boast of the Communists:

RUSSIANS HAIL END
OF SOCIAL CLASSES

First of Soviet Aims Largely Achieved,
Andreieff Tells Communist
Youth

PRODUCTION GOAL IS NEAR

Private Industry Will Turn Out Only 1.5
Per Cent of Union's Goods This Year

By HAROLD DENNY

Special Cable to The New York Times

MOSCOW, April 21—The Soviet State has now largely achieved the first goal in its march toward communism, Andrei Andreieff, secretary of the central committee of the Communist party of the Union of Soviet Socialist Republics, told the Young Communist League [Comsomol] conference here today. The productive means of the country are now almost entirely socialized and class divisions have been wiped out, he asserted.

Of all goods produced in the U.S.S.R. this year 98.5 per cent will be produced by the State, leaving only 1.5 per cent made up of small handicraft trades, such as dressmakers, milliners, and shoemakers, non-socialized, Mr. Andreieff asserted. Although Mr. Andreieff did not mention it, these also are rapidly being driven out of business by the prohibitive taxes now being applied to them.

With the socialization of industry and the almost complete collectivization of agriculture, there is now only one class—the workers, Mr. Andreieff declared.

Only 1.5 per cent of non-socialized industry remaining in the Soviet Union! And that, understand, is not capitalist industry in the usual sense, because in it the producers work for themselves—there is no hiring of other people to do the work. All the rest of the productive apparatus of the country is collectively owned, and is managed by the government.

Now, the big economic questions facing the government of the U.S.S.R. in its capacity of owner of the means of production, are what shall be produced, how much shall be produced, and who shall get what is produced? These are decisions that have to be made for the country as a whole. In capitalist countries, each capitalist, before he invests his capital in an undertaking, has to make some similar decisions. Shall he put his money into an automobile factory, or build a railway, or manufacture cloth? And how much shall he manufacture, and how much shall he pay his workmen? The result of thousands and millions of such small decisions makes up the totality of production. But there is no guarantee that the particular parts are going to fit into each other, and you and I know from experience that every few years there is a breakdown when the parts do not fit.

The government in a socialist state is in the position of the capitalist, but magnified a thousandfold—that is to say it is the sole owner of capital and has to make *every* decision. The socialist government attempts to get all the different parts, all the thousand and one varied and complicated economic activities, to join up together harmoniously and fit one another so that the whole thing works smoothly. In order to do this well

Russia Has a Plan.

"The most significant socially of all the trends in Soviet Communism [is] the deliberate planning of all the nation's production, distribution and exchange, not for swelling the profit of the few, but for increasing the consumption of the whole community. . . .

"Once private ownership, with its profit-seeking motive of production for the competitive market, is abandoned, specific directions must be given as to what each establishment has to produce. It is this necessity . . . that makes indispensable, in a collectivist state, some sort of General Plan."

You have heard time and again of Russia's Five-Year Plan. When they completed that one, they started their Second Five-Year Plan. And so it will go, for ever and ever, so long as Russia is socialized. For, as Sidney and Beatrice Webb point out in the quotation above, a collectivist state *has* to have a plan. Socialist economy is, of necessity, planned economy.

Since Russia is the only country in the world that has a planned economy, to understand how such an economy works, we must examine the Russian model.

What does a plan involve? When you or I make a plan, when anybody makes a plan, there are two parts to it—a *for* and a *how*, an aim and a method. The goal is one part of our plan and the way to get there is the other part.

This is true of socialist planning. It has an aim and a method. But it is important to note at the outset that the aim of socialist planning is entirely different from the ends sought in capitalist countries. This is well put by the Webbs in their excellent study of the U.S.S.R. *Soviet Communism: A New Civilization?* "In a capitalist society, the purpose of even the largest private enterprise is the pecuniary profit to be gained by its owners or shareholders. . . . In the U.S.S.R., with what is called the Dictatorship of the Proletariat, the end to be planned for is quite different. There are no owners or shareholders to be benefited, and there is no consideration of pecuniary profit. The sole object aimed at is the maximum safety and well-being, in the long run, of the entire community."

Well and good. There's the broad general aim. It has to be made concrete. Specific policies in line with that desired goal must be adopted. But policy must be based on possibility. And the possibility can be gauged only by getting a complete accurate picture of the country.

That is the job of the State Planning Commission (Gosplan).

Its first task is to find out who and what and where and how about everything in the U.S.S.R. What is the size of the labour force? What is the condition of the collective plant? What are the natural resources? What has been done? What can be done? What is available? What is needed?

Facts. Figures. Statistics. Mountains of them.

From every institution in the vast territory of the U.S.S.R., from every factory, farm, mill, mine, hospital, school, research institute, trade union, coöperative society, theatre group; from all of these everywhere, from every far-away corner of this tremendous area come the answers to the questions: What did you do last year? What are you doing this year? What do you hope to do next year? What help do you need? What help can you give? And a hundred others.

All this information pours into the offices of Gosplan, where it is assembled, organized, digested, by experts. "The whole staff of the U.S.S.R. Gosplan now amounts to something approaching a couple of thousand expert statisticians and scientific technicians of various kinds, with as many more clerical subordinates—certainly the best equipped as well as the most extensive permanent machine of statistical inquiry in the world."

When these experts have finished their job of sorting, arranging, and checking the collected data, they have their picture of Things As They Are. But that's only part of their job. They must now put their minds to the question of Things As They Might Be. At this point the planners must meet with the heads of the government. "The conclusions of the State Planning Commission and its projects were subject to endorsement by the government, the planning function was separated from the function of leadership, and the latter was not subordinate to the former."

Planning, of course, does not do away with the necessity to make the decisions of policy which the plan is to carry out. Policy is determined by the heads of the government, and the job of the planners is to work out the most efficient way of carrying out that policy on the basis of the material they have assembled. Out of the discussions between Gosplan and the leaders comes the first draft of The Plan.

But only the first draft. This is not yet The Plan. For in a socialist planned economy the plan of a Brain Trust by itself is not enough. It must be submitted to all the people. That is the next step. Here is how I. Maiski, the Russian ambassador to England, describes this second stage in the preparation of The Plan: "The 'control figures' are submitted for perusal and comment to the various people's Commissariats and other central bodies dealing with the national economy, as, for instance, the Peoples' Commissariat of Heavy Industry, Light Industry, Commerce, Transport, Foreign Trade, etc. Each central authority refers the various parts of its Plan to the body next below it in authority, so that finally the appropriate part of the Plan comes down to the individual factory or farm. At every stage the 'control figures' are subject to a very thorough scrutiny and consideration. When they reach the last halt on the journey from the State Planning Committee, the factory or collective farm, all the keen workers and peasants take an active part in the discussion and consideration of the Plan, making proposals and suggestions.

After this the 'control figures' are sent up along the same line until they finally return, in their amended or supplemented form, to the State Planning Committee."

Workers in the factory and peasants on the farm voicing their opinions on the merits and demerits of the Plan. This is a picture of which the Russians are justly proud. Often, it happens, these workers and peasants disagree with the control figures for their particular place of work. Often they submit a counter-plan in which they give their own figures to show that they can *increase* the production expected of them. In this discussion and debate on the provisional Plan by millions of Soviet citizens everywhere, the Russians see real democracy. The plan of work to be done, of goals to be achieved, is not imposed from above. Workers and peasants have a voice in it. With what result? A competent observer gives this answer: "Wherever you go, at least in the parts of Russia which I saw, you will find workers saying proudly to you, 'This is *our* factory; this is *our* hospital; this is *our* rest-house'; not meaning that they, individually, own the particular object in question; but that it was functioning and producing . . . directly for their benefit, and that they were aware of it, and aware, moreover, that they were, at any rate in part, responsible for seeing that it was kept up to the mark."

The third stage in the preparation of the Plan is the final examination of the returned figures. Gosplan and the government heads go over the suggestions and amendments, make the necessary changes, and then the Plan is ready. In final form it is sent back to workers and peasants everywhere, and the whole nation bends all its energies to completing the task. Collective action for collective good becomes a reality.

But what is the collective good? What policies did the heads of the government think were essential first? Certain general objectives suggested themselves immediately. Most of the inhabitants of the U.S.S.R. were illiterate, uneducated. So a universal program of education must be part of the Plan. Free education for all—with free maintenance for students while attending the universities, was provided. Most of the inhabitants of the U.S.S.R. knew little or nothing about health and hygiene. So a campaign to raise the living standards, furthered by provision for hospitals, maternity centres, nurseries, etc., staffed by competent doctors, nurses, and teachers, must be part of the Plan. Rest homes for workers, parks, museums, clubhouses—these and similar services must be part of the Plan. Institutes and laboratories for scientific research must be part of the Plan. About these and a host of other obvious needs there could be no doubt—so they became part of the Plan. But what answer was to be given to questions such as these:

1. Would it be better policy to concentrate on producing goods for people to eat and wear and enjoy now? Or would it be advisable to give special attention to the building of factories, power plants, railways, etc., which would mean that the people would have less now, but more in the future? To develop the consumers' goods plant meant well-being today; to develop the producers' goods plant meant well-being tomorrow. Which was best?

2. Would it be better policy to concentrate on the production of those supplies which it could do best and import what it was bad at or deficient in? Or would it be more sensible to try to get its own supplies from within its own borders?

The Soviet answer to these questions was determined, in great measure, by the fact that as a socialist country it was afraid of the danger of attack by the capitalist world. This was no pessimistic guess. It had happened. From 1918 to 1920 a half-dozen capitalist countries, including the United States, had tried to overthrow the Bolsheviks by armed force. And the Russians were sure it would happen again, particularly if they were successful in building socialism. Because, then, the capitalists everywhere would be more than ever afraid that the working class in their particular country would follow the example of the Russian working class, and kick them out of the seats of power.

For this and other reasons—for example, the fact that an agricultural community cannot provide as high a standard of living as an industrialized one—the Russians set themselves to the task of industrialization.

It was not easy. This decision was, in effect, a sacrifice of present comfort for the sake of the future. It meant the allocation of a huge part of the resources to capital goods equipment which wouldn't immediately give people houses and things to eat and clothes to wear. A country has a certain amount of labour and capital to use in, say, a year. It can put all its workers to making bricks and building houses, to raising wheat and baking bread, to growing cotton and manufacturing clothes—and there'll be a lot for everybody. *But there'll never be any more than there is now.* If it wants to have more, it has got to put some of its workers to making machinery, laying rails, building factories, etc.—in short, into producers' goods equipment. This will enable it in the next year, or in the next few years, to turn out more bread, more clothes, more houses. The rate at which you decide to invest for the future, determines the amount you have to eat and wear in the present. Russia found that it could have more coal for heating houses, or more coal for feeding blast furnaces which would make steel which would make machinery which would make automatic looms for turning out cloth quickly and abundantly—but it couldn't have both. It chose the latter. Producers' goods were developed at the expense of consumers' goods. This was the path of industrialization. It was not easy.

In the interview he granted to Roy Howard of the Scripps-Howard Press, on March 1, 1936, Joseph Stalin suggested that, though the path of industrialization was hard, nevertheless it pointed toward the Soviet goal. "If you are going to build a house you must economize and make sacrifices. Even more is it true if you are building a new society.

"It is necessary for us temporarily to limit certain of our demands to accumulate the necessary resources. We have made this sacrifice with the definite objective of developing real freedom in the best sense of the term."

What were some of the "sacrifices" which followed when Russians decided to cut down production for immediate consumption and enlarge production of capital goods? For one thing, it meant that there wasn't enough labour and capital to produce enough things for the present. There was an acute shortage of all consumption goods in Russia—a fact which, as you know, did not go unnoticed by unfriendly visitors to the Soviet Union. It was easier to get a tractor than a teapot, or a railway sleeper than a blanket. Unfortunately, the Russians couldn't make tea in a tractor, or cover themselves with a railway sleeper. So they had to pull in their belts to the last hole—and in some cases they were still too loose—to pay for all the tractors and factories and locomotives and power stations that they were building.

Now, however, according to the *New York Times* of March 27, 1936, there are signs that good times are ahead for Soviet citizens. "This year, for the first time since the Revolution, it is pointed out, greater relative stress is being placed on the production of consumer goods than on means of production, to which everything else was subordinated in the earlier phases of the building of Socialist economy.

"This year's plan . . . provides for a 23-per-cent increase in consumer goods and a 22-per-cent increase in means of production."

Keep one fact clear. The past emphasis on producers' goods instead of consumers' goods is not inherent in national planning. It would not, for example, be at all necessary in the United States if ever it went in for socialized national planning. It was an essential part of the Soviet Plan only because of conditions peculiar to the Soviet Union. In America we are rich in capital goods equipment, so their construction at feverish haste and with great sacrifices would not be part of any Plan we might evolve.

Russia, however, was poor in railways, machinery, factories, plants of every description. The little it had before the World War was almost entirely destroyed during that war, the civil war, and the intervention period. So after the Revolution, Russia had to start practically from scratch. It had a good long way to go before it could catch up to countries like Italy, Sweden, and Australia, let alone England, Germany, and America. Such a long way, in fact, that it seemed almost impossible for them ever to catch up. But the Russians decided that Russia would catch up, and quickly, too. It hasn't done it yet, of course, but impartial observers everywhere agree that it is on the way. This was the view of an outstanding Cambridge economist, who said, back in 1932 (that would be long, long ago at the speed with which Russia is moving): "What it aimed to do was so stupendous as to be greeted with scorn and laughter by the whole of the capitalist world. By the standards of achievement of the capitalist world its aims necessarily seemed a mad Utopian dream. A rich country like pre-war Britain used to invest as new capital some 14 per cent of her national income before the war. Under the Five-Year Plan Soviet Russia planned to invest (per annum on the average of the five years) some 30 per cent of her national income—a stupendous income for a relatively poor country. The annual increase of world production, considered 'normal' to capitalist industry, was estimated at about 3 per cent. In the six years between 1907 and 1913 this annual rate of increase in Britain amounted to less than 1½ per cent. In the four 'boom' years of 1925-1929 it was no higher than 9 per cent even in rapidly expanding countries like Poland and France, and under 4 per cent in the United States and Britain. The Five-Year Plan provided for an annual increase in the output of large-scale State industry at the rate of over 20 per cent, and of all industry (large and small) of some 17 to 18 per cent."

This is all the more remarkable when we realize that during this period of industrialization, loans and credits from other countries were not forthcoming in the usual way. Practically every other country in the world on the path of industrialization has been helped along by foreign capital which enabled it to buy steel, machines, etc., while it was beginning to construct its own plants for the making of these things. In the industrialization of the United States, British capital played a large part. In South America, British, German, and American loans were forthcoming. Surplus capital, as we saw in Chapter XIX, was on the lookout everywhere for places to invest—that is, everywhere but Russia. For the wicked Bolsheviks capitalists had no use and no money. When the Russians did finally manage to break through the boycott and arrange for some needed credit, the terms were stiff—and how!

In what ways, then, were the necessary materials from abroad paid for? What was the source of the capital accumulation that was so sorely needed for the building of industry in the U.S.S.R.? That's an important question—and it has an important answer.

Part of the money came from Soviet industry itself.

In capitalist society accumulation is individual (here "individual" also includes group—e.g. reserve funds of corporations, banks, etc.), whereas in socialist society accumulation, like production, is social. A certain part of the net output of each industry is transferred to the central financial institutions, which thus have single unified control over the entire resources available for expansion. In the Plan of the U.S.S.R. there is no place for the coupon-clipper, so familiar to capitalist society—the life-long *rentier* who is kept by the profits of industry. In the Soviet Union the state itself gathers in the profits of economic activity and directs these funds to the channels where they will be most useful, according to the Plan.

"A part of the development of each industry is automatic, and is provided for by the portion of profits retained by each industry; but the remainder of the profits made by each industry is mobilized and can be used (together with other centrally-accumulated funds) for a consciously-directed development of the whole system of production and distribution. This control of economic development is one of the most important aspects of the organization of central planning."

There is, of course, a small amount of individual saving, but as most saving comes from profits, and there are no profits in the individual sense, saving in the U.S.S.R. is a community function, not a capitalist strangle-hold.

This was one source of capital accumulation. Another important way of getting money for necessary industrial supplies was through foreign trade.

The autos, tractors, locomotives, and machines for making machines, which were so necessary if Russia was to become self-sufficient, could be obtained abroad by exchanging for them Russian wheat, oil, minerals, timber, and furs. Intensive industrialization did not mean that Russians were to stop growing wheat, or tapping the earth for oil and minerals, or felling timber, or trapping fur-bearing animals. On the contrary, these activities were extended and large-scale improvements made. Inefficient nineteenth-century methods were replaced by up-to-date twentieth-century techniques. The mechanization and scientific procedure that were introduced into industry came to agriculture and mining also. Everywhere along the line energies were bent to increasing production. It was through the exporting of Russia's "natural" products that the importing of industrial necessities was made possible.

This means, of course, that foreign trade had to be controlled and made part of the general Plan. It was.

Gosplan decides absolutely and completely what comes into the U.S.S.R. from foreign countries, and what goes out of it to foreign countries. If collective farms were to buy agricultural machinery from the United States, if the electrical industry were to get its equipment from Germany, if the cotton mills were to purchase their spindles from England, just as they liked, without reference to the whole, then everything would go completely to pot. Gosplan has a plan of production and foreign trade is an integral part of that plan; it cannot be left to a lot of individual groups, each buying what it needs and selling what it can, irrespective of the requirements of the national economy. Therefore, just as control of the banks, the railways, the means of production in general, are provided in the Plan, so is state monopoly of foreign trade.

It is an interesting fact that Babeuf, in his plans for a communist state, formulated at the time of the French Revolution, saw the need of state monopoly of foreign trade: "All private trade with foreign countries is forbidden; commodities entering the country in this way will be confiscated for the benefit of the national community. . . . The republic shall acquire for the national community those objects of which it has need by exchanging its surplus . . . products against those of other nations."

However, even with its monopoly of foreign trade as a fundamental part of its socialist-planned economy, the government of the U.S.S.R. is not altogether in command of the kind and amount of its imports and exports. Nor will it ever be, so long as it has to do business with the unplanned economic systems of foreign countries. While the Russians can control what happens in their world, they cannot control what happens in the rest of the world. This was brought home to them during the course of the Five-Year Plan.

Gosplan had decided to make certain purchases of machinery abroad. It had given the orders for these at the prices prevailing at the time, and it had allocated, over a number of years, a certain part of the home production for exports to pay for this machinery.

Well and good. They had signed the contracts for what they wanted, and they had provided for the means of payment. Everything looked rosy.

But—while the contracts were still running, the crisis of 1929 came to the capitalist countries of the world. Which meant that the prices of the goods which Russia was exporting, fell catastrophically. Let us suppose that Gosplan had contracted to pay $10,000,000 for the machinery it had ordered; suppose further that Gosplan had decided to export in exchange

2,000,000 bushels of wheat @ $1.00 per bushel........		$ 2,000,000
1,000,000 fur skins @ 3.00 each..............		3,000,000
2,500,000 barrels of oil @ 2.00 each..............		5,000,000
	Total.............	$10,000,000

Now, because of the crisis, wheat drops to 50 cents, people won't buy furs unless they are practically given away, and oil slumps to an unheard-of low price.

What was the Soviet government to do? It needed the machinery and it had to pay for it by exports. (Even had there been no contracts at the former high prices, nevertheless, industrial prices did not drop so fast or so far as the products Russia had to sell.) It had to export about twice as much as it had planned for. It had to say to the Russian people: "You've got to pull your belts tighter still. Those capitalists have made such a mess of things that world prices have gone down with a bang, and they'll give only half as much for our wheat as before. So we'll have to export twice as much to meet our commitments."

That is, roughly, what happened. The Soviet Union, having planned against crisis in its own country, nevertheless found itself suffering from the effects of the crisis in capitalist countries. Crisis outside Russia was an external factor making for disequilibrium in the Plan.

Much more important are the upsets that may occur due to internal factors—some controllable and some beyond control. Because deliberate planning of all economic activities means that every part is geared to every other, the smashing of one cog in a wheel must of necessity affect every other wheel. Suppose the Russian counterpart of the boll weevil destroys the major part of the cotton crop. This has immediate repercussions on the textile plants; it will affect foreign trade if the Plan called for the export of cotton; it will affect the wage-price relationship if there isn't as much cotton goods on the market as had been anticipated. Soviet economists have learned from experience that, "As a consequence of the close interconnection between all the elements of national economy, a breach in the line or a retreat from the plan on one sector affects a number of other sectors, no matter how well they themselves may be working. Every serious deviation from the plan in one place requires that coordinating measures be taken in another."

There's the danger—and the remedy. The planners must have a reserve which will cushion the blow when it comes. They must allow for accidents. They must collect statistics which will show the top and the bottom of past event, and they must, on the basis of this information, be able to guess what will probably happen. But that's not enough. They must be prepared, in case the probable does not happen, to take "coordinating measures."

They're easy to take—on paper. But coordination in reality is difficult and the Russians paid the price for lack of it time and again. The Webbs give one instance: "After a widely advertised opening of the factory [for making automobiles, at Gorki] on May 1, 1932, the whole enterprise obstinately stuck! The huge buildings copied from Ford's works at Detroit were filled with expensive machinery. Tens of thousands of workmen had been collected and placed upon the pay-roll. But the conveyor . . . refused to move. . . . The bed on which it rested had, in various places, sagged owing to insecure foundations. . . . And even if the conveyor could be made to move, there was nothing like a complete stock of the varied series of components which had to be successively affixed one by one, as the great belt passed along."

Here is a prime example of inefficiency, of lack of direction and coordination. But is it fair to blame this on national planning? Shouldn't it rather be ascribed to the inexperience of the Russians in industry? The Webbs go on to state that the lesson was learned in due time and new factories in Russia now function properly in the first day of operation. If national planning were to come to the United States, it is safe to assume that there would be no lack of coordinating ability. That it already exists in great measure is evidenced in the statement, by the editors of *Fortune*, that just two of the steel companies belonging to the U. S. Steel Corporation "can make as much steel as England and Germany together produced in 1934." Obviously this couldn't be done if there were not in the U. S. Steel Corporation coordinating ability equal to the most difficult problem of industrial organization. One cannot, then, argue that national planning is impossible because getting all the parts together is too big a job.

But there are other arguments. One is directed against the word "socialized" in the phrase, "socialized national planning," and the other against the words "national planning."

It is argued that socialism couldn't work because, the motive of profit being absent, people would have no incentive to do their best, to try new methods, to take risks. As a result economic life would stagnate.

The Russians answer that this is so much nonsense. They point to the fact that in capitalist society most of the work is done by people who are not in a position to make a profit—by people who work day in and day out for wages alone. Most people work because they have to earn a living. This applies everywhere—in Russian as well as in the capitalist world. In addition, in Russia, social pressure, social esteem, and the honour in which good workers are held, all help to induce the worker to do his best. The socialists claim that their incentives are much more productive than the incentives under capitalism. The Russians point with justifiable pride to the various ranks of labourers who work voluntarily and for nothing to help at any weak spot on the economic front. Lenin, in 1919, was impressed by the "subbotniks" who did this: "The communist 'subbotniks' have an enormous historical importance. . . . Labour productivity is, in the final analysis, the prime and most important factor in the triumph of the new social order. Capitalism has created a degree of labour productivity unknown to serfdom. Capitalism can be finally overthrown, and will be finally overthrown, by the fact that socialism will create a new and much higher productivity of labour. This is a very difficult matter and will take a long time. . . . Communism means a higher labour productivity, as compared with that of capitalism, on the part of voluntary, conscious, united workers employing progressive technique."

"Socialist competition" is another way of increasing productivity of labour. Teams of workers vie with each other in friendly rivalry in increasing output. When the competition is over the winning team does what no other winning side anywhere has ever done—goes out to help the losers, to show them how to be winners next time. People will work when money profits are not forthcoming! Anyway, say the Russians, there is no reason in a socialist-planned economy why good efforts should not be rewarded by bonuses, premiums, free holidays, etc. All these are common in Russian economic life.

The *Manchester Guardian*, at least, is convinced that the Russians are succeeding in their effort to get people to work without the incentive of profit. On February 20, 1936, an editorial said: "A sceptical world has to admit that collective ownership is surviving, that it has created a new kind of patriotism and new incentives . . . to labour. It may not be the Socialism of the fathers or the prophets, but it works."

To the other argument, that in the absence of competition there would be no incentive to experiment, to take risks, to try new methods, the Russians say, simply, "Look at the record." They argue that nowhere in the world is more money and effort being spent on experimentation in every field. They hold that *because* they have complete control of economic life they can afford to take chances with new ideas and methods which competing industries in capitalist countries often do not dare to do. They are backed up in their arguments on this score by the following sweeping statement of the Webbs: "Far from showing any lack of initiative in great matters or in small; far from any refusal to incur risks in new developments, Soviet Communism has proved to be, in all fields, almost wildly initiating. . . . No student of the U. S. S. R. can fail to be impressed by what seems to be even excess in the desire for change and in the spirit of adventure, in industry, in science, in various forms of art, and in social institutions, as compared even with the United States."

The economists' objection to national planning is along different lines. They argue that where there is national planning there is no free market; the absence of a free market makes a pricing system impossible; the absence of a pricing system means good-bye to a rational economy, because without prices, which register the relative scarcity of goods in relation to the demand for them, your choice of the goods to be produced is bound to be arbitrary and chaotic, and hence uneconomic—you will spend your resources on some things which are less urgently required than other things, because you haven't prices to guide you. Under capitalism, the market price directs, in the long run, the channels of production. Prices go up when more of anything is required, and down when less is required. Which means that things are made or not made, in accordance with people's needs. In the absence of such a pricing system, the economists ask, how are you going to decide where to invest your capital to satisfy the wants of the people?

The national planners answer this criticism by first denying that the price system does what is claimed for it. Prices do not, they argue, move in accordance with what all the people need, but rather in accordance with what some people can pay. The function of the price system, they contend, is merely to satisfy the needs of only those people who have the money to pay for what they want.

The next answer the national planners make is that the market price—most rational use of resources—is considerably upset under capitalism, anyway, what with artificial and controlled prices caused by high tariffs, subsidies, monopolies, etc. So the pure capitalism where everything works smoothly and perfectly under the price mechanism never exists in real life, but only in the books of bourgeois economists. If it did work so nicely there would never be crises.

On the positive side, the national planners argue that they do have a way of having supply meet demand. Gosplan gets monthly, weekly, even daily reports from all over the country, and these register the relationship between what the people need and what they are getting. Suppose the Plan calls for the production of two million pairs of shoes and one-half million new houses. Suppose complaints poured in that there weren't enough shoes while the people were not troubling to move into the new houses. The Plan has a lot of "give," it need not be adhered to rigidly. Labour and capital could be switched from the making of houses to the making of shoes—not all at once, of course, but as fast as in capitalist society.

Nevertheless, there is a point to the question the capitalist critics ask. What will make Gosplan decide to introduce electric coal-cutters rather than automatic looms, when they haven't enough capital for both? The central authority *must* decide the problem of distributing limited resources among competing purposes. The Russians have to admit this. But they contend that even if you can't have both socialist national planning and a free market, and even if the absence of a free-market price doesn't give the most economic use of resources, it gives you a lot of other things. They put security and equality and the absence of exploitation, for the many, over the acquisition of profits, however enormous, for the few; they think a more equal distribution of wealth is better than the "two nations"; they prefer safe, sane, well-ordered living under a planned system to the crises and booms of an unplanned economy.

The breakdown that came in 1929 is often referred to as a world crisis. We are told that the paralysis of production, with its accompanying unemployment and misery of the masses of people, infected every part of the globe. The Russians, however, argue that this is not true. The crisis swept like a tidal wave over all countries but one; it washed against the borders of the Soviet Union—and receded. The Russians were secure behind their dyke of a socialist planned economy.

.   .   .   .

While this chapter was being written, news came of the completion of the new Constitution of the U. S. S. R. The new Constitution was not put into effect immediately. It had first to be submitted to all the people throughout the Soviet Union for discussion, criticism, and amendment. Here are some of the important provisions in the first draft:

"Article 1: The Union of Soviet Socialist Republics is a socialist state of workers and peasants.

"Article 4: The economic foundation of the U. S. S. R. consists in the Socialist ownership of the implements and means of production, firmly established as a result of the liquidation of the capitalist system of economy, the abolition of private ownership of the instruments and means of production, and the abolition of exploitation of man by man.

"Article 11: The economic life of the U. S. S. R. is determined and directed by the national economic State plan for the purposes of increasing public wealth, of a steady rise in the material and cultural level of the toilers, of strengthening the independence of the U. S. S. R. and its defence capacity.

"Article 118: Citizens of the U. S. S. R. have the right to work—
the right to receive guaranteed work, with payment for their work
in accordance with its quantity and quality.

"The right to work is ensured by the socialist organization of national economy, the steady growth of the productive forces of Soviet
society, the absence of economic crises, and the abolition of unemployment."

XXII

Will They Give Up the Sugar?

THE Western World was faced with the paradox of poverty in plenty.

What to do about it?

Something had to be done to bring order out of the chaos created by the breakdown of capitalism. The breakdown was too complete —the credit structure smashed, industry paralyzed, millions of unemployed, farmers down and out, poverty in the midst of plenty— yes, of course, something *had* to be done. The old order was based on *laissez-faire*; the old order had crashed. Changes were called for. Instead of *laissez-faire*—organized regulation and control. Economic life, left to itself, had ended in disaster. It must no longer be left to itself. It must be taken in hand and guided.

"We must plan!"

Faced with the paradox of poverty in plenty, the Western World, like Russia, turned to planning. But there was a difference.

In the Soviet Union there is production for use; in capitalist countries there is production for profit. In the Soviet Union private property in the means of production has been abolished; in capitalist countries private property in the means of production is sacred. In the Soviet Union planning is comprehensive, embracing every sphere of economic activity; in capitalist countries planning is piece-meal, touching one sphere independently of others. In the Soviet

Union planning is designed by consumers for consumers; in capitalist countries planning is designed by producers for producers.

Confronted with the paradox of poverty in plenty, capitalist countries devised a plan for tackling the problem.

The plan was *to abolish the plenty*.

You remember the headlines: "Cotton Plowed Under," "Thousands of Little Pigs Slaughtered," "Wheat Acreage Reduced," "Sugar Plantations Cut Production." All this was done according to plan. The Agricultural Adjustment Administration (AAA) entered into contracts with the thousands of producers of cotton, wheat, corn, hogs, tobacco, sugar, etc., all over the United States; payments were made to these producers if they would curtail their production —that is, if they would fall in with the plan *to abolish the plenty*.

In other countries similar "plans" for destruction or restriction were put into effect. On July 3, 1936, the *New York Times* carried this story from our South American neighbour:

BRAZIL TO DESTROY
30% OF COFFEE CROP
GROWERS TO RECEIVE 5 MILREIS A BAG FOR 6,600,000 SACKS TAKEN BY GOVERNMENT
RIO DE JANEIRO, July 2—Estimating at 22,000,000 bags the 1936-37 coffee crop, plus 4,000,000 to 5,000,000 bags left over from last year's crop, the National Coffee Department has established a quota of thirty per cent to be destroyed. It is paying growers five milreis a bag for coffee destroyed.

Across the ocean, in Europe, the same story. This one, from England, was first-page news:

BRITISH TO CUT PRODUCTION IN U. S. MANNER; BILL CURBS TEXTILE OUTPUT TO RAISE PRICES
by CHARLES A. SELDEN.
LONDON, Feb. 4—With the passage in the House of Commons tonight on the second reading of a bill to eliminate superfluous cotton spindles . . . Great Britain is now setting out on President Roosevelt's policy of reducing production by law, for the sake of better prices. . . .
There have been other attempts in this country to get rid of surplus—in shipping and in the coal industry, for example—but the previous efforts had no statutory force behind them. This is now provided by the Cotton Spindles Bill, which sets up a government board with the right to buy and take out of commission spindles that are in excess of what is deemed

> necessary for the best interests of the cotton industry as a whole. . . .
>
> According to tentative estimates, about 10,-000,000 spindles, or about a quarter of those now in use, will be eliminated. . . .
>
> Most Lancashire manufacturers favor the bill, but it is opposed by workers and by Labor members of Parliament, on the ground that it makes no provision for those who are in danger of losing their jobs by its operation.

But why?

What is the purpose of all these plans to abolish plenty?

Laissez-faire capitalism, you remember, had for its purpose the making of profits. *Laissez-faire* capitalism broke down and attempts at planning were made. The purpose of planned capitalism is the same—the making of profits. In an economy of abundance, where production outstrips consumption, this can be done only by restricting supply. The creation of more goods for consumption would lower prices; restriction of production, on the other hand, raises prices and so increases profits. So capitalist planning is scarcity planning.

Because that is true there is some justification in this crack at the New Deal by Stolberg and Vinton: "There is nothing the New Deal has so far done that could not have been done better by an earthquake. A first-rate earthquake, from coast to coast, could have reestablished scarcity much more effectively, and put all the survivors to work for the greater glory of Big Business—with far more speed and far less noise than the New Deal."

Capitalist planning has another distinguishing characteristic. It is piecemeal planning.

While the NRA was functioning in Washington there was an amusing—and instructive—story going the rounds about Oscar Ameringer, the astute editor of *The American Guardian*. He was an interested observer of the morning's work in the office of one of the important officials of the NRA. He watched a steady stream of industrialists pour in with their stories of business collapse; he listened to the "plans" that were formulated to put life into the corpse. After watching this in silence for a few hours, he could contain himself no longer. He jumped up and shouted to the planning official, "The patient is suffering with the smallpox and you are treating each individual pimple!"

Mr. Ameringer felt that there was a need for comprehensive planning of the entire national economy. Instead, he found that there was a "plan to aid the shipping industry," a "plan to help the farmers," a "plan to increase the purchasing power of the workers." There was nothing in America—or in any other country—even remotely resembling the Russian Plan which consciously attempts to fit all the thousand and one economic activities of the nation into one self-consistent whole.

This is possible in Russia only because private property in the means of production has been abolished. Where a planning authority has no right to do this, that, or the other thing, because by so doing it will tread on the toes of Mr. Property-owner, comprehensive planning is impossible. A decision made by Gosplan in the Soviet Union is effective because it is made on behalf of one organization, the entire Soviet national economy, which has no competitors or rivals. A decision made by a planning authority in a capitalist country is ineffective because if it favours one group of property-owners, say the importers of sugar from Cuba, it is opposed by another group of property-owners, the growers of American sugar. And since the state authority has no power to compel obedience, it must wobble about, now giving a bite to one group, now to another.

Mrs. Barbara Wootton in her *Plan or No Plan* shows what happens to planning when the means of production remain private property: "So long as the instruments of production and the products thereof are the property of private persons interested in the financial results of operating those instruments and selling those products, the major economic decisions must be made, firm by firm, or industry by industry, in accordance with the view taken by those persons of the course most advantageous to their own industry or firm. . . . The output of steel will be planned to make a paradise for the steel plants, the output of beer will be planned to make a brewers' paradise, the output of pictures will be planned to make heaven on earth for the artists, and the final upshot may fairly be described as a community more planned against than planning."

If private property stands in the way of central planning when it is in the interests of the capitalists themselves, how much more liable is it to prevent planning action in the interests of the whole nation! Take as one example the matter of slum clearance. Everybody is agreed that the slums ought to be done away with. Well then, why aren't they? What stands in the way of this obvious public necessity? The answer is simple. Private property—individual profit. There are some landlords who make money out of the rents of slum dwellings; there are other landlords whose rents would go down if new and better houses were erected for the occupants of slums. So slum clearance is blocked. Or if it is undertaken, it is done haltingly, slowly, never completely. Thus community benefit is hindered by private-property interests.

How differently this works out in the planned economy of socialist society! The planners have before them a map of a city. One section is shaded—the slums where people live in wretched unhealthy conditions. What is to be done? The slums must be removed. O.K. Run a pencil across the shaded area. Cross it out. Down with the slums! The work begins at once. Where private property does not stand in the way action can follow as soon as the need is felt and the plans are made.

Where private property does stand in the way, then what is to its interest is put first and what is to the national interest can go hang. This was deplored by the *London Times* in an editorial on August 28, 1935. The *Times* was concerned about the fact that manufacturing industry was moving from the north of England where there were plenty of unemployed in need of jobs, to the south, where "rural beauties" would be ruined by the encroachment of new factories "on field and farm and wood." Here is the *Times'* lament: "There is no unifying direction to establish where the fundamental, although obscured, national interest lies when industrial places and populations are left economically desolate while other places and other populations are being enriched and increased by new industrialization. . . .

"If inventive genius should make possible the development of a new industry capable of employing a large number of men and not tied to a locality by the conditions of production, then it would be socially advantageous for the industry to find its home in the depressed areas. *Social advantages, however, might have no weight with those who would in fact decide where the industry should be established."*

There's the rub. On every front what is for the good of the community may be hamstrung by the interests of private property. To some people this doesn't matter. They argue that the advantages of private ownership and control of the means of production outweigh the disadvantages. They point to capitalism's amazing success in the last 150 years in producing such an enormous quantity and variety of goods, and in establishing (particularly in the United States) such an unprecedented high living standard for the mass of the population. In the following ringing declaration, part of its "Platform for American Industry," the National Association of Manufacturers ties its flag to the mast of private property: "Private ownership and control of the facilities of production, distribution and living are recognized as essential to the preservation of individual liberty and progress. Ownership or control of these facilities by government make for a planned economy, a static society and autocracy. . . .

"National economic planning by government seeks to balance production and consumption by centralizing decisions in the hands of a few. Economic and social progress has made the greatest advance where enterprise has been directed by an infinite number of individual judgments and decisions, thus utilizing the skill, intelligence, and knowledge of the whole people. No small group of men can possess the wisdom, foresight, and discernment required to plan, direct, and stimulate successfully the activities of all the people. . . ."

That last sentence, coming, as it does, from manufacturers who within their own industries are acknowledged as perhaps the greatest planners in the world, is indeed a surprise. Here are captains of industry who have performed miracles of organization and planning in businesses which, taken separately, have more capital resources than many nations of the world, businesses whose ramifications spread over the globe; here they are—the leading planning experts in the leading capitalist country, arguing so strenuously against doing for all the nation's industry what they have so skilfully done for their own.

Why are capitalists so opposed to a national planned economy?

Is it because they realize that a national planned economy means inevitably the abolition of private property—their private property? This is what Mr. G. D. H. Cole suggests in his book on *The Principles of Economic Planning*: "A great many capitalists . . . regard those of their fellow-capitalists who do advocate a planned system as dangerous heretics. . . . Most articulate capitalist leaders vigorously defend a planless economy because they regard it, whatever its faults, as the only reliable upholder of the rights of property."

And Stolberg and Vinton drive home the same point in their caustic style: "To rest secure in its anti-social control of industry in order to be free to make decisions against the rest of us in its own favour, Big Ownership cannot possibly arbitrate its control of society. . . . The Weirs, the Teagles, and the Sloans realize that they must sabotage even the most confused efforts toward 'social planning.' For all their social brutishness and economic ignorance, they sense—and are quite right—that authentic social planning means socialist construction, not capitalist 'recovery.'"

Perhaps another explanation of capitalist opposition to national planning is that such planning must, of necessity, make the question of the distribution of income a live issue. In capitalist theory the distribution of income, no matter how unequal was justified as a result of "natural law." Of this we were assured by one of the leading American economists, Professor John Bates Clark. In the Preface to his famous book, *The Distribution of Wealth,* Professor Clark wrote: "It is the purpose of this work to show that the distribution of the income of society is controlled by a natural law, and that this law, if it worked without friction, would give to every agent of production the amount of wealth which that agent creates. . . .

"Free competition tends to give to labour what labour creates, to capitalists what capital creates, and to entrepreneurs what the co-ordinating function creates. . . . To each agent a distinguishable share in production, to each a corresponding reward—such is the natural law of distribution."

Confronted with the charge that the distribution of income was grossly unfair, capitalists could shrug their shoulders and say, "Why pick on us? Everyone gets what he earns. It's a natural law." But in a national planned economy the question of the distribution of income is not so lightly dismissed. It becomes a red-hot issue, no longer determined by impersonal forces, but an important task of the central coordinating authority. And in democratic countries where that authority would be influenced by the sentiment of the mass of people, there is no doubt that the wide gap in income distribution in existence today would be considerably lessened. For the masses more income; for the capitalists less income—according to plan.

For these reasons it is not to be wondered that the leaders of the opposition to any such development are the capitalists.

Yet in certain countries they cannot help themselves; the break-down of economic life is so extensive and the onward march of the working class becomes so threatening, that the capitalists see the need for a central coordinating authority—but they make sure that it is *their* authority, acting in *their* interests. This can be accomplished only by crushing the militant forces of the working class. Hence the capitalists resort to Fascism.

In Russia the working-class revolution had been successful. But the disillusionment, starvation, and misery following the disastrous World War drove many new recruits into the ranks of the revolutionary-minded, everywhere. With opportunities for improving their lot decreasing rapidly, the middle classes, too, became discontented.

The established order, though not overthrown, was definitely tottering.

This was particularly true in Italy and Germany. The capitalists in these countries were faced with a revolutionary working class which threatened their power. So they gave money and aid to Mussolini's Blackshirts and Hitler's Brownshirts—in return for favours to come. The big favour was to be the crushing of the organized working-class movement. And both leaders delivered the goods. The Fascism that came to Italy and the National Socialism that came to Germany were thus counter-revolutionary movements. The established order—capitalist power and privilege—was secure.

It was a difficult job. The propaganda which was to sidetrack the socialist-minded mass had to be skilful. It was. The line of the National Socialist German Workers' Party was baited with socialist catchwords to hook the discontented. Here, for example, are three extracts from the famous Nazi program of 25 points:

"Point 11. Abolition of incomes unearned by work.

"Point 12. Ruthless confiscation of all war gains.

"Point 13. We demand nationalization of all businesses which have been up to the present formed into companies (Trusts)."

That was the promise. Was it carried out? Let us look at the answer given by the Berlin correspondent of *The Economist* (London) on February 1, 1936: "The relative tranquillity of the past year, however, was attained by an attitude of masterly inactivity toward the Party program, the vigorous prosecution of which would have precipitated dangerous conflicts between interests. . . . The issue of Socialism v. Capitalism, which once attracted to the Party a great many have-nots, has degenerated into a mere exchange of unmeaning catchwords. On the one hand, it is affirmed that Socialism is under way (indeed this week it is officially stated to have already replaced Capitalism), while at the same time it is asserted that private capital, in land as well as in industry, must not only remain intact, but must be made profit-making."

It can be stated in defence of the Nazi regime that three years of power are too short to put into effect the sweeping promises of their program. That is a legitimate argument. But the drift is unmistakable. Three years of power was time enough for the Nazis to smash the trade unions, seize their funds, and clap their leaders into jail. Three years of power was time enough for the Nazis to reduce wages and cut social services—in short, to distribute the national income in accordance with the desires of Big Business.

From Italy comes a similar story. Here is Mussolini's latest pronouncement on the glories of Fascism. There have been similar ones before: "In this economy the workers are to become collaborators of capital with equal rights and equal duties."

These are the words. What is the reality? Let us turn to John Gunther's *Inside Europe* for a clue. "Indeed, one may assemble a seemingly impressive list of anti-capitalist forces in the corporate state. No employer may discharge labour without government consent. No capitalist may undertake such comparatively minor independent activity as, say, enlarging his factory, without state approval. Wages are determined by the government. . . . A factory-owner may not liquidate his business without state permission; the government controls his sources of credit; and it takes a large share of his income in Draconian taxation.

"On the other hand, the disadvantages to labour under Fascism are infinitely more severe. Workers have lost their right to bargain; their trade unions have been dissolved . . . their wages may be (and have been) mercilessly deflated by decree; above all, they have lost the right to strike. The capitalist, on the other hand, even if he has suffered inconvenience, maintains his fundamental privilege, that of earning private profits. Fascism as Mussolini introduced it was not, probably, a *deliberate* artifice for propping up the capitalist structure, but it had that effect. The restriction on the mobility of capitalism was in effect 'a premium which the capitalists were willing to pay in order to get full security against the demands of labour.' The whole colour and tempo of the Fascist revolution, in contrast to that in Russia, is backward."

Mussolini blusters phrases about "equal rights and equal duties," but Mr. Gunther's picture of actual happenings is quite different.

Some capitalist privileges have been curtailed—but the fundamental right to earn private profits remains. Labour, on the other hand, has had its trade unions dissolved, its right to strike abolished, and its wages lowered.

Nevertheless, it is obvious that something significant is happening in both Italy and Germany to Capital, as well as to Labour. In both countries a strong state authority is dictating to capitalists in an unusual fashion. Though private property has not been abolished and industry still has profit as its guiding motive, it is true that individual capitalists are, in a sense, having their wings clipped. To what end are capitalist privileges being restricted? What is behind the aid to agriculture, the drive for self-sufficiency, the rigid control of imports, the subsidizing of exports, and the commandeering of banking resources that has been going on in both Fascist countries? The answer is short and horrible—WAR.

It is obvious to everybody that rearmament, preparation for war, is the driving motive behind the feverish activity of the state authority; this is not denied by the leaders of either Fascist government—on the contrary, it is an open boast.

Both Mussolini and Hitler are on record as admirers of war. Listen to Mussolini on the subject: "Above all, Fascism . . . believes neither in the possibility nor in the utility of perpetual peace. . . . War alone brings up to its highest tension all human energy, and puts the stamp of nobility upon the peoples who have the courage to meet it. . . . Thus a doctrine which is founded upon this harmful postulate of peace is hostile to Fascism."

But those are words again, and we have learned to be distrustful of writings from this source. What does the record show?

That was written in 1933. In 1935 and 1936 Fascist armies were invading Ethiopia. *This* promise was performed.

Now listen to Hitler on the same subject: "In eternal warfare mankind has become great—in eternal peace mankind would be ruined."

At the moment of writing, the Nazi armies are not on the march, but that they will be before long is evident to everyone. Germany presents the frightening spectacle of a nation forced to bend every effort, to undergo painful sacrifices, to direct every activity, toward rearmament—and the war to follow. The correspondent of the *New York Times* put the whole thing in a nutshell in a dispatch to his paper on March 22, 1936: "Fundamentally the German economic situation revolves around the issue of how to finance rearmament. . . ."

Fascism means war.

It means war not merely because the leaders in both Fascist countries like to fight; it means war because Fascist economy is capitalist economy with the same necessity for expansion, the same drive for markets, which is characteristic of capitalism in its period of imperialism.

When capitalist economy breaks down and the working class marches toward power, then the capitalists turn to Fascism as the way out. But Fascism cannot solve their problem, because in it, from an economic point of view, nothing fundamental is changed. In Fascist economy, as in capitalist economy, private ownership of the means of production, and the profit motive, are basic.

Is there a moral for capitalists in Arthur Morgan's story of how the East Indians catch monkeys? "According to the story, they take a coconut and cut a hole in it barely big enough for the monkey's empty hand to pass through. In it they place some lumps of sugar and then fasten the coconut to a tree. The monkey squeezes his hand inside the coconut and grasps the sugar and then tries to draw out his fist. But the hole is not large enough for his closed fist to go through, and greed is his undoing, for he will never give up the prize."

Appendix

CHAPTER I

Page 4, line 2. P. Boissonnade, *Life and Work in Medieval Europe (fifth to fifteenth centuries)*, p. 146. Alfred A. Knopf, N. Y., 1927.
Page 6, line 35. *Ibid.*, p. 146.
Page 7, line 25. *Ibid.*, p. 136.
Page 9, line 3. J. W. Thompson, *An Economic and Social History of the Middle Ages, 300-1300*, p. 730. The Century Company, N. Y., 1928.
    Line 8. *English Economic History, Select Documents*, p. 72. Compiled and edited by A. E. Bland, P. A. Brown, and R. H. Tawney. G. Bell & Sons, London, 1914.
    Line 18. *Ibid.*, p. 66.
Page 10, line 26. *Translations and Reprints from the Original Sources of European History*, vol. IV, Section III, p. 22. Series for 1897. Department of History of the University of Pennsylvania, Philadelphia, 1898.
Page 11, line 28. J. H. Robinson, *Readings in European History*, vol. I, p. 177. Ginn and Company, Boston, 1904.
Page 12, line 7. *Translations and Reprints, op. cit., p.* 31.
    Line 29. *Translations and Reprints, op. cit.,* p. 24.
Page 13, line 2. Bland, Brown, and Tawney, *op. cit.,* p. 29.
    Line 7. *Translations and Reprints, op. cit.,* p. 26.
    Line 24. *Translations and Reprints, op. cit.,* p. 21.
Page 14, line 20. J. H. Robinson, *op. cit.,* vol. I, p. 178.
    Line 26. *Ibid.*
Page 15, line 4. Cf. J. W. Thompson, *op. cit.,* pp. 656 ff.
    Line 12. G. G. Coulton, quoted in J. W. Thompson, *op. cit.,* p. 652.
    Line 19. *Ibid.*, p. 681.
Page 16, line 5. P. Boissonnade, *op. cit.,* p. 131.

CHAPTER II

Page 19, line 1. J. W. Thompson, *op. cit.,* p. 710.
    Line 29. Cf. H. W. C. Davis, *Medieval Europe*, pp. 184-187. Thornton Butterworth, Ltd., London. 11th edition, 1930.
Page 20, line 17. J. H. Robinson, *op. cit.,* p. 314, footnote.
Page 22, line 8. *Translations and Reprints, op. cit.,* vol. III, Section I. Series for 1896.
Page 23, line 34. A. Thierry, *Recueil des Monuments Inédits de l'histoire du tiers état*, vol. III, p. 643. Paris, 1856.
Page 24, line 22. *Ordonnances des Roys de France de la Troisième Race. Recueillies pa. ordre chronologique*, vol. II, p. 309. A Paris, de l'imprimerie royale, 1729.
Page 25, line 30. S. Poignant, *La Foire de Lille*, p. 179. E. Raoust, Lille, 1932.

Chapter III

Page 28, line 22. Cf. H. Pirenne, "The Stages in the Social History of Capitalism," in *The American Historical Review*, vol. XIX, April 1914. The Macmillan Company, N. Y., 1914.
Page 29, line 32. *A Source Book of Medieval History*, pp. 328 ff., edited by F. A. Ogg. American Book Company, N. Y., 1907.
Page 30, line 11. *Ibid.*
Page 31, line 26. *Dortmunder Urkundenbuch*, Bd. 1, pp. 33, 269-271, bearbeitet von Karl Rübel. Dortmund, 1881.
Page 32, line 32. H. Pirenne, *Medieval Cities*, p. 177. Princeton University Press, 1925. I have followed this book closely for much of the material on towns.
Page 33, line 22. A. Luchaire, *Les communes française a l'epoque des Capetiens Directs*, p. 112. Hachette et Cie., Paris, 1890.
Page 34, line 7. A. Thierry, *op. cit.*, vol. IV, pp. 170, 171.
Line 27. Charles Gross, *The Gild Merchant*, vol. I, pp. 39-40. 2 vols. Clarendon Press, Oxford, 1890.
Page 35, line 2. *Ibid.*, vol. I, p. 48.
Line 27. *Ibid.*, vol. II, p. 195.
Page 36, line 7. *Ibid.*, vol. I, p. 36, footnote.

Chapter IV

Page 39, line 18. *Tudor Economic Documents*, vol. II, p. 142. Edited by R. H. Tawney and E. Power. 3 vols. Longmans, Green and Company, London, 1924.
Page 40, line 26. Matthew 16:26.
Page 41, line 11. *Ibid.*, 19:24.
Page 41, line 17. Quoted in R. H. Tawney, *Religion and the Rise of Capitalism*, p. 36. Harcourt, Brace and Company, N. Y., 1926.
Page 43, line 28. *Early Economic Thought*, pp. 113, 114. Edited by A. E. Monroe. Harvard University Press, 1924.

Chapter V

Page 45, line 9. E. O. Schulze, *Kolonisierung und Germanisierung der Gebiete Zwischen Saale und Elbe*, p. 125. Hirzel, Leipzig, 1896.
Line 24. P. Boissonnade, *op. cit.*, p. 229.
Page 46, line 24. O. J. Thatcher and E. H. McNeal, *Source Book for Medieval History*, pp. 572, 573. Charles Scribner's Sons, N. Y., 1905.
Page 48, line 29. T. W. Page, *End of Villainage in England*, pp. 54, 55. American Economic Association, N. Y., 1900.
Line 35. *Ibid.*, p. 41.
Page 49, line 20. C. G. Coulton, *The Medieval Village*, pp. 147, 148. Cambridge University Press, 1925.
Line 25. *Ibid.*, p. 148.
Page 50, line 2. F. Pollock and F. W. Maitland, *History of English Law Before the Time of Edward I*, vol. I, pp. 378, 379. Cambridge University Press.
Page 51, line 16. *Stories of Boccaccio, The Decameron*, pp. 1, 2. Translated into English by John Payne. The Bibliophilist Library, 1903.

Line 31. Quoted in J. Kulischer, *Allgemeine Wirtschaftsgeschichte des Mittelalters und der Neuzeit*, vol. I, p. 129. Oldenbourg, Berlin, 1928. (My italics.)
Page 54, line 6. Bland, Brown, and Tawney, *op. cit.*, p. 105.
Line 31. Page, *op. cit.*, p. 85.

CHAPTER VI

Page 59, line 7. Bland, Brown, and Tawney, *op. cit.*, p. 136.
Line 34. Cf. J. Kulischer, *op. cit.*, vol. I, p. 192.
Page 60, line 12. F. Philippi, *Die Aeltesten Osnabrückischen Gildeurkunden (bis 1500)*, pp. 75-76. Kisling, Osnabrück, 1890.
Line 32. G. Renard, *Guilds in the Middle Ages*, p. 36. G. Bell & Sons, Ltd., London, 1918.
Page 61, line 9. Thierry, *op. cit.*, p. 540.
Line 28. *Memorials of London and London Life in the XIIIth, XIVth, and XVth Centuries*, p. 146. Selected, translated and edited by H. T. Riley. Longmans, Green and Company, London, 1868.
Page 62, line 25. Monroe, *op. cit.*, p. 54, 55.
Page 63, line 5. R. H. Tawney, *op. cit.*, p. 55.
Line 19. W. J. Ashley, *An Introduction to English Economic History and Theory*, Book II, p. 60. 2 vols. G. P. Putnam's Sons, N. Y., 1913.
Page 65, line 13. V. Brants, *Les Théories Economiques aux XIIIᵉ et XIVᵉ Siècles*, p. 69, Peeters, Louvain, 1895.
Page 66, line 12. G. Renard, *op. cit.*, p. 29.
Line 26. K. von Hegel, *Städte und Gilden der germanischen Völker im Mittelalter* vol. II, p. 315. 2 vols. Duncker u. Humblot, Leipzig, 1891.
Line 31. *Ibid.*, p. 452.
Page 67, line 14. Thierry, *op. cit.*, vol. 2, p. 5.
Line 17. Renard, *op. cit.*, p. 39.
Line 29. *Ibid.*, p. 19.
Page 68, line 11. Bland, Brown, and Tawney, *op. cit.*, pp. 139-141.
Line 20. *Recueil Général des anciennes Lois Françaises*, vol. XII, Part 2, pp. 763-765. Edited by MM. Jourdan, Decrusy, Isambert. Plon Frères, Paris.
Line 30. *Ibid.*
Page 69, line 9. Bland, Brown, and Tawney, *op. cit.*, pp. 165, 166.
Line 18. *Ordonnances, op. cit.*, p. 367.

CHAPTER VII

Page 75, line 8. *Memorials of London and London Life, op. cit.*, pp. 208-210.
Line 17. *The Statutes of the Realm from Original Records and Authentic Manuscripts*. vol. II, p. 63. London, 1816.
Page 76, line 7. *Ordonnances des Roys de France de la Troisième Race, op. cit.*, vol. XI (1782), pp. 306-313.
Line 30. G. Schmoller, *The Mercantile System and Its Historical Significance*, p. 22. The Macmillan Company, N. Y., 1910.
Page 77, line 12. *Statutes of the Realm, op. cit.*, vol. II, pp. 298-299.
Line 25. *Documents Relatifs a l'histoire de L'Industrie et du Commerce en France*, vol. II, pp. 123-124. Publiés par M. G. Fagniez. Picard, Paris, 1898. vol. II, 1900.
Page 78, line 22. P. Boissonnade, *Le Socialisme d'Etat (1453-1661)*, pp. 9-10. Champion, Paris, 1927.

APPENDIX

Page 79, line 12. *Tudor Economic Documents, op. cit.,* vol. II, p. 31.

Line 35. Lang, *The Maid of France,* p. 165. Longmans, Green and Company, London, 1929.

Page 80, line 7. *Ibid.,* p. 110.

Line 27. G. B. Shaw, *Saint Joan,* Scene 4.

Page 81, line 29. G. G. Coulton, *Encyclopaedia Britannica,* vol. XIX, p. 34. 14th Edition. Article on the Reformation.

Line 35. *Ibid.*

Page 82, line 3. G. G. Coulton, *op. cit.,* p. 301.

Page 83, line 2. J. H. Robinson, *op. cit.,* vol. I, pp. 375-377.

Line 25. J. S. Shapiro, *Social Reform and the Reformation,* p. 78. Columbia University Press, 1909.

Line 29. *Ibid.,* p. 80.

Line 35. *Ibid.,* pp. 85, 86.

Page 84, line 15. *Address to the German Nobility.* Buchheim's translation in Harvard Classics, vol. 36, p. 281.

Line 27. *Ibid.,* pp. 292, 293.

Page 85, line 11. Cf. W. Cunningham, *Western Civilization in Its Economic Aspects (Medieval and Modern Times).* Cambridge University Press, 1913.

Line 21. Cf. F. Engels, *Socialism, Utopian and Scientific,* pp. 24, 25. Kerr edition.

Chapter VIII

Page 87, line 26. E. Levasseur, *Histoire des classes ourvrières et de L'industrie en France avant 1789.* 2 vols. vol. I, p. 685. Rousseau, Paris, 1900, 1901.

Page 88, line 6. Monroe, pp. 92, 95.

Line 12. R. Cantillon, *Essai sur la Nature du Commerce en Général* (1755), p. 113. Edited with an English translation by H. Higgs. Macmillan & Company, Ltd., London, 1931.

Line 24. *Traictie de la première Invention des Monnoies de Nicole Oresme et Traité de la Monnoie de Copernic,* publiés et annotés par M. L. Wolowski, p. 49. Guillaumin, Paris, 1864.

Page 89, line 7. Monroe, *op. cit.,* pp. 97-98.

Line 32. Statutes of the Realm, *op. cit.,* vol. II, p. 454.

Page 90, line 7. Recueil Général, *op. cit.,* vol. XII, part 1, pp. 179-183.

Page 94, line 3. Cf. W. R. Scott, *The Constitution and Finance of English, Scottish and Irish Joint Stock Companies to 1720.* 3 vols. vol. I, p. 81. Cambridge, 1910-1912.

Line 13. *The Fugger News Letters.* Edited by V. Von Klarwill. Translated by P. de Chary. 1st series, 1924; 2nd series, 1926. 2nd series, No. 11. Bodley Head, London.

Page 95, line 11. W. Cunningham, *op. cit.,* vol. II, p. 175.

Page 96, line 14. R. Ehrenberg, *Capital and Finance in the Age of the Renaissance,* p. 80. Harcourt, Brace and Company, Inc., N. Y.

Page 97, line 11. C. J. Hayes, *A Political and Social History of Modern Europe.* 2 vols. p. 66, footnote. The Macmillan Company, N. Y. Revised edition, 1921.

Page 98, line 31. Levasseur, *op. cit.,* vol. II, p. 45.

Page 99, line 3. Cantillon, *op. cit.,* p. 257.

Chapter IX

Page 100, line 10. G. Renard and G. Weulersse, *Life and Work in Modern Europe (Fifteenth to Eighteenth Centuries),* p. 287. Alfred A. Knopf, N. Y., 1926.

Page 101, line 2. Quoted in Hayes, *op. cit.*, p. 229.

Page 103, line 7. *La Réponse de Jean Bodin à M. de Malestroit* (1568). Nouvelle edition par H. Hauser. Colin, Paris, 1932. Introduction, p. 16.

Line 34. *A Discourse of the Common Weal of This Realm of England* (1581), p. 19. Edited by Elizabeth Lamond. Cambridge Univ. Press, 1893.

Page 104, line 9. Bodin, *op. cit.*, p. 9.

Line 20. *Tudor Economic Documents, op. cit.*, vol. III, pp. 386, 387.

Line 30. Cantillon, *op. cit.*, pp. 159, 161.

Page 106, line 2. J. E. Thorold Rogers. *Six Centuries of Work and Wages*, pp. 389-392. G. P. Putnam's Sons, N. Y., 1884.

Line 15. *Urkundenbuch der Stadt Halberstadt*, vol. I, p. 523, Bearbeitet von G. Schmidt. Halle, 1878.

Page 109, line 5. Bland, Brown, and Tawney, *op. cit.*, pp. 255-258.

Page 110, line 10. *Ibid.*, pp. 252-253.

Line 17. Quoted in E. P. Cheyney, *Social Changes in England in the 16th Century*, p. 45. Ginn and Company, Boston, 1895.

Line 28. R. Crowley, *Select Works*. Introduction, p. XXII. Ed. by J. M. Cowper, Early English Text Society. London, 1872.

CHAPTER X

Page 112, line 23. Cf. G. Unwin, *Industrial Organization in the Sixteenth and Seventeenth Centuries*, p. 10. Clarendon Press, Oxford, 1904.

Page 113, line 23. W. Petty, *Economic Writings,* vol. I, p. 260. Edited by C. H. Hull, 2 vols. Cambridge University Press, 1899.

Page 115, line 10. M. Dobb, *Capitalist Enterprise and Social Progress*, p. 310. Routledge & Sons, London, 1925.

Line 21. E. Thurkauf, *Verlag und Heimarbeit in der Basler Seidenbandindustrie*, pp. 12-13. Kohlhammer, Stuttgart, 1909.

Page 116, line 13. Daniel Defoe, *A Tour Thro' the Whole Island of Great Britain* (1724-1726), 2. vols. vol. II, p. 602. Peter Davies, London, 1927.

Line 27. Defoe, *op. cit.*, vol. I, pp. 282, 290.

Page 120, line 46. *Report on Homework in the Fabricated Metal Industry in Connecticut*, State Department of Labor, Minimum Wage Division. Hartford, Conn. September, 1934.

CHAPTER XI

Page 123, line 25. Adam Smith, *Inquiry into the Nature and Causes of the Wealth of Nations* (1776), vol. I, p. 396. Edited with an Introduction by E. Cannan. 2 vols. Methuen & Co., London, 1930.

Line 32. Quoted by J. Viner in "English Theories of Foreign Trade Before Adam Smith" in *The Journal of Political Economy*, vol. 38, June, 1930, No. 3, p. 277. University of Chicago Press.

Page 124, line 8. *Tudor Economic Documents, op. cit.*, vol. II, pp. 177, 178.

Line 20. *The Fugger News Letters, op. cit.*, 1st series, nos. 176, 209.

Page 125, line 7. *Tudor Economic Documents, op. cit.*, p. 321.

Line 33. T. Mun, *England's Treasure by Forraign Trade* (1664), pp. 7-8, 52. The Macmillan Company, N. Y., 1895.

Page 126, line 16. L. Memmert, *Die öffentliche Forderung der gewerblichen Produktionsmethoden zur Zeit des Merkantilismus in Bayern*, p. 28. Noske, Leipzig, 1930.

APPENDIX

Page 127, line 5. Quoted by J. Viner, *op. cit.*, August, 1930, p. 417.

Line 29. P. Boissonnade, *Colbert*, p. 292. Rivière, Paris, 1932.

Page 128, line 26. *Tudor Economic Documents*, *op. cit.*, vol. I, p. 249.

Page 129, line 3. *Recueil Général*, *op. cit.*, vol. 16, pp. 18-21.

Page 130, line 7. *Recueil Général*, *op. cit.*, vol. 15, pp. 283-287.

Line 16. T. Manley, *A Discourse Shewing That the Exportation of Wooll is Destructive to this Kingdom*, p. 3. London, 1677.

Page 132, line 19. Bland, Brown, and Tawney, *op. cit.*, pp. 670, 671.

Page 134, line 6. Quoted in Charles and Mary Beard, *The Rise of American Civilization*. The Macmillan Company, N. Y., 1933. (My italics.) Revised edition, vol. I, p. 115.

Page 135, line 18. Savary des Bruslons, *Universal Dictionary of Trade and Commerce, translated from the French with Additions and Improvements by Malachy Postelthwayt*, 2nd ed. 2 vols. vol. II, p. 6, article on labor. London, 1757.

Line 26. A. J. Sargent, *Economic Policy of Colbert*, pp. 78, 79. Longmans, Green and Co., London, 1899.

Page 136, line 6. Quoted in C. J. H. Hayes, *Essays on Nationalism*, p. 37. The Macmillan Company, N. Y., 1926.

CHAPTER XII

Page 138, line 23. G. Hinrichs, *Die Wollindustrie in Peussen*, pp. 377, 378. Parey, Berlin, 1933.

Page 139, line 20. Journals of the House of Commons, vol. 75, 1819-1820, May 8, 1920.

Page 140, line 8. N. Barbon, *A Discourse of Trade* (1690), p. 35. Reprinted and edited by J. H. Hollander. Johns Hopkins Press, Baltimore, 1905.

Line 22. D. North, *Discourses Upon Trade* (1691), pp. 12-13. Reprint edited by J. H. Hollander. Baltimore, 1907.

Line 29. J. Tucker, *Brief Essay on the Advantages and Disadvantages Which Respectively Attend France and Great Britain with Regard to Trade*, p. 25. London, 1749.

Page 141, line 4. *Ibid.*, p. 28.

Line 17. D. Hume, *Essays Moral, Political and Literary*. Edited by T. H. Green and T. H. Grose, p. 309. Longmans, Green and Co., London, 1875. Essays first published in 1742.

Page 142, line 33. Cf. Renard and Weubersse, *op. cit.*, pp. 180-182.

Page 143, line 19. E. Cannan, *A Review of Economic Theory*, pp. 26-27. P. S. King & Co., London, 1929.

Page 144, line 4. *Carl Friedrichs von Baden brieflicker Verkehr mit Mirabeau und Du Pont*, vol. I, p. 27. Bearbeitet von C. Knies, Heidelberg, 1892.

Line 26. Le Mercier de la Rivière, *L'Ordre Naturel et Essentiel des Sociétés Politiques*, 1767, p. 24. Publié par E. Depetre. Geuthner, Paris, 1910.

Line 35. C. Knies, *op. cit.*, p. 32.

Page 145, line 30. *Wealth of Nations*, *op. cit.*, vol. 2, p. 176.

Page 146, line 10. *Ibid.*, vol. 1, p. 407.

Line 17. *Ibid.*, vol. 2, p. 111.

Page 147, line 23. *Ibid.*, vol. 1, pp. 6, 7.

Page 148, line 2. *Ibid.*, vol. 1, p. 19.

Page 149, line 10. *Ibid.*, vol. 2, p. 184.

CHAPTER XIII

Page 151, line 15. C. D. Hazen, *The French Revolution*, vol. I, pp. 128, 129. Henry Holt and Company, Inc., N. Y., 1932.

Page 152, line 11. Cf. *Cambridge Modern History*, vol. VIII, p. 72.

Page 153, line 9. A. de Tocqueville, *The State of Society in France before the Revolution of 1789*, pp. 54, 55. Translated by H. Reeve. Murray, London, 1856.

Page 154, line 22. Cf. L. Madelin, *The French Revolution*, 3rd edition, 1922, p. 11. William Heinemann, London.

Page 156, line 3. A. Mathiez, *The French Revolution*, p. 13. Alfred A. Knopf, N. Y., 1928. Line 29. L. Madelin, *op. cit.*, pp. 11, 12.

Page 157, line 7. E. J. Sieyès, *Qu'Est-ce Que Le Tiers État?* (1789). Published by Société de L'Histoire De La Révolution Française. Paris, 1888.
Line 33. History of the Working Class, Lesson I, Course 2 (pamphlet), pp. 40, 41. International Publishers, N. Y.

Page 159, line 4. Karl Marx, *The Eighteenth Brumaire of Louis Bonaparte* (1852), p. 24. Translated by Eden and Cedar Paul. Allen and Unwin, London, 1926.

Page 160, line 2. Ralph Broome, *Strictures on Mr. Burke's Two Letters*, p. 4. Printed by John Thompson, Philadelphia, 1797.

CHAPTER XIV

Page 165, line 15. J. A. Hobson, *The Evolution of Modern Capitalism* (1894). Revised edition 1926, p. 11. Walter Scott Publishing Co., Ltd., London.
Line 32. Karl Marx, *Capital* (1867), translated from the third German edition by Samuel Moore and Edward Aveling, and edited by Frederick Engels, vol. I, p. 775. Wm. Glaisher, Ltd., London, 1918.

Page 166, line 18. Quoted in K. Marx, *op. cit.*, p. 776.
Line 28. Karl Marx, *op. cit.*, p. 777.

Page 167, line 11. W. Howitt, *Colonization and Christianity*, pp. 296, 297. Longman, Orme, Brown, Green and Longmans, London, 1838.
Line 31. H. Merivale, *Lectures on Colonization and Colonies* (delivered in 1839, 1840 and 1841), p. 302. Oxford University Press, 1928.

Page 168, line 8. *Documents Illustrative of the History of the Slave Trade to America*, edited by Elizabeth Donnan. 3 vols., 1930, 1931, 1932. Vol. 2, pp. 574, 575. Published by the Carnegie Institute of Washington.

Page 169, line 5. *Documents of the Slave Trade, op. cit.*, vol. I, pp. 45-47, footnote.
Line 15. Karl Marx, *Capital, op. cit.*, vol. I, p. 786.

Page 170, line 3. Merivale, *op. cit.*, p. 256.

Page 171, line 6. Marx, *Capital, op. cit.*, vol. I, p. 738.

Page 172, line 9. *Collections de Documents Inédits Sur l'Histoire Economique de la Révolution Française. Les Comités des Droits Feodaux et le Législation et l'Abolition du Régence Seigneurial, 1789-1793*, pp. 142, 143. Documents Publiés par P. Sagnac et P. Caren. Imprimerie Nationale, Paris, 1907.
Line 34. Arthur Young, *Tours in England and Wales* (1768-1808), pp. 134, 137. Reprint No. 14, London School of Economics. London, 1932.

Page 173, line 18. Marx, *Capital, op. cit.*, vol. I, pp. 752-754.
Line 33. *Ibid.*, vol. I, p. 750.

Page 174, line 16. Report from the Committee Appointed to Consider the State of the Woolen Manufacture of England. Journals of the House of Commons, 1806, vol. 61, p. 698.

Page 175, line 2. "Reports from Assistant Hand-Loom Weavers' Commissioners." Part II, 1840, p. 217, Journals of the House of Commons, vol. 75, 1819-1820.
Line 18. Gaskell, *Artisans and Machinery*, pp. 35-38. Parker, London, 1836.

Page 176, line 23. Max Weber, *The Protestant Ethic and the Spirit of Capitalism*, p. 162. Allen and Unwin, London, 1930.
Line 27. *Ibid.*, p. 175.

APPENDIX

Page 177, line 2. R. H. Tawney, *Religion and the Rise of Capitalism, op. cit.*, p. 105.

Line 23. B. Franklin, *Poor Richard's Almanack* (1732-1757), pp. 70, 76. Edited by B. E. Smith, Century Co., N. Y., 1898.

Line 28. B. Franklin, *The Way to Wealth. To which are Added his Advice to Young Tradesmen* (1757), p. 30. Windsor, Vt., 1826.

Page 178, line 11. J. M. Keynes, *A Tract on Monetary Reform*, p. 7. Macmillan & Co., Ltd., London, 1923.

CHAPTER XV

Page 179, line 12. *A Century of Birmingham Life from 1741-1841*, Compiled and edited by J. A. Langford. 2 vols. Vol. I, p. 221. Osborne, Birmingham, 1868.

Line 16. Cf. J. Lord, *Capital and Steam Power, 1750-1800*, p. 175. P. S. King and Son. London, 1923.

Page 180, line 21. Cf. D. George, *London Life in the 18th Century*, p. 336. Kegan Paul, Trench, Trubner and Co., Ltd., London, 1930.

Page 181, line 24. Cf. A. Toynbee, *Lectures on the Industrial Revolution of the 18th Century in England* (1884), p. 19. Longmans, Green and Co., 1913.

CHAPTER XVI

Page 183, line 12. J. L. and B. Hammond, *The Town Labourer, 1760-1832*, p. 65. Longmans, Green and Co., 1932.

Page 184, line 16. P. Gaskell, *op. cit.*, Preface. Parker, London, 1836.

Line 33. B. Disraeli, *Sybil or the Two Nations* (1845), p. 74, Macmillan & Company, Ltd., London, 1895.

Page 185, line 14. *Reports from Assistant Hand-Loom Weavers' Commissioners, op. cit.*, Part II, p. 232. 1840.

Page 186, line 12. J. L. and Barbara Hammond, *op. cit.*, pp. 19, 20.

Page 187, line 20. *Report of the Minutes of Evidence Taken Before the Select Committee on the State of the Children Employed in the Manufactories, 1816*, pp. 178-180.

Line 35. *First Report of the Central Board of His Majesty's Commissioners on Employment of Children in Factories, 1833*. pp. 31, 32.

Page 188, line 16. J. L. and B. Hammond, *op. cit.*, p. 160.

Line 32. Th. Rothstein, *From Chartism to Labourism*, p. 9. Martin Lawrence, Ltd., 1929.

Page 189, line 11. Quoted in F. Engels, *The Condition of the Working Class in England in 1844*, pp. 63, 64. Allen and Unwin, London, 1920.

Line 27. *Ibid.*, p. 107.

Line 35. St. John 12:8.

Page 190, line 9. Hammond, *op. cit.*, p. 163.

Line 20. *Ibid.*, p. 57.

Line 34. A. Ure, *The Philosophy of Manufactures* (1835), 3rd ed., p. 17. London, 1861.

Page 191, line 16. W. Paley, *Reasons for Contentment; Addressed to the Labouring Part of the British Public*, pp. 11, 12. London, 1793.

Line 27. *Ibid.*, p. 16.

Page 192, line 7. *Ibid.*, pp. 20, 22.

Line 28. Ure, *op. cit.*, p. 297.

Page 193, line 17. Adam Smith, *op. cit.*, vol. I, p. 123.

Page 194, line 22. F. Peel, *The Risings of the Luddites, Chartists, and Plug-drawers*, 2nd ed., p. 284. Heckmondwike, 1888.

APPENDIX

Page 195, line 16. *Ibid.*, pp. 71-72, 75.
Page 196, line 3. J. L. and B. Hammond, *The Skilled Labourer, 1760-1832*, p. 110. Longmans, Green and Co., London, 1919.
Page 197, line 3. J. L. and B. Hammond, *op. cit.*, pp. 66, 67.
Line 11. Adam Smith, *op. cit.*, vol. II, p. 207.
Page 198, line 13. Quoted in Engels, *op. cit.*, p. 230.
Page 199, line 19. Engels, *op. cit.*, p. 122.
Page 200, line 7. Adam Smith, *op. cit.*, vol. I, pp. 68, 69.
Line 24. Hammond, *The Town Labourer*, p. 209, footnote.
Page 201, line 7. E. Levasseur, *op. cit.*, vol. II, p. 241.
Line 21. H. Muller, *Geschichte der deutschen Gewerkschaften bis zum Jahre 1878*, Verlag Vorwärts, Berlin, 1918.
Page 202, line 3. Methodist Federation for Social Service, *The Social Questions Bulletin*, January, 1936.
Page 203, line 8. *Shelley Complete Poetical Works*, edited by G. E. Woodberry, pp. 364, 365. Houghton Mifflin Company, 1901.

CHAPTER XVII

Page 206, line 2. Adam Smith, *op. cit.*, vol. I, p. 419.
Page 207, line 20. T. R. Malthus, *An Essay on the Principle of Population*, 1st ed., pp. 176, 177. J. Johnson, London, 1798.
Page 208, line 9. *Ibid.*, pp. 14, 23, 24.
Line 15. *Ibid.*, p. 141.
Line 23. *Ibid.*, p. 346.
Page 209, line 3. *Ibid.*, 2nd ed., p. 549.
Page 210, line 2. M. Turgot, *Reflections on the Formation and Distribution of Wealth* (1766), E. Spragg, London, 1793.
Line 10. D. Ricardo, *The Principles of Political Economy and Taxation* (1817), p. 52. J. M. Dent & Sons, 1926.
Line 19. *Ibid.*, p. 53.
Line 32. *Ibid.*, p. 52.
Page 211, line 29. *Ibid.*, p. 225.
Page 212, line 12. *Ibid.*, p. 35.
Line 30. *Ibid.*, p. 225.
Page 213, line 7. *Ibid.*, p. 225.
Page 214, line 2. N. W. Senior, *Letters on the Factory Act as It Affects the Cotton Manufacture* (1837), 3rd ed., pp. 4, 5. London, 1844.
Line 26. J. S. Mill, *Principles of Political Economy* (1848), 2 vols., 3rd ed., vol. I, p. 409. Parker & Son, London, 1852.
Page 215, line 2. Prof. Perry quoted in *The Wages Question*, by Francis A. Walker, p. 143. Henry Holt and Company, Inc., N. Y., 1891 (first published 1876).
Page 216, line 2. N. W. Senior, *Three Lectures on the Rate of Wages*, 2nd ed., preface. John Murray, London, 1831.
Line 28. Walker, *op. cit.*, pp. 128-130.
Page 217, line 3. F. Utley, *Lancashire and the Far East*, pp. 110, 387. Allen & Unwin, Ltd., London, 1931.
Line 20. J. S. Mill, *Principles of Political Economy*, edited by W. J. Ashley, p. 993. Longmans, Green and Co., London, 1909.
Page 218, line 21. J. E. Cairnes, *Essays in Political Economy*, pp. 260, 261. Macmillan & Company, London, 1873.
Page 219, line 20. Ricardo, *op. cit.*, p. 81.

Page 220, line 15. F. List, *National System of Political Economy*, Preface. Longmans, Green and Co., London, 1904 (first published 1841).

Line 25. *Ibid.*, p. 108.

Line 31. *Ibid.*, p. 295.

CHAPTER XVIII

Page 224, line 34. *Capital*, vol. I, p. 19, footnote.

Page 225, line 5. *Ibid.*, p. 1.

Line 13. *Ibid.*, p. 8.

Line 32. *Ibid.*, p. 6.

Page 226, line 26. K. Marx, *Value, Price and Profit* (1865), edited by Eleanor Aveling, p. 33. International Publishers, N. Y., 1935.

Page 227, line 34. *Capital, op. cit.*, vol. I, p. 147.

Page 228, line 30. *Ibid.*, pp. 149, 150.

Page 229, line 28. *Value, Price, and Profit, op. cit.*, pp. 44, 45.

Page 231, line 2. Nicolay and Hay, *Abraham Lincoln, Complete Works*, vol. I, p. 92. Century Company, N. Y., 1920.

Line 11. H. W. Laidler, *A History of Socialist Thought*, p. 56. Thomas Y. Crowell Company, N. Y., 1927.

Line 29. Robert Owen, *Book of the New Moral World*, p. 58. London, 1836.

Page 232, line 3. H. W. Laidler, *op. cit.*, p. 70.

Line 10. E. Levasseur, *op. cit.*, vol. II, p. 18.

Line 31. K. Marx and F. Engels, *Manifesto of the Communist Party* (1848), edited by Engels. Kerr edition, pp. 54, 56.

Page 233, line 13. Martin Lawrence, *Karl Marx and Friedrich Engels Correspondence, 1846-1895*, pp. 376, 377. London, 1934.

Page 234, line 6. F. Engels, *Socialism, Utopian and Scientific*, Kerr edition, p. 85.

Line 29. K. Marx, *A Contribution to the Critique of "Political Economy"* (1859), Kerr edition, 1904, Preface, p. 11.

Page 236, line 3. *Communist Manifesto*, p. 19.

Page 237, line 22. *Capital*, vol. I, pp. 788, 789.

Page 238, line 20. K. Marx, *Letters to Dr. Kugelmann*, Marx-Engels-Lenin Institute translation, p. 26. Martin Lawrence, London.

Line 25. *K. M. and F. E. Correspondence*, p. 336.

Page 239, line 24. *Communist Manifesto*, pp. 30-35.

Page 240, line 3. *Ibid.*, p. 58.

Line 13. *Abraham Lincoln, Complete Works*, vol. I, p. 105.

Line 20. *Communist Manifesto*, p. 15.

Line 32. *Ibid.*, p. 42.

Page 241, line 9. *Wealth of Nations*, vol. II, p. 143.

Line 21. Woodrow Wilson, *The New Freedom*, pp. 57, 189, 190. Doubleday, Page and Co., N. Y., 1913.

Page 242, line 34. *New York Herald Tribune*, Sept. 27, 1932 (my italics).

Page 243, line 6. *Socialism, Utopian and Scientific, op. cit.*, pp. 134, 135.

CHAPTER XIX

Page 245, line 8. W. S. Jevons, *Theory of Political Economy*, p. 2. Macmillan & Company, Ltd., London, 1871.

Page 246, line 24. E. Cannan, *op. cit.*, p. 201.

Page 249, line 6. Jevons, *op. cit.*, p. 52.

Line 35. Cannan, *Review of Economic Theory*, pp. 203-204.

Page 252, line 30. *Capital*, vol. I, pp. 640, 641.

Page 253, line 18. Ida M. Tarbell, *The History of the Standard Oil Company*, 2 vols. The Macmillan Company, 1925.

Page 254, line 2. J. W. Jenks, W. E. Clark, *The Trust Problem*, 5th ed., p. 29. Doubleday, Doran & Company, Inc., 1929.

Line 11. *The Encyclopaedia of Social Sciences*, vol. 3, p. 234, article by R. Liefmann. The Macmillan Company, N. Y.

Line 29. J. Morgan Rees, *Trusts in British Industry, 1914-1921*, p. 12. King & Son, London, 1923.

Page 257, line 5. V. I. Lenin, *Imperialism* (1916), revised translation, 2nd ed., p. 42. Martin tion H.M.S.O., 1919.

Line 13. *Ibid.*, p. 2.

Line 34. *Capital*, vol. I, p. 641.

Page 256, line 20. Quoted in *Other People's Money* (1914), by L. D. Brandeis, p. 1. National Home Library Assn. Washington, D. C., 1933.

Page 257, line 5. V. I. Lenin, *Imperialism* (1916), revised translation, 2nd ed., p. 42. Martin Lawrence, London, 1934.

Line 21. *Other People's Money*, p. 3.

Page 258, line 13. Quoted in *Imperialism and World Politics*, by P. T. Moon, p. 27. The Macmillan Company, N. Y., 1932.

Page 259, line 11. *Ibid.*, p. 66.

Line 29. Quoted in *The American Observer*, March 16, 1936.

Page 261, line 24. Lenin, *op. cit.*, pp. 57, 58.

Page 262, line 17. J. A. Hobson, *Imperialism*, p. 91. J. Pott & Company, N. Y., 1902.

Page 263, line 3. Leonard Woolf, *Imperialism and Civilization*, pp. 73, 74. Hogarth Press, London, 1933.

Line 12. *The Last Will and Testament of Cecil John Rhodes*, pp. 58, 98. Edited by W. T. Stead, *Review of Reviews* office, London, 1902.

Page 264, line 5. G. Gorer, *Africa Dances*, p. 122. Faber and Faber, London, 1935.

Line 15. L. Woolf, *Economic Imperialism*, p. 102. Swarthmore Press, London, 1920.

Page 265, line 3. J. Morgan Rees, *op. cit.*, p. 245.

Line 10. Quoted in *Economic Imperialism and International Relations during the Last Fifty Years*, by A. Viallate, p. 62. The Macmillan Company, N. Y., 1923.

Page 266, line 2. *Common Sense*, Nov., 1935.

Line 17. A. A. Berle and G. C. Means, *The Modern Corporation and Private Property*, p. 19. The Macmillan Company, N. Y., 1933.

Page 267, line 29. *Ibid.*, pp. 24, 25.

Page 268, line 5. Lenin, *op. cit.*, p. 68.

Page 269, line 2. Rhodes, *op. cit.*, p. 190.

CHAPTER XX

Page 270, line 10. *Communist Manifesto, op. cit.*, pp. 20, 21.

Page 272, line 6. F. A. von Hayek, *Monetary Theory and the Trade Cycle*, p. 68. Jonathan Cape, London, 1933.

Line 18. K. Marx and F. Engels, *Correspondence, op. cit.*, p. 199.

Line 29. Thorstein Veblen, *The Vested Interests and the Common Man*, pp. 92 ff. B. W. Huebsch, N. Y., 1920.

Page 273, line 2. Wesley C. Mitchell, *Business Cycles*, pp. 65, 66. National Bureau of Economic Research. 1927.

Line 25. *Ibid.*, pp. 9, 10.

Page 274, line 17. A. C. Pigou, *Industrial Fluctuations*, p. 33. Macmillan & Company, Ltd., London. 2nd ed., 1929.

Line 32. *Ibid.*, pp. 90, 91.

Page 275, line 10. *Ibid.*, p. 34.

Line 19. J. M. Keynes, *A Tract on Monetary Reform, op. cit.*, Preface, p. 5.

Page 277, line 28. *Ibid.*, pp. 38, 40.

Page 278, line 2. F. A. von Hayek, *Prices and Production*, p. 89. Routledge & Sons, London, 1931.

Page 279, line 13. J. A. Hobson, *Poverty in Plenty*, pp. 54, 63, 64, 67. Allen & Unwin, London, 1931.

Line 33. F. A. von Hayek, *op. cit.*, pp. 85, 86, 111, 112. Routledge & Sons, London, 1931.

Page 280, line 15. Cf. John Strachey, *The Nature of the Capitalist Crisis* (Covici Friede, N. Y., 1935), for a more detailed exposition of this point.

Page 282, line 9. Karl Marx, *Capital*, edited by F. Engels, vol. III, p. 248. Kerr and Co., Chicago, 1909.

Page 284, line 6. Thomas Carlyle, *Past and Present*, bk. I, ch. III. Chapman & Hall, London, 1843.

CHAPTER XXI

Page 286, line 8. V. I. Lenin, *Toward the Seizure of Power,* vol. I, pp. 224, 225. International Publishers, N. Y., 1932.

Page 287, line 10. *Ibid.*, vol. II, pp. 40-41.

Line 27. John Reed, *Ten Days That Shook the World* (1919), p. 126. International Publishers, N. Y., 1926.

Page 288, line 6. *New York Times Magazine,* Nov. 6, 1932.

Page 289, line 33. *New York Times,* April 22, 1936.

Page 290, line 20. Sidney and Beatrice Webb, *Soviet Communism: A New Civilization?* 2 vols., vol. II, pp. 602, 630. Charles Scribner's Sons, N. Y., 1936.

Page 291, line 10. *Ibid.*, p. 631.

Page 292, line 2. *Ibid.*, p. 625.

Line 11. *Socialist Planned Economy in the Soviet Union,* p. 24. Martin Lawrence, London, 1932.

Page 293, line 3. Quoted in *Social and Economic Planning,* by C. A. Macartney, p. 19. League of Nations Union, London, 1935.

Line 22. "Life in Soviet Russia." M. I. Cole in *The Highway,* Dec., 1932, p. 15.

Page 295, line 33. *New York World-Telegram,* March 4, 1936.

Page 296, line 20. *New York Times,* March 27, 1936.

Page 297, line 24. "Economist" in *The Highway,* Dec., 1932, p. 19.

Page 298, line 27. Emile Burns, *Russia's Productive System,* p. 234. Gollancz, London, 1930.

Page 300, line 2. E. Belfort Bax, *The Last Episode of the French Revolution, Being a History of Gracchus, Babeuf and the Conspiracy of Equals,* p. 132. Grant Richards, London, 1911.

Page 301, line 27. *Socialist Planned Economy, op. cit.*, pp. 46, 47.

Page 302, line 12. Webbs, *op. cit.*, vol. II, p. 786.

Line 24. *Fortune*, March, 1936, p. 200.

Page 303, line 23. Quoted in Webbs, *op. cit.*, vol. II, p. 758.

Page 304, line 5. *Manchester Guardian*, Feb. 20, 1936.

Line 22. Webbs, *op. cit.*, pp. 794, 795.

Page 307, line 7. *New York Times*, June 26, 1936.

CHAPTER XXII

Page 309, line 27. *New York Times,* July 3, 1936.
Page 310, line 10. *New York Times,* February 5, 1936.
    Line 27. B. Stolberg and W. J. Vinton, *The Economic Consequences of the New Deal* p. 85. Harcourt, Brace and Company, N. Y., 1935.
Page 312, line 2. Barbara Wooton, *Plan or No Plan,* p. 320. Gollancz, London, 1934.
Page 313, line 9. London *Times,* August 28, 1935 (my italics).
    Line 34. *New York Times,* Dec. 6, 1935.
Page 314, line 18. G. D. H. Cole, *Principles of Economic Planning,* p. 222. Macmillan & Company, Ltd., London, 1935.
    Line 27. Stolberg and Vinton, *op. cit.,* pp. 20, 21.
Page 315, line 9. J. B. Clark, *The Distribution of Wealth,* Preface, p. 3. The Macmillan Company, N. Y., 1899.
Page 316, line 20. G. Feder, *The Programme of the N.S.D.A.P. and Its General Conceptions,* p. 19. Translated by E. T. S. Dugdale, Munich, 1932.
    Line 33. *The Economist,* February 1, 1936.
Page 317, line 10. *New York Times,* March 24, 1936.
    Line 33. John Gunther, *Inside Europe,* Harper & Brothers, 1936, p. 189.
Page 318, line 26. Benito Mussolini, *The Political and Social Doctrine of Fascism. Political Quarterly* (London), July-September, 1933, pp. 344, 345.
    Line 33. Adolf Hitler, *Mein Kampf,* p. 149. Verlag Franz Eber Nachfolger. München 2 No. 1930 (VI Auflage).
Page 319, line 7. *New York Times,* March 22, 1936.
    Line 28. Arthur Morgan, "Power and the New Deal," *The Forum,* March, 1935.

Bibliography

ASHLEY, SIR WILLIAM, *The Economic Organisation of England*. Longmans, Green and Co., London, 1933. Eight lectures admirable for their brevity, clarity, and fine scholarship.
An Introduction to English Economic History and Theory, 2 vols. G. P. Putnam's Sons, N. Y., 1913. Excellent. Simply written.

AULARD, A., *La Révolution Française et le Régime Féodal*, Bibliothèque d'Histoire Contemporaine. Alcan, Paris, 1919. Brief survey of the position of the peasantry before and during the revolution.

BADEN, CARL FRIEDRICHS VON, *Brieflicher Verkehr mit Mirabeau und Du Pont*. Bearbeitet von C. Knies, vol. I. Heidelberg, 1892. Has good introduction.

BARBON, NICHOLAS, *A Discourse of Trade* (1690), reprinted and edited by J. H. Hollander. Johns Hopkins Press, Baltimore, 1905. Very good edition.

BAX, E. BELFORT, *The Last Episode of the French Revolution Being a History of Gracchus Babeuf and the Conspiracy of the Equals*. Grant Richards, Ltd., London, 1911. Very interesting.

BEALES, H. L., *The Industrial Revolution*. Longmans, Green and Co., London, 1928. One of the best short accounts.

BEARD, CHARLES AND MARY, *The Rise of American Civilization*. The Macmillan Company, N. Y., 1933. Far and away the best complete history of the U. S.

BEER, M., *A History of British Socialism*, 2 vols. G. Bell & Sons, London, 1920, 1921. Authoritative survey by a first rate scholar.
The Life and Teaching of Karl Marx. International Publishers, N. Y., 1929. Well-written short account (159 pages).

BERLE, ADOLF AND MEANS, GARDINER C., *The Modern Corporation and Private Property*. The Macmillan Company, N. Y., 1933. Important, well-documented study dealing with the divorce of ownership from control in our corporate structure.

BLAND, H. E., BROWN, P. A., AND TAWNEY, R. H., *English Economic History, Select Documents*. G. Bell & Sons, London, 1914. An invaluable collection of source material.

BODIN, JEAN, *La Réponse de Jean Bodin à M. de Malestroit* (1568). Nouvelle Edition par H. Hauser. Colin, Paris, 1932.

BOHM-BAWERK, EUGEN V., *Karl Marx and the Close of His System*, translated by A. M. Macdonald. Fisher Unwin, London, 1898. A critical study of Marx's economic doctrines by an opponent.

BOISSONNADE, P., *Colbert*. Rivière, Paris, 1932. First-rate. Of great use in study of mercantilism.
Le Socialisme d'Etat (1453-1661). Champion, Paris, 1927. Thorough account of the rise of the national state.
Life and Work in Medieval Europe (fifth to fifteenth centuries). Alfred A. Knopf, N. Y., 1927. A masterly and interesting survey.

BRANDEIS, LOUIS D., *Other People's Money* (1914). National Home Library Association, Washington, D. C., 1933. Spotlight on the growth and power of finance capital.

BRANTS, V., *Les Théories Economiques aux XIIIe et XIVe Siècles*. Peeters, Louvain, 1895. A Catholic interpretation. Helpful study.

BRETTE, A., *Recueil de Documents Relatifs à la Convocation des Etats Généraux de 1789*, 3 vols. Imprimerie Nationale, Paris, 1894, 1896, 1904. A comprehensive collection of local and national documents with lists of deputies, constituencies, etc.

BROOME, RALPH, *Strictures on Mr. Burke's Two Letters*. John Thompson, Philadelphia, 1797.

334   BIBLIOGRAPHY

BRUSLONS, SAVARY DES, *Universal Dictionary of Trade and Commerce*, translated from the French with Additions and Improvements, by Malachy Postlethwayt, 2 vols. London, 1757. Very useful.

BRUTZKUS, B., *Economic Planning in Soviet Russia*. George Routledge & Sons, London, 1935. An exiled Russian professor says socialist planning is economically impossible.

BUCHHEIM (Translator), *Address to the German Nobility. Harvard Classics*, vol. XXXVI.

BURNS, EMILE, *Russia's Productive System*. Victor Gollancz, Ltd., London, 1930. A clear description of the organisation and administration of industry, agriculture, and transport.

CAIRNES, JOHN ELLIOT, *Essays in Political Economy*. The Macmillan Company, London, 1873.

Cambridge Modern History. The Macmillan Company, N. Y., 1907.

CANNAN, EDWIN, *History of the Theories of Production and Distribution in English Political Economy from 1776 to 1848*. P. S. King & Son, Ltd., London, 1903. First class book by an eminent British economist.

A Review of Economic Theory. P. S. King & Son, Ltd., London, 1929. Excellent critical analysis of the development of economic theories.

CANTILLON, RICHARD, *Essai sur la Nature du Commerce en Général* (1755), edited with an English translation by Henry Higgs. Macmillan & Company, Ltd., London, 1931. Interesting essay by a merchant of the period.

CARLYLE, THOMAS, *Past and Present*. Chapman and Hall, London, 1843.

CHASE, STUART, *Parade of the Gravediggers. Harper's Magazine*, August, 1935. A well-written summary of the views of seven economists who submit six reasons why capitalism must collapse.

CHEYNEY, E. P., *European Background of American History*. Harper & Brothers, N. Y., 1904. Excellent. Crammed full of useful information written in simple style.

Social Changes in England in the 16th Century. Ginn and Company, Boston, 1895. Very good.

CLARK, JOHN BATES, *The Distribution of Wealth*. The Macmillan Company, N. Y., 1899. Contribution by one of the leading American economists of his period.

COLE, G. D. H., *Principles of Economic Planning*. Macmillan & Company, Ltd., London, 1935. A useful book by the most prolific English Socialist.

What Marx Really Meant. Alfred A. Knopf, N. Y., 1934. Well-written, simple and generally helpful—though the author occasionally stands alone on "what Marx really meant."

COREY, LEWIS, *The Decline of American Capitalism*. Covici Friede, N. Y., 1934. Corey is, perhaps, America's leading Marxist. His style, however, is difficult.

COULTON, G. G., *The Medieval Village*. Cambridge University Press, 1925. Fascinating book on rural social life in the middle ages by a great authority.

Article on the Reformation in *Encyclopaedia Britannica*, 14th Edition, vol. 19. Excellent summary.

CROWLEY, R., *Select Works*, edited by J. M. Cowper. Early English Text Society, London, 1872. Contemporary writings on the condition of England in the 16th century.

CUNNINGHAM, W., *Western Civilization in Its Economic Aspects (Medical and Modern Times)*. University Press, Cambridge, 1913. A masterly work by the father of economic history in England.

DAVIS, H. W. C., *Medieval Europe*. Thornton Butterworth, Ltd., London, 11th Edition, 1930. Brief but fascinating survey, best read after the student is familiar with the history of the period.

DEFOE, DANIEL, *A Tour Thro' the Whole Island of Great Britain* (1724, 1725, 1726, 3 vols.), 2 vols. Peter Davies, London, 1927. A star reporter writes a lively and informative account of the England in which he lived.

DISRAELI, B., *Sybil or the Two Nations* (1845). Macmillan & Company, Ltd., London, 1895.

DOBB, MAURICE, *Capitalist Enterprise and Social Progress*. George Routledge & Sons, Ltd., London, 1925. For advanced students only; a Marxist looks at modern economic history.

An Introduction to Economics. Victor Gollancz, Ltd., London, 1932. Excellent—but for the student, not the layman.

BIBLIOGRAPHY 335

Russian Economic Development Since the Revolution. Labor Research Department, London, 1928. Extremely useful.

DONNAN, ELIZABETH (Editor), *Documents Illustrative of the History of the Slave Trade to America,* 3 vols. Carnegie Institute of Washington, 1930, 1931, 1932. An invaluable collection.

DUTT, R. PALME, *Fascism and Social Revolution.* International Publishers, N. Y., 1935. Definitive work on Fascism from the Marxist point of view.

EHRENBERG, RICHARD, *Capital and Finance in the Age of the Renaissance,* translated by H. M. Lucas. Harcourt, Brace and Company, N. Y. An extremely bad translation of an excellent book.

EINZIG, PAUL, *The Economic Foundations of Fascism.* Macmillan & Company, Ltd., London, 1934. Sympathetic appraisal with the emphasis on Italy rather than Germany.

Encyclopaedia of the Social Sciences, article by R. Liefman, vol. 3. The Macmillan Company, N. Y. This encyclopaedia is indispensable to students of the social sciences.

ENGELS, FRIEDRICH, *The Condition of the Working Class in England in 1844.* George Allen and Unwin, Ltd., London, 1920. An excellent study written when Engels was only twenty-four.

Germany: Revolution and Counter-Revolution. International Publishers, N. Y., 1933. A series of brilliant articles which appeared in the *New York Tribune,* 1851-1852.

Socialism, Utopian and Scientific. Kerr edition, 1908. Excellent. Simple exposition of difficult concepts.

FAGNIEZ, M. G. (Editor), *Documents Relatifs à l'histoire de l'Industrie et du Commerce en France.* Picard, Paris, 1898, vol. II, 1900. Valuable.

FEDER, GOTTFRIED, *The Programme of the N. S. D. A. P. and Its General Conceptions,* translated by E. T. S. Dugdale. Munich, 1932. This contains the famous 25 points of the Nazi program. N. S. D. A. P. stands for National-Sozialistische Deutsche Arbeiter Partei (National-Socialist German Workers' Party).

FINER, H., *Mussolini's Italy.* Victor Gollancz, Ltd., London, 1935. Comprehensive factual account.

First Report of the Central Board of His Majesty's Commissioners on Employment of Children in Factories. 1833.

FISHER, IRVING, *Booms and Depressions.* Adelphi Company, N. Y., 1932. One of the foremost exponents of the monetary explanation of crises puts his case.

FOREMAN, CLARK, *The New Internationalism.* W. W. Norton & Company, Inc., N. Y., 1934. Compact account of the growth and breakdown of international capitalism.

FRANKLIN, BENJAMIN, *Poor Richard's Almanack* (1732-1759), edited by B. E. Smith. The Century Company, N. Y., 1898.

The Way to Wealth. To which is added his advice to young Tradesmen (1757). Windsor, Vermont, 1826.

GASKELL, P., *Artisans and Machinery.* Parker, London, 1836. One of the best and most famous contemporary accounts of the condition of the working classes.

GEORGE, DOROTHY, *London Life in the Eighteenth Century.* Kegan, Paul, Trench, Trubner & Company, Ltd., London, 1930. Excellent study, full of information and very readable.

GIDE, CHARLES AND RIST, CHARLES, *A History of Economic Doctrines.* D. C. Heath & Co., London. Useful.

GIRY, A. AND REVILLE, A., *Emancipation of the Medieval Towns,* translated and edited by F. G. Bates and P. E. Titsworth. Henry Holt and Company, Inc., N. Y., 1907. A concise and interesting study of the struggle for urban independence.

GORER, GEOFFREY, *Africa Dances.* Faber and Faber, London, 1935. Lucid and engaging account of the French West African colonies.

GREGORY, T. E., *Gold, Unemployment and Capitalism.* P. S. King & Son, Ltd., London, 1933. In the last two chapters, Professor Gregory examines the case for planning, and comes out against it.

GROSS, CHARLES, *The Gild Merchant,* 2 vols. Clarendon Press, Oxford, 1890. Standard work.

336   BIBLIOGRAPHY

GUNTHER, JOHN, *Inside Europe*. Harper & Brothers, N. Y., 1936. A shrewd reporter writes a best-seller on important men and affairs in Europe.
HACKER, LOUIS, *A Short History of the New Deal*. Crofts, N. Y., 1934. Excellent summary of what happened and why.
HAMMOND, J. L. AND BARBARA, *Lord Shaftesbury*. Constable & Co., London, 1923. The life story of one of the leading humanitarians of the 19th century. Extremely well done and excellent reading.
The Skilled Labourer, 1760-1832. Longmans, Green and Company, London, 1929. Justly famous studies by experts who write simply and brilliantly.
The Town Labourer, 1760-1832 (1917). Longmans, Green and Company, 1932. See above.
HAYEK, F. A. VON, *Monetary Theory and the Trade Cycle,* translated from the German by N. Kaldor and H. M. Croome. Jonathan Cape, London, 1933. This is much simpler than *Prices and Production,* but still too difficult for the uninitiated.
Prices and Production, foreword by Professor L. Robbins. George Routledge & Sons, Ltd., London, 1931. An exposition of the latest monetary theories, but very difficult for the beginner.
HAYES, CARLETON J. H., *Essays on Nationalism*. The Macmillan Company, N. Y., 1926. Well-written.
A Political and Social History of Modern Europe, 2 vols. The Macmillan Company, N. Y., revised edition, 1921. Standard text.
HAZEN, C. D., *The French Revolution*. Henry Holt & Company, N. Y., 1932. Standard text.
HEGEL, K. VON, *Städte und Gilden der germanischen Völker im Mittelalter,* 2 vols. Duncker u. Humblot, Leipzig, 1891. Excellent and comprehensive study of towns and gilds in England, Germany, the Netherlands, and Scandinavia by an eminent German historian.
HEIDEN, KONRAD, *A History of National Socialism*. Methuen, London, 1934. Well-informed account by an eye-witness.
HELD, A., *Zwei Bücher zur Socialen Geschichte Englands*. Duncker u. Humblot, Leipzig, 1881. A well-documented and comprehensive account of the economic, social and political literature and developments of the period of the industrial revolution in England.
HIGGS, H., *The Physiocrats*. Macmillan & Company, Ltd., London, 1897. Standard English work on the subject.
HINRICHS, G., *Die wollindustrie in Preussen*. Parey, Berlin, 1933. For advanced study only.
History of the Working Class. International Publishers, N. Y. Marxist slant.
HITLER, ADOLF, *Mein Kampf*. Verlag Franz Eher Nachfolger, Munchen 2 No. 1930, VI Auflage. The Fuehrer's credo.
HOBSON, JOHN A., *The Evolution of Modern Capitalism* (1894). Walter Scott Publishing Co., Ltd., revised edition, 1926. Established classic which should be read.
Imperialism. J. Plott and Company, N. Y., 1902. See above.
Poverty in Plenty. George Allen & Unwin, Ltd., London, 1931. A brief but cogent examination of the ethics of the inequitable distribution of income and its disastrous consequences.
HODGSKIN, TH., *Labour Defended Against the Claims of Capital* (1825), with an Introduction by G. D. H. Cole. Labour Publishing Company, London, 1922. A classic of early British socialism.
HOOK, SIDNEY, *Towards the Understanding of Karl Marx*. John Day, N. Y., 1933. A clear exposition by an able scholar.
HORROCKS, J. W., *Short History of Mercantilism*. Methuen, London, 1925. A standard English work.
HEWITT, W., *Colonization and Christianity*. Longman, Orme, Brown, Green & Longmans, London, 1838. Exciting reading, by a person who found the methods of colonization shocking.
HUME, DAVID, *Essays Moral, Political and Literary,* edited by T. H. Green and T. H. Grose. Longmans, Green and Company, London, 1875. A good edition of the essays of this famous English philosopher, first published in 1742.
ILIN, M., *New Russia's Primer*. Houghton Mifflin Company, N. Y., 1931. The author is a

genius in the art of simple writing. Though intended for children, this book should not be missed by any adult interested in the Soviet Union.

JENKS, J. W. AND CLARK, W. E., *The Trust Problem*. Doubleday, Doran & Company, Inc., 1929. Good.

JEVONS, WILLIAM STANLEY, *Theory of Political Economy*. Macmillan & Company, Inc., London, 1871. Simply written account of the difficult concept of marginal utility.

JOURDAN, DECRUSY, ISAMBERT (Editors), *Recueil Général des anciennes Lois Françaises*. Plon Freres, Paris. Valuable.

Journal d'un Bourgeois de Paris, 1405-1449, edited by A. Tuetey. Champion, Paris, 1881. An interesting record.

Journals of the House of Commons, 1806-1820.

KAUTSKY, KARL, *Economic Doctrines of Karl Marx*, translated by H. J. Stenning. Black, Ltd., London, 1925. Outstanding Social-Democrat.

KEYNES, J. M., *The General Theory of Employment Interest and Money*. Macmillan & Co., Ltd., London, 1936. Important book, although too difficult for non-specialist adult reader.

A Tract on Monetary Reform. Macmillan & Company, Ltd., London, 1923. A brilliant analysis of the influence of price fluctuations and suggestions for their control.

KLARWILL, V. VON (Editor), *The Fugger News Letters*, translated by P. de Chary. Bodley Head, London, 1st series, 1924, 2nd series, 1926. Exciting, important source material.

KNOWLES, L. C. A., *The Industrial and Commercial Revolutions in Great Britain during the 19th Century*. George Routledge & Sons, London, 1921. Very useful for reference. Excellent section on transport.

KULISCHER, J., *Allgemeine Wertschaftsgeschichte des Mittelalters und der Neuzeit*, 2 vols. Oldenbourg, Berlin, 1928-1929. A detailed, comprehensive, and masterly study, unfortunately not yet translated into English.

LAIDLER, H. W., *Concentration of Control in American Industry*. Thomas Y. Crowell Company, N. Y., 1931. Valuable close-up picture of corporate development of American business.

A History of Socialist Thought. Thomas Y. Crowell Company, N. Y., 1927. Useful bird's-eye view.

LAMOND, ELIZABETH (Editor), *A Discourse of the Common Weal of This Realm of England* (1581). Cambridge University Press, 1893. Excellent edition of this famous book.

LANG, ANDREW, *The Maid of France*. Longmans, Green and Co., London, 1929. A well-written biography by an admirer of Joan of Arc.

LANGFORD, J. A. (Editor), *A Century of Birmingham Life, from 1741-1841*, 2 vols. Osborne, Birmingham, 1868. Contains a great deal of material, but there is practically no attempt at selection or arrangement.

LASKI, HAROLD J., *The State in Theory and Practice*. The Viking Press, N. Y., 1935. Brilliant analysis by an authority.

LENIN, V. I., *Collected Works*. Marx-Engels-Lenin Institute edition, International Publishers, N. Y. *The Iskra Period*, 2 vols., 1929. *The Imperialist War*, 1930. *The Revolution of 1917*, 2 vols., 1929. *Toward the Seizure of Power*, 2 vols., 1932. A wealth of material for students of history by one of the greatest makers of history.

The State and Revolution (1917). The Vanguard Press, N. Y., 1926. The rôle of the State as seen by a Marxist.

Imperialism, the Highest Stage of Capitalism (1916), revised translation. Martin Lawrence, Ltd., London, 2nd edition, 1934. The economic nature of imperialism placed under the microscope by a great student of the subject.

LEONARD, E. M., *Early History of English Poor Relief*. University Press, Cambridge, 1900. Good standard work.

LEVASSEUR, E., *Histoire des classes ouvrières et de l'Industrie en France avant 1789*, 2 vols. Rousseau, Paris, 1900-1907. An excellent detailed and comprehensive standard work.

LIEFMANN, R., *International Cartels, Combines and Trusts*. Europa Publishing Company,

London [1927]. A record of discussions on Cartels at the International Economic Conference. Short and good.

LIPSON, E., *An Introduction to the Economic History of England*. A. & C. Black, Ltd., London, 1915. One of the best from every point of view.

LIST, FRIEDRICH, *National System of Political Economy* (1841). Longmans, Green and Co., London, 1904. Interesting forerunner of the economic nationalism of today.

LORD, JOHN, *Capital and Steam Power, 1750-1800*. P. S. King & Son, London, 1923. Short, clear account, based largely on unpublished stories and papers of Boulton and Watt.

LUCHAIRE, A., *Les Communes françaises á l'époque des Capétiens Directs*. Hachette et Cie, Paris, 1890. Full of meat for the more advanced student.

MACARTNEY, C. A., *Social and Economic Planning*. League of Nations Union, London, 1935. Interesting digest of the speeches at a meeting of experts.

MADELIN, L., *The French Revolution*. William Heinemann, London, 3rd edition, 1922. Good.

MALTHUS, THOMAS ROBERT, *An Essay on the Principle of Population*. J. Johnson, London, 1798, 1st edition. The father of the idea wrote beautifully—far better than his disciples.

MANLEY, T., *A Discourse Shewing that the Exportation of Wooll is destructive to this Kingdom*. London, 1677. Mercantilist source.

MANTOUX, P. J., *The Industrial Revolution in the Eighteenth Century*, translated by M. Vernon. Revised edition. Jonathan Cape, London, 1928. Standard work.

MARX, KARL, *Address and Provisional Rules of the International Working Men's Association*. Established September 28, 1864. Speech at the founding of the First International in London.

Capital, vol. I (1867). Translated from the 3rd German edition by Samuel Moore and Edward Aveling and edited by F. Engels, Wm. Glaisher, Ltd., London, 1928. Vols. II and III (1894), edited by F. Engels, Kerr edition, Chicago, 1909. An epoch-making work by a great thinker.

The Civil War in France (1871), with an Introduction by Friedrich Engels. Martin Lawrence, Ltd., London, 1933. The Paris Commune is the subject of this vivid polemic.

A Contribution to the Critique of Political Economy (1859), translated by N. I. Stone. Kerr & Co., Chicago, 1904. Indispensable for an understanding of Marxism.

Critique of the Gotha Programme (1875). International Publishers, N. Y., 1933. Left criticism of the program of the leaders of German Social Democracy.

The Eighteenth Brumaire of Louis Bonaparte (1852), translated by Eden and Cedar Paul. George Allen and Unwin, London, 1926. Polemic writing at its best.

Letters to Dr. Kugelmann. Marx-Engels-Lenin Institute translation. Martin Lawrence, London. Very useful.

The Poverty of Philosophy. Kerr edition. Scathing criticism of the political and economic theories of Proudhon, the French Socialist.

Value, Price and Profit (1865), edited by Eleanor Aveling. International Publishers, N. Y., 1935. In this address to workingmen in London, Marx popularizes his economic theories.

Wage, Labour and Capital (1849, with an Introduction by Friedrich Engels). International Publishers, N. Y., 1933. Based on lectures delivered before the German Workingmen's Club of Brussels, this, too, is in popular style.

MARX, KARL AND ENGELS, FRIEDRICH, *Correspondence, 1846-1895*. Martin Lawrence, London, 1934. A very useful selection, in English, from the voluminous correspondence of Marx and Engels to each other and to friends and acquaintances.

MARX-ENGELS GESAMTAUSGABE, *Der Briefwechsel zwischen Marx und Engels*. Dritte Abteilung, 4 vols. Im auftrage des Marx-Engels Institute, Moskau, herausgegeben von D. Rjazanov, 1929, 1930, 1930, 1931. The complete and authoritative edition of this extremely interesting correspondence, which is invaluable for a study of Marxism.

MARX, KARL AND ENGELS, FRIEDRICH, *Manifesto of the Communist Party* (1848). Kerr Edition. One of the most important books ever published.

MATHIEZ, A., *The French Revolution*. Alfred A. Knopf, N. Y., 1928. Excellent.

BIBLIOGRAPHY

MEHRING, F., *Karl Marx, the Story of His Life*. Covici, Friede, N. Y., 1935. Excellent, authoritative biography.

MEMMERT, L., *Die öffentliche Förderung der gewerblichen Produktionsmethoden zur Zeit des Merkantilismus in Bayern*. Noske, Leipzig, 1930. Very good for detailed study of mercantilism.

MERIVALE, H., *Lectures on Colonization and Colonies* (Delivered in 1839, 1840 and 1841). Oxford University Press, 1929. Clear and useful analysis.

Methodist Federation for Social Service, The Social Questions Bulletin, January, 1936. Excellent.

MEYER, GUSTAV, *Friedrich Engels*. Alfred A. Knopf, N. Y., 1936. First and only biography in English of the collaborator of Karl Marx.

MILL, JOHN STUART, *Principles of Political Economy* (1848), edited by W. J. Ashley. Longmans, Green and Co., 1909. Standard edition.

MITCHELL, WESLEY C., *Business Cycles. The Problem and Its Setting*. National Bureau of Economic Research, Inc., N. Y., 1927. A famous book by one of America's foremost economists.

MONROE, A. E. (Editor), *Early Economic Thought. Selections from Economic Literature Prior to Adam Smith*. Harvard University Press, 1924. A very useful collection of outstanding passages from early economic writings.

MOON, P. T., *Imperialism and World Politics*. The Macmillan Company, N. Y., 1932. Standard work well-written.

MORGAN, ARTHUR, *Power and the New Deal. The Forum*, March, 1935. The director of T. V. A. discusses an important present-day problem.

MORRIS, G. W. AND WOOD, L. S., *The Golden Fleece*. Oxford University Press, 1931. The great part played by wool in English history made clear by sound scholarship and good writing.

MULLER, H., *Geschichte der deutschen Gewerkschaffen bis zum Jahre 1878*. Verlag Vorwärts, Berlin, 1918. A brief but comprehensive and reliable survey of the Germany T. U. movement.

MUN, THOMAS, *England's Treasure by Forraign Trade* (1664). The Macmillan Company, N. Y., 1895. Justly famous source.

MUSSOLINI, BENITO, *The Political and Social Doctrine of Fascism*, in the *Political Quarterly*, London, July-September, 1933. Mussolini's theoretical justification of the fascist hostility to peace, socialism, and liberalism.

NICOLAY AND HAY (Editors), *Complete Works of Abraham Lincoln*. The Century Company, N. Y., 1920.

NORTH, DUDLEY, *Discourses upon Trade* (1691). Reprint edited by J. H. Hollander, Baltimore, 1907. Very good edition of one of the most famous economic writings before Adam Smith.

NUSSBAUM, F. L., *History of the Economic Institutions of Modern Europe*. Crofts, N. Y., 1933. Useful well-written work by a disciple of Sombart.

OGG, F. A., *A Source Book of Medieval History*. American Book Company, N. Y., 1907. Good.

Ordonnances des Roys de France de la Troisième Race. Imprimerie Royale, Paris, vol. II, 1729, vol. XIII, 1782, vol. XIV, 1790. Valuable collection.

OWEN, ROBERT, *Book of the New Moral World*. London, 1836. Utopian hope for the future.

PAGE, T. W., *End of Villainage in England*. American Economic Association, N. Y., 1900. Brief, readable, and well-documented.

PALEY, WILLIAM, *Reasons for Contentment; Addressed to the Labouring Part of the British Public*. London, 1793. The Archdeacon of Carlisle reflects the ideas of the English ruling classes at the time of the French Revolution.

PEEL, FRANK, *The Risings of the Luddites, Chartists, and Plugdrawers*. Heckmondwike, 2nd edition, 1888. Based largely on personal conversations with old workers, etc., and local newspaper reports.

PETTY, SIR WILLIAM, *Economic Writings.* Edited by C. H. Hull, 2 vols. Cambridge University Press, 1899. A good edition of the writings of this famous English administrator.

PHILIPPI, F., *Die ältesten Osnabrückischen Gilde urkunden (bis 1500).* Kisling, Osnabruck, 1890. Good.

PIGOU, A. C., *Industrial Fluctuations.* Macmillan & Company, Ltd., London, 2nd edition, 1929. The father of the Cambridge School Investigates crises.

PIRENNE, HENRI, The Stages in the Social History of Capitalism, in The American Historical Review, Vol. XIX, April, 1914. The Macmillan Company, N. Y., 1914. Interesting point of view brilliantly expounded.

Medieval Cities. Princeton University Press, Princeton, 1925. Simple, interesting, authoritative.

PITIGLIANI, F., *The Italian Corporative State.* P. S. King & Son, London, 1933. The Fascist side of the structure of the corporate state.

POIGNANT, S., *La Foire de Lille.* Raoust, Lille, 1932. A brief and well-documented study of the Lille fairs.

POLLOCK, F. AND MAITLAND, F. W., *History of English Law before the time of Edward I,* vol I. Cambridge University Press, 1923. The classic exposition of the legal aspects of feudalism.

POSTGATE, R. W. (Editor), *Revolution from 1789 to 1906.* Grant Richards, Ltd., London, 1920. Valuable collection of documents.

POWER, EILEEN, *The Industrial Revolution, 1750-1850.* Economic History Society, London. Select bibliography compiled by a first-rate scholar; particularly valuable for teachers of the subject.

QUESNAY, F., *Oeuvres Economiques et Philosophiques.* Publiées avec une Introduction par A. Oucken, Baer, Francfort, 1888. The best edition of the works of the founder of the Physiocratic school.

REED, JOHN, *Ten Days that Shook the World* (1919), with an introduction by Lenin. International Publishers, N. Y., 1926. History is fortunate that one of the eye-witnesses of so eventful a period was one of the greatest reporters of all time.

REES, J. MORGAN, *Trusts in British Industry, 1914-1921.* P. S. King & Son, London, 1923. Useful account of the development towards concentration, and an able argument for public control. Good.

RENARD, G., *Guilds in the Middle Ages.* G. Bell & Sons, Ltd., London, 1918. The shortest and best book on the Gilds. Simply written by an expert.

RENARD, G., AND WEULERSSE, G., *Life and Work in Modern Europe (Fifteenth to Eighteenth Centuries).* Alfred A. Knopf, N. Y., 1926. Very good.

Reports from Assistant Hand-Loom Weavers' Commissioners, 1840.

Report of the Commissioners Appointed to Inquire into the Condition of the Framework Knitters, 1845.

Report of Committee on Trusts, Ministry of Reconstruction, H.M.S.O., 1919, Cd. 9236. Contains a great deal of excellent material.

Report on "Homework in the Fabricated Metal Industry in Connecticut," State Department of Labor, Minimum Wage Division, Hartford, Conn., Sept., 1934. A thorough, interesting, factual account of deplorable conditions. Excellent job.

Reports of Inspectors of Factories for the Half Year Ending 31 December, 1841.

Report of the Minutes of Evidence Taken before the Select Committee on the State of the Children Employed in the Manufactories of the United Kingdom, 1816.

RIAZONOV, D., *Karl Marx and Friedrich Engels.* International Publishers, N. Y., 1927. Simple, vivid and easy reading.

RICARDO, D., *Works,* edited by J. R. McCulloch. Murray, London, 1888. Writings of the "founder of the science of economics."

RILEY, H. T. (Translator and Editor), *Memorials of London and London Life in the XIIIth, XIVth and XVth Centuries.* Longmans, Green and Company, London, 1868. Useful.

RIVIERE, LE MERCIER DE LA, *L'Ordre Naturel et Essentiel des Sociétés Politiques* (1767).

Publié par E. Depetre, Geuthner, Paris, 1910. A comprehensive study of the ideas of the Physiocrats by a disciple of Quesnay.

ROBINSON, JAMES HARVEY, *Readings in European History.* Ginn and Company, Boston, 1904, vol. I. Good.

ROGERS, J. E. THOROLD, *Six Centuries of Work and Wages; The History of English Labour.* J. P. Putnam's Sons, N. Y., 1884. A classic.

ROTHSTEIN, TH., *From Chartism to Labourism.* Martin Lawrence, Ltd., London, 1929. Essays on the English working class movement with a Marxist slant.

RUBEL, K. (Editor), Dortmunder Urkundenbuch, vol. I. Bearbeitet von K. Rubel, Dortmund, 1881. Useful.

SAGNAC, P., *La Legislation Civile de la Révolution Française, 1789-1804.* Hachette et Cie., Paris, 1898. A well-documented historical study of the legislation of the time, with particular attention to landed property. For the advanced student.

SAGNAC, P. AND CAREN, P. (Editors), *Collections de Documents Inédits sur l'Histoire Economique de la Révolution Française. Les Comités des Droit Féodaux et le Législation et l'abolition du Régime Seigneurial, 1789-1793.* Imprimerie Nationale, Paris, 1907. Extremely valuable and instructive collection.

SALVEMINI, G., *Under the Axe of Fascism.* Viking, N. Y., 1936. Well documented account of the gap between the promise and the performance of Mussolini's Italy.

SARGENT, A. J., *Economic Policy of Colbert.* Longmans, Green and Co., London, 1899. Excellent introduction to mercantilism.

SCHANZ, G., *Zur Geschichte der deutschen Gesellen-Verbände.* Duncker u. Humblot, Leipzig, 1877. Famous work.

SCHAPIRO, J. SALWYN, *Social Reform and the Reformation.* Columbia University Press, 1909. Extremely good account of the social origins and setting of the Reformation.

SCHMIDT, G. (Editor), *Urkundenbuch der Stadt Halberstadt.* Halle, 1878. Valuable.

SCHMOLLER, G., *The Mercantile System and Its Historical Significance.* The Macmillan Company, N. Y., 1910. Early classic.

SCHULZE, E. O., *Kolonisierung und Germanisierung der Gebiete zwischen Saale und Elbe.* Hirzel, Leipzig, 1896. Carefully documented study.

SCOTT, W. R., *The Constitution and Finance of English, Scottish and Irish Joint Stock Companies to 1720,* 3 vols. Cambridge, 1910-1912. The standard work on this subject.

SEE, H., "Dans Quelle Mesure Puritains et Juifs ont-ils contribué aux Progrès du Capitalisme Moderne?" in *Revue Historique,* Tome 155, Mai-Août, 1927. Paris, 1927. Ten excellent pages on Weber's and Sombart's ideas concerning the influence of Puritans and Jews on the growth of capitalism.

SEE, H. E., *Modern Capitalism,* translated by H. B. Vanderblue and G. F. Donot, Adelphi Company, N. Y., 1928. A clear, comprehensive account of the historical origins and development.

Select Documents Illustrating the History of Trade Unionism. The Tailoring Trade, edited with an Introduction by F. W. Galton. Longmans, Green and Company, London, 1896. One of the best collections on this subject.

SENIOR, NASSAU, *Letters on the Factory Act, as it affects the Cotton Manufacture* (1837), 3rd edition. London, 1844.

Three Lectures on the Rate of Wages. John Murray, London, 1831, 2nd edition.

SHAW, GEORGE BERNARD, *Saint Joan.* Dodd, Mead & Company, N. Y. Saint Joan treated as protagonist for Protestantism and the national state.

SIEYES, E. J., Qu'est-ce Que Le Tiers Etat? Société de l'Histoire de la Révolution Française. Paris, 1888. Beautifully written.

SMITH, ADAM, *Inquiry into the Nature and Causes of the Wealth of Nations,* edited with an Introduction by E. Cannan, 2 vols. Methuen and Company, London, 1930. The best edition of this classic.

Socialist Planned Economy in the Soviet Union. Martin Lawrence, Ltd., London, 1932. Contributions by different Russian economists on the theory and practice of planning in the U.S.S.R.

342 BIBLIOGRAPHY

SOMBART, W., *Jews and Modern Capitalism,* translated by M. Epstein. Fisher Unwin, London, 1913.
   The Quintessence of Capitalism. A Study of the History and Psychology of the Modern Business Man, translated by M. Epstein. E. P. Dutton & Company, N. Y., 1915. Two important works by the famous German historian.

STANFIELD, JOHN, *Plan We Must.* Hamish Hamilton, London, 1934. Brief and bright argument for the necessity of planning.

Statutes of the Realm, from Original Records and Authentic Manuscripts, vol. II, London, 1816. Valuable.

STEAD, W. T. (Editor), *The Last Will and Testament of Cecil John Rhodes.* Review of Reviews Office, London, 1902. Interesting document with useful comments and chapters by the editor.

STOLBERG, BENJAMIN AND VINTON, WARREN J., *Economic Consequences of the New Deal.* Harcourt, Brace and Company, N. Y. Short, lively, and readable criticism of the New Deal.

Stories of Boccaccio, The Decameron. The Bibliophilist Library, 1903.

STRACHEY, JOHN, *The Coming Struggle for Power.* Covici Friede, N. Y., 1933. Forceful Marxist analysis in support of the communist program.
   The Nature of the Capitalist Crisis. Covici Friede, N. Y., 1935. Remarkably lucid treatment of the conflicting views on causes of crises by one of the clearest Marxist writers.

TARBELL, IDA M., *The History of the Standard Oil Company.* The Macmillan Company, 1925. Pioneer work in the field of trustification.

TAWNEY, R. H., *Agrarian Problem in the Sixteenth Century.* Longmans, Green and Company, London, 1912. Clear, well documented study by an eminent English historian.
   Religion and the Rise of Capitalism. Harcourt, Brace and Company, N. Y., 1926. Stimulating work brilliantly written.

THATCHER, O. J. AND McNEAL, E. H., *Source Book for Medieval History.* Charles Scribner's Sons, N. Y., 1905. Good.

THELWALL, J. W. F., *Economic Conditions in Germany to June, 1934.* Department of Overseas Trade, His Majesty's Stationery Office, London, 1934. Thelwall was Commercial Counsellor to H. M. Embassy in Berlin, and the Report, though far too detailed for general reading, is excellent and has a good general introduction.

THIERRY, A., *Recueil des monuments inedits de l'histoire du tiers état,* 4 vols. Paris, 1850-1870. Valuable collection.

THOMPSON, JAMES WESTFALL, *An Economic and Social History of the Middle Ages, 300-1300.* The Century Company, N. Y., 1928. Comprehensive, well-written, extremely useful.

THOMPSON, WILLIAM, *Labor Rewarded. The Claims of Labor and Capital Conciliated By One of the Idle Classes.* London, 1827.
   An Inquiry into the Principles of the Distributions of Wealth most Conducive to Human Happiness (1824). Orr & Co., *London,* 1850. Among the most important early socialist and cooperative writings.

THURKAUF, EMIL, *Verlag und Heimarbeit in der Basler Seidenbandindustrie.* Kohlhammer, Stuttgart, 1909. A study for advanced readers, of the putting out system in Basle.

TOCQUEVILLE, ALEXIS DE, *The State of Society in France Before the Revolution of 1789,* translated by H. Reeve. Murray, London, 1856. Justly famous.

TOYNBEE, ARNOLD, *Lectures on the Industrial Revolution of the 18th Century in England* (1884). Longmans, Green and Co., 1913. Stimulating essays by the humane economist who first used the term "Industrial Revolution."

Translations and Reprints from the Original Sources of European History. Published by the Department of History of the University of Pennsylvania, Philadelphia, 1898. Very good.

TUCKER, JOSEPH, *Brief Essay on the Advantages and Disadvantages which Respectively Attend France and Great Britain with Regard to Trade. London,* 1749.

Tudor Economic Documents, edited by R. H. Tawney and Eileen Power, 3 vols. Longmans, Green and Co., London, 1924. Invaluable.

TURGOT, M., *Reflections on the Formation and Distribution of Wealth* (1766). E. Spragg, London, 1793. Aid to an understanding of Physiocratic doctrine.

TROTSKY, LEON, *History of the Russian Revolution*, 3 vols. Simon and Schuster, N. Y., 1932-1933. The play vividly described by one of the leading actors who is no longer a member of the cast.

UNWIN, GEORGE, *Industrial Organization in the Sixteenth and Seventeenth Centuries*. Clarendon Press, Oxford, 1904. Pioneer work.

URE, DR. ANDREW, *The Philosophy of Manufactures* (1835), 3rd edition. London, 1861. Extreme example of capitalist self-righteousness.

UTLEY, FREDA, *Lancashire and the Far East*. George Allen and Unwin, Ltd., London, 1931. Excellent study, carefully documented, of the workings of imperialist competition in the cotton textile industry.

VEBLEN, THORSTEIN, *The Theory of the Leisure Class*. Vanguard Press, N. Y., 1926. A truly great book.

The Vested Interests and the Common Man. B. W. Huebsch, N. Y., 1920. Profound essays by one of our greatest social thinkers.

VIALLATE, A., *Economic Imperialism and International Relations during the Last Fifty Years*. The Macmillan Company, N. Y., 1923.

VINER, JACOB, *English Theories of Foreign Trade before Adam Smith*. Journal of Political Economy, June, August, 1930, vol. 38. Interesting articles by an expert in the field.

VINOGRADOFF, P., *Villainage in England*. Clarendon Press, Oxford, 1892.

Growth of the Manor. George Allen & Unwin, London, 1920. Two well-known, indispensable books on English feudalism.

WALKER, FRANCIS A., *The Wages Question*. Henry Holt & Company, N. Y., 1876. One of the better-known early American economists.

WALLACE, HENRY R., *America Must Choose*. World Affairs Pamphlets, No. 3, 1934. A brief but clear and interesting account of the social and economic problems involved in the control of American agriculture and foreign trade.

WATERS, CHARLOTTE M., *A Short Economic History of England*. Oxford University Press, 1922. Unusually fine high school text. Scholarly, simple, never dull, and well illustrated.

WEBB, SIDNEY AND BEATRICE, *Soviet Communism: A New Civilisation?* 2 vols. Charles Scribner's Sons, N. Y., 1936. Invaluable for reference. A remarkably clear exposition.

WEBER, MAX, *The Protestant Ethic and the Spirit of Capitalism*. George Allen and Unwin, London, 1930. Pioneer study of great value.

WEULERSSE, G., *Les Physiocrates*. Doin, Paris, 1931. Standard work by an expert.

WILSON, WOODROW, *The New Freedom*. Doubleday, Page and Company, N. Y., 1913. Important collected essays.

WOLOWSKI, M. L. (Publiés et annotés par), *Traictie de la première Invention des Monnoies de Nicole Oresme et Traité de la Monnoie de Copernic*. Guillaumin, Paris, 1864. The best modern edition of these two famous treatises, with excellent introduction and notes.

WOOLF, LEONARD, *Economic Imperialism*. Swarthmore Press, London, 1920. A keen student of the subject marshalls the facts and presents them in interesting fashion.

Empire and Commerce in Africa. George Allen and Unwin, London, 1920. See above.

Imperialism and Civilization. Hogarth Press, London, 1933. See above.

WOOTTON, BARBARA, *Plan or No Plan*. Victor Gollancz, Ltd., London, 1934. A simple, well-written analysis of planned and unplanned economic systems.

YOUNG, ARTHUR, *Tours in England and Wales* (1768-1808). Reprint No. 14, London School of Economics, London, 1932. Interesting observations by an agricultural expert of the period.

Index